A BEAUTIFUL THING

For Dwight A. Moody
Preacher, Mentor, Friend

A BEAUTIFUL THING

Sermons from the Inaugural Festival of Young Preachers

LEE HUCKLEBERRY, EDITOR

Foreword by Dwight A. Moody

ST. LOUIS, MISSOURI

Visit Chalice Press on the World Wide Web at
www.chalicepress.com

Paperback: 978-08272-02726

Hardcover: 978-08272-02757

EPUB: 978-08272-02733

EPDF: 978-08272-02740

Printed in the United States of America

Table Of Contents

LIFE & MINISTRY

PASSION & DEATH

Preface

On January 7, 2010, a beautiful thing took place in Louisville, Kentucky. Ninety-two aspiring young preachers gathered at St. Matthews Baptist Church to participate in the inaugural Festival of Young Preachers. They came from east and west, north and south. They came from small towns and large cities. They came from high schools, colleges, universities, and seminaries. They came from nearly twenty denominations. They came with a passion for Jesus and a commitment to gospel preaching. It was one of the most unique, inspiring, and hopeful events I have ever attended.

The Festival was created and launched by my longtime mentor and friend, Dwight A. Moody. In the summer of 2008, Dwight invited me to work with him on a new project known as the Academy of Preachers. With some generous seed money from the Lilly Endowment of Indianapolis and a few untested ideas, we began the challenging work of identifying, networking, inspiring, and supporting young people who discern a call to preach. We invited students in high school, college, university, and seminary–between the ages of 16 and 28–to engage with one another in their common calling through a variety of opportunities, one of which was the Festival.

To the best of our knowledge, the 2010 Festival was a historic, ground-breaking event. At no other time in our nation's history have so many young people gathered in one place for the sole purpose of preaching. Every year there are dozens of conferences and gatherings for ordained clergy and academicians that feature outstanding preachers, but none that exclusively feature young preachers.

Upon registering for the Festival, each participant was asked to select a sermon text from one of four categories: the birth of Jesus, the life and ministry of Jesus, the passion and death of Jesus, and the resurrection of Jesus. Included in each category were gospel stories as well as Old Testament texts that informed Jesus' teachings. He or she was also asked to enlist a preaching mentor, a pastor or teacher who would help them prepare the sermon, accompany them to the Festival, and introduce them before they preached. Every sermon was videotaped and uploaded to YouTube, and every participant was invited to submit a manuscript.

This collection features 59 sermons from the 2010 Festival of Young Preachers. In the pages that follow, you will be impressed with the talent, passion, intelligence, and authenticity of these fresh, emerging voices in American Christianity. Each sermon is a gift to the church in that it signifies the promise of a new day in preaching for the glory of God and the common good.

I wish to acknowledge and thank Dr. Craig Dykstra and Dr. Chris Coble of the Lilly Endowment for embracing the vision and mission of the Academy. Their wise counsel and enthusiastic support have helped this promising idea to flourish, and I am grateful.

Russ White, President and Publisher of Chalice Press, also deserves great thanks. From the beginning, he has been an invaluable supporter and friend of the Academy, and his editorial team (Gail, Connie and Lynne) did outstanding work on this book.

I offer thanks to Lucas Rice who preached a splendid sermon at the Festival on Jesus' anointing at Bethany (Matthew 26:6-13). His sermon title, "A Beautiful Thing," was selected as the title of this volume, and it is an apt description of what transpires when we present our very best to God. I am also grateful to Isaac Moody for the five original drawings he created for this volume. His work is a perfect complement to the sermons themselves: simple, attractive, and inspiring.

My wife, Angie Bailey, deserves much adulation for her patience and encouragement as I worked on this project. Her love and support is "a beautiful thing" I behold each and every day.

Finally, I dedicate this volume to Dwight A. Moody who has been my preacher, mentor, and friend for nearly eighteen years. I will never forget his first words of advice to me about preaching: "Have something to say, and say it in an interesting way." These are good words for young and not-so-young gospel preachers everywhere.

Lee Huckleberry, Executive Director
Academy of Preachers

Foreword

Early in the summer of 1996, I took my 15-year old daughter to the RiverPark Center in Owensboro, Kentucky to audition for the community theater. The show was "Fiddler on the Roof," and we both ended up getting parts. She and I danced together, sang together and had a terrific experience. It helped her clarify her passion for the stage. School courses, Governor's School of the Arts, the National Institute of Theater, and finally an M.F.A. in stage performance at age 26 gave her the training and opportunity she needed to launch her own career.

Too bad I did not have this same kind of support when I walked the center aisle at the Baptist church in Murray, Kentucky to announce my call to gospel ministry. The pastor then and there led the church to "license" me to the ministry, but he never said another word to me about it. I was on my own: no school courses (except speech), no summer programs, no internships, nothing except a father and a mother who gave me encouragement and guidance.

Today gospel preaching is one of the few vocational tracks that offer young people no support. Programs are scattered here and there: the high school preaching competition for those in the independent Christian church, the triennial sermon competition sponsored by the African American Pulpit, and that is about it. Even in the programs for high school and colleges funded by the Lilly Endowment of Indianapolis, there is little if any attention given to preaching. This includes the one I designed and administered while Dean of the Chapel at Georgetown College in Kentucky.

For future farmers, lawyers, musicians, athletes, and tradesmen of all sorts there are opportunities to test interest, learn skills, and meet people. Junior Achievement, for example, is an international organization mobilizing 330,377 volunteers to teach 379,968 classes to 9,795,485 students a year. It is "a partnership between the business community, educators and volunteers–all working together to inspire young people to dream big and reach their potential. JA's hands-on, experiential programs teach the key concepts of work readiness, entrepreneurship and financial literacy to young people all over the world" (www.ja.org). Too bad there has been no such network of support for young preachers…until now!

In 2008 the Lilly Endowment of Indianapolis approved a grant to launch the Academy of Preachers. How this happened is worth telling. For 11 years I served as Dean of the Chapel at Georgetown College. In that capacity, I taught in the religion department and led the chapel services. I also received and managed a Lilly Endowment grant, part of their 88-school project supporting programs for the theological exploration of vocation. Part of our campus strategy was launching a ministerial student formation program; I directed this for a few years. In that process I became concerned, first, that there were no larger, richer programs supporting young preachers, and second, that too many of our entering ministerial students were siphoned off to other vocational tracks.

I became convinced that our young ministerial students were losing confidence in preaching as a socially significant vocation. They were bright, talented, and committed to making a difference in the world, but just not convinced that preaching was an attractive way into that future. So they were drawn to social justice, music and worship, law and public policy, higher education, or medicine and research. All of these are noble callings, but something needed to be done to advocate gospel preaching as a transformational vocation.

The idea of an academy of young preachers began to percolate in my imagination. I discussed it with ministerial friends around the college and even wrote an email or two to some in the administration. However, concurrent with this emerging conviction, I began to sense within my own soul a vocational restlessness. I was personally ready for a change of venue and portfolio. I imagined a resuscitation of a radio program I had launched and shelved a few years earlier. So I wrote my friends at the Lilly Endowment, asked for an audience, and scheduled a meeting. I wrote the letter on April 24, 2008 and scheduled the meeting for June 23, 2008. In between these dates, I resigned my position at the college, and continued preparing for my interview at the Endowment.

When I sat down with Craig Dykstra and Chris Coble, their first question caught me unprepared: "How are things at Georgetown College?"

"I don't know," I responded. "I am not there anymore."

"What are you going to do?" Dykstra asked.

"I don't know," I answered. "I am like a man going fishing. I have five fishing poles. I will put them in the water and see what happens."

Dykstra then said to me something so simple, so wise, and eventually, so pivotal to my life: *"Tell us about these fishing poles."*

I began to rattle off to him and Chris the various vocational options that this 58-year-old, unemployed Baptist preacher had discussed with his wife. These included returning to the pastorate and launching a ministerial coaching initiative. Of course, I had in front of me a large, leather folder crammed full of ideas, statistics, interviews, and proposals ready to present to the nation's number one religion philanthropist. We never made it to the prepared material because the third idea I rolled off the top of my head in response to his fishing pole appeal was the idea of the Academy of Preachers.

I simply described to them my experience, my observations, and my ideas; and they liked them, much to my surprise. I was caught off-guard when they asked, "What can we do to make this happen?" When I stumbled with an answer, they said, "Why don't we just give you a grant and let you do it?" So I spent the summer writing the grant for a pilot project. I called everybody I could think of, from Bob Russell in Louisville to Brad Braxton in Nashville to John Killinger in New York to Martha Simmons in Atlanta. I consulted with my friend Lee Huckleberry and my colleague Mac Warford. In the end, I designed an 18-month pilot project, housed at St. Matthews Baptist Church in Louisville, Kentucky, and centered on congregations, institutions, and organizations within a 150 mile radius of Louisville, Kentucky. I recruited Lee to assist me, promising him the extraordinary title of Senior Consultant. The grant was submitted in September of 2008, was approved in November of that year, and Lee and I began our work officially in January of 2009.

Three ideas dominated that first proposal, and over the last 15 months we have given them a good test. I recruited an 18-member young preacher's leadership team, brought them to a retreat, and with them planned the inaugural Festival of Young Preachers. The team also gathered for a preaching camp, during which we introduced them to a self-managed strategy of certification as a gospel preacher. And finally, in January of 2010, they gathered with scores of other young preachers to launch a national festival of preaching for young people.

At the initial retreat, these young leaders revised all of my plans. I proposed a festival hosted in four different churches; they voted for all under one roof. I suggested segregating the anticipated 104 preachers by age and experience; they opted for mixed groups. I envisioned recognizing the best preachers in each category; they demanded a "no competition" clause in the description of the event. In all of these ways, these young preachers were right, and I learned quickly to respect their judgment on many things.

The preaching camp was truly remarkable: primarily, that it even occurred. Each summer multitudes of young people go to camp. At my college, more than 8,000 young people flock to campus to learn everything from balancing equations to twirling a baton. Leadership, athletics, music, mathematics, and religion of all types: everything, except preaching. Not at Georgetown College, and nowhere else in America, as far as we can tell, can a young preacher spend a week honing skills and cultivating interest.

That made our camp all the more significant. We had 12 young people who preached every morning; each had a coach, and the whole group had a guest presenter each day. But the remarkable thing that occurred each night, after all the old dudes went to bed, was the peer coaching that happened from 9 p.m. to 2 a.m. They bonded and blended and blessed each other, and thus opened a way into the future for preaching camps around the country.

What didn't go so well was the certification program. First, several specialists in the field warned us against using the "certification" language. "You can't guarantee or certify anything," they said to us. And we could get few of even our young preacher's leadership team to take seriously the 11 elements of this guideline for making progress as a gospel preacher. Hence, we have retooled this idea and embedded it our leadership team strategy for year two; we shall see what happens.

The one piece of this preaching project that did fit nicely into place was the Festival. We opened registration to any young person in the country who wanted to come and preach, and in the end we had 107 registrants. Of these, some withdrew and others failed to follow through, and only 96 were given preaching slots. Of these, all but four arrived in Louisville on time and ready to preach. (Two became ill, one was drawn away by a family emergency, and one was hindered by the icy weather that surrounded our festival.) But 92 young people came, from 41 schools in 21 states, ranging in age from 15 to 29 (plus one 33 year-old man who slipped through undetected!), from almost every denomination you could imagine: liberal and conservative, male and female, black and white, and including Roman Catholics, Church of Christ, Christian, Nazarene, Brethren, Orthodox, Pentecostal, Presbyterian, Disciple, Methodist, and Baptists–plenty of every type of Baptist. Missing were Lutherans and Episcopalians; and I surmise this is because neither of these faith groups have institutions within the target area of the pilot project. But next year, for sure!

These 92 young preachers gathered for a unique and historic event. We know of nothing like it: not just in current American Christianity but also not in the history of the church. Time will tell whether it ignites a fresh and persistent attention to young preachers, but we are already deep into the planning for national festivals in 2011 and 2012.

These young preachers were directed to preach from one of four broad categories: the birth of Jesus, the life of Jesus, the death of Jesus, and the resurrection of Jesus. On each of these we presented six biblical texts, including from the Hebrew Bible, the Gospels, and the other apostolic writings. We selected these basic themes and listed these texts because we wished to keep these young preachers focused on the central theme of the gospel. The prospect that some or many might use the occasion to launch into rhetorical attacks on ideas or people or institutions represented at the festival made us very wary. The list of sermon texts was one way to limit that, as well as a pre-festival piece about developing a sense of occasion in the work of the preacher.

As it turned out, there was little in the way of wayward rhetoric. The fact is, most of the young preachers selected the life of Jesus as their preaching theme, and the most preached text at the inaugural Festival was, surprisingly, the "take up your cross and follow me" text from the eighth chapter of the Gospel of Mark. A strong call to radical discipleship was easily the dominant preaching theme of this first Festival, and this focus cut across all theological and denominational lines of demarcation.

Young preachers were required to be endorsed by a congregation and accompanied by a mentor; sermon times were limited to 16 minutes. Each was placed in one of four venues: Sanctuary, Fellowship Hall, Choir Suite, and Chapel. The preaching began in four places simultaneously at 1 p.m. on Thursday and concluded at 11:30 a.m. on Saturday. Mixed in and around these 92 sermons were three plenary worship sessions, two conversation circles, several meals, and plenty of time to stroll through the 27 exhibitors who had set up shop in the vestibule of the church.

Some sermons were better than others, of course. Some of these young people were preaching their very first sermon. In fact, one young lady signed in with trepidation. "This is not me," she said to her pastor. "I don't know why I am here." But listening to six sermons on Thursday afternoon transformed her fear into confidence. "I can do this," she said. And on Saturday morning she did, and did so in such a way that the following Sunday morning she walked the aisle of her home church and announced her call to gospel ministry.

During the Festival I managed to hear only a dozen or so sermons. But in the weeks after, I watched all 92 of them in DVD format; you can now do the same on our Academy of Preachers site on YouTube! My listening and watching leads me to conclude that much of the quality difference relates to preparation; some of these young preachers simply did not prepare well and others had little coaching in preparation for the event. Both of these dynamics are being addressed as we prepare for the second Festival scheduled for January of 2011.

These sermons, many of which are collected in this volume, lack imagination, as might be expected of young and inexperienced preachers. They demonstrate weakness in the dynamics of appeal in public speech, of calling the listener to respond in specific ways. Experience and coaching will help them progress. Also missing from many of these sermons is the careful use of compelling illustrations. They do give encouraging evidence, however, of extraordinary talent and also of uncompromising commitment to Jesus Christ as Lord and Savior.

What is perhaps the most powerful dynamic at work within the Academy of Preachers and certainly evident at the Festival of Young Preachers is the sense of community, of comradery, of collegiality that has taken root among many of these young preachers. Most are developing in their gospel vocation within a very narrow range of ideology and communion; this exposure to one another at an early age not only helps to confirm and enrich their sense of call but also expands and deepens their appreciation for others who are walking, in a sense, a path parallel to their own.

"I arrived at the Festival," one young preacher said to me weeks later, "unsure of what to expect. Would I be free to be myself, I wondered? Would others respect my Brethren ways?"

I am sure he was not the only one who brought those same questions to Louisville, Kentucky in January of 2010. But he continued, and his testimony was also common to many. "It did not take long for me to learn otherwise," he said. "I was warmly received. The young preachers were interested in my Brethren tradition. And I enjoyed very much hanging out with the Roman Catholic preachers who were there. It was a memorable occasion for me and I am eager to come back next year."

Friendships were formed at the Festival, friendships that will last a lifetime, friendships that will continue to be avenues of gospel grace in the lives and ministries of these young preachers who gathered in Louisville in January of 2010. I am glad I was there.

Dwight A. Moody, Founder and President
Academy of Preachers

Birth

1

"WILDERNESS IMAGINATION"
Mark 1:1-8

John Jay Alvaro

A voice from the wilderness cries out, "Come home! Gather together in your hearts the old stories of God. Listen well. The time you have been waiting for is here. The great and terrible day of the LORD has arrived!"

The writer of Mark has need of few words as he opens his account of Jesus the Messiah. His first sentence is not even a real sentence. It is a fragment of thought. "The beginning of the good news of Jesus Christ, the Son of God" (Mark 1:1). The writer forces us to envision the larger image given here in glimpses. The term *gospel*, good news, is loaded with conflict. For those living under the shadow of Rome, gospel was imperial language. The good news proclaimed in Roman culture was that Caesar and Rome had conquered in battle. Power had been consolidated. The region was stabilized by the violence of war, and Caesar had brought peace by the sword. And the title "Son of God" also belonged to this tradition. Who was the Son of God? Caesar Augustus, of course. Poets would write of his birth as "good tidings of great joy ... a savior is born!" This Son of God has brought peace, imperial peace.

So when the writer of Mark places this imperial language at the front end of his account of Jesus, he is inviting a comparison between the way the world understands salvation and the way God imagines it. The sword or an execution stake? This good news concerns the powers that sit on the throne. It concerns all those who claim to be savior, Son of God, but only to say "NO!" to their legitimacy. This story is about the arrival of Messiah Jesus. All those non-powers, those non-gods are in the process of being dethroned. The "NO!" of the gospel, this over against nature of redemption, must be acknowledged.

There is much to which we must say "NO!" before we can say "YES!" From the very first words of Mark's story, we hear bundled up with the goodness of this news an implicit critique of all other claims to power. If Mark is right, if the Kingdom of God has come near, then God has unseated all other non-powers. Is it any wonder these people got themselves killed? This good news is both great and terrible.

It is a cry from the wilderness that invites the people to get ready. If the power structures of the world are about to be disrupted by the coming Reign of God, it is going to take a new set of eyes for people to see what God is up to. So they follow the messenger's voice into the wilderness to turn back to God. This is not the first time the people of God have challenged those who sit on the throne, non-gods dressed up in divine language. The wilderness is once again calling the people of God to believe impossible tales of rescue and redemption. When Israel was too crushed by the heel of Pharaoh to hope for anything other than a back full of bricks and a sea full of dead babies, God calls them into the wilderness. Here God says, "You are no longer Egyptian slaves, I have adopted you. I will be your God for all time." In that place God covenants with them. In the wilderness, they regain the ability to imagine life outside of Egypt, outside of slavery.

What is the movement of the people in this text? The people come from the Judean countryside and from Jerusalem to the wilderness. Why would they do this? Why leave Jerusalem? The Jews had been waiting a long time for a new deliverance, one that would finally bring peace, *shalom.* It had always been assumed that when the Messiah came, he would defeat all the Jewish oppressors (in this case Rome) and set up a throne in the Temple from which to issue justice. The Temple is in Jerusalem, so that is where any good Jew would look for the Messiah. But the voice comes from the wilderness. And what does the writer tell us about this voice? We find in the second and third verses a combination of Hebrew scriptures from Isaiah and Malachi. The writer of Mark quotes, "See, I am sending my messenger ahead of you, who will prepare your way" (Mark 1:2). In Malachi, God says:

> See, I am sending my messenger to prepare the way before me...For I the LORD do not change; therefore you, O children of Jacob, have not perished. Ever since the days of your ancestors you have turned aside from my statutes and have not kept them. Return to me, and I will return to you,

> says the LORD of hosts...See, the day is coming, burning like an oven...but for you who revere my name the sun of righteousness shall rise with healing in its wings...Lo, I will send the prophet Elijah before the great and terrible day of the LORD comes (Malachi 3:1a, 6-7, 4:1-2, 5).

The writer of Mark then tells us that John the Baptist appeared in the wilderness dressed how? In camel's hair with a leather belt. Any Jew knows that is what Elijah wore. And what is he eating out there in the wilderness? Honey and locusts, food for one like Elijah. And what is his message? What is he crying from the wilderness? "Repent! Turn back to God! That great and terrible day spoken of by the prophets is at hand. For one is coming who is greater than me, and when he shows up, you better be ready." The great and terrible day is here. Mark is casting John the Baptist in the role of Elijah, carefully connecting the prophetic dots, and what his emerging picture suggests is that the arrival of Jesus is the arrival of the long awaited day of the LORD. And we get that this is a great day. But how is it terrible?

For those who have more than they need but fail to share with those who have nothing–this is a terrible day. For those who continue to take advantage of the poor and vulnerable with heavy economic burdens–this is a terrible day. For those who continue to use their power to subdue and oppress the powerless–this is a terrible day. For those who pretend that religion is a social club for the elite, who assume that their meager contribution to God will cover the blood on their hands–this is a terrible day. For those selling a lie that salvation comes in the form of a political platform, a moral majority that promises peace and security if we only bomb this place, those people–this is a terrible day.

But Malachi says that the day of the LORD is also great. Mark calls it good news and gives us more than just Malachi with his harsh words. Mark gives us Isaiah 40, that beautiful chapter of poetry where God says, "Enough!" to Israel's suffering. For thirty-nine chapters Isaiah has spoken against Israel:

> How the faithful city has become a whore!
> She that was full of justice,
> righteousness lodged in her–
> but now murderers!
> Your silver has become dross,

your wine is mixed with water.
Your princes are rebels
and companions of thieves.
Everyone loves a bribe
and runs after gifts.
They do not defend the orphan,
and the widow's cause does not
come before them…
The LORD rises to argue his case;
he stands to judge the peoples.
The LORD enters into judgment
with the elders and princes of his people:
"It is you who have devoured the vineyard;
the spoil of the poor is in your houses.
What do you mean by crushing my people,
by grinding the face of the poor?" (Isaiah 1:21-23, 3:13-15).

Isaiah describes unfaithful Israel and lyrically leads them into exile. They are in a foreign land, in Babylon. The Psalmist says that they cannot even sing the songs of Zion (Psalm 137). In exile, they hang up their harps and weep, all the while being mocked by their oppressors, "Sing us a song! One of those peppy ones about Zion!" They answer, "How can we sing in a foreign land?" However, in Isaiah 40 the prophet paints a different picture, and the writer of Mark uses this text to set up his gospel. You see, when you are in exile long enough, when the only reality you can imagine is oppression, slavery, and homelessness, something happens to your understanding of God. For Israel during the Babylonian exile, God was still considered a tribal deity. Even though they had plenty of scripture to the contrary, that is just how things were understood. "Sure, our God is God in Israel, but here in Babylon, we are all alone. How could God follow us into exile? How can we worship and sing to our God in this foreign land?" But in chapter 40 the prophet says it is time to go home, reassuring the people that there is not a time or place where God is not the God of all creation:

Comfort, O comfort my people,
says your God.
Speak tenderly to Jerusalem…
A voice cries out:
"In the wilderness prepare the way

of the LORD,
make straight in the desert a
highway for our God.
Every valley shall be lifted up,
and every mountain and hill be
made low;
the uneven ground shall become level,
and the rough places a plain.
Then the glory of the LORD shall
be revealed,
and all people shall see it together …
Why do you say, O Jacob,
and speak, O Israel,
"My way is hidden from the LORD,
and my right is disregarded by
my God?"
Have you not known? Have you not heard?
The LORD is the everlasting God,
the Creator of the ends of the earth.
He does not faint or grow weary;
his understanding is unsearchable.
He gives power to the faint,
and strengthens the powerless (Isaiah 40:1-2*a*, 3-5, 27-29).

As I have been sitting with these texts, they have worked their way into my life. Each night my little boy asks me for a story. He loves any excavator, backhoe, or dump truck he sees, so I started to tell him about this image given in Isaiah 40. I tell him that the people of God got lost and ended up far away from home in a place called Babylon. In that strange land they would dream of home, but they knew that between Babylon and Jerusalem was a vast expanse of dangerous land. The land contained mountains and valleys with no safe road to get from here to there. So the prophet talks about angelic backhoes and bulldozers clearing a path. The mountains are torn down and the depressions filled in. Then the angelic scraper and grader come through and carve a road home. And it occurred to me in the telling what this image could do for a little Jewish boy living in Babylon. What if my son and I were in exile? What would it do for him to hear about divine bulldozers making a way home? Abraham Joshua Heschel, a Jewish theologian, says of Isaiah 40,

"No words have ever gone further in offering comfort when the sick world cries."[1] Here is the genius of Mark's opening to his gospel. He knows that he is speaking to a sick world crying out for rescue. He knows that Rome sure feels a lot like Babylon. But he also knows that something new is being born from the old.

For a young church trying to make sense of the events of Jesus' life, coming to terms with the Roman reality of persecution, moving forward without the person of Jesus among them, the writer of Mark recalls old stories and characters, clothes John the messenger in Elijah's garb, and this seemingly crazy man speaks these seemingly crazy words about another one coming who is more powerful. One who will bind up the brokenhearted. One who will call home the exiles. One who will put it all back together. Mark's terse prose is like a whisper, giving glances and nods. We have to listen well, like kids tucked into beds in a foreign land, being told the stories of the prophets and the exodus, dreaming of home. Mark builds the tension and thrill in these first eight verses of his story. With all this expectation being born in our hearts, listen closely to where Mark is taking us. Another voice comes from the wilderness … not John's … not Elijah's. And this voice whispers to our weary hearts the good news of God, "The time is fulfilled, and the kingdom of God has come near" (Mark 1:15*a*).

---

[1]Abraham Joshua Heschel, *The Prophets* (Peabody: Hendrickson, 2007), 145.

2

"OVERLOOKED AT CHRISTMAS"
Luke 2:25-38

Jake Caldwell

It had been a hard couple of years since her husband died. They were married fifty years. He always took care of the finances. But after he died, it was too hard for her to make ends meet. So at seventy-two she entered the workforce. She had given her best years to raising a family, but that didn't count for much when it came to looking for a job. Finally, she was offered a position as a cashier at a local grocery chain. She took it. She needed the money bad enough that she was willing to put up with her boss. He speaks to her loudly and slowly, because he assumes that at her age, she probably can't hear him or understand his instructions. He berates her because she can only scan twenty items per minute–half as many as their younger clerks. He counts the money in her till twice because he assumes she has made a mistake. In truth, her failing eyesight and her arthritic hands do make it difficult for her to shuffle the crisp bills. She puts up with it until he explains to her that they're letting her go because of the downturn in the economy–"business has been slow," he says. But she knows it's because they can get someone to do the job more efficiently–someone who doesn't need to take time off for doctors appointments and doesn't rely on the bus to get to work on time.

A few months go by, and she arrives an hour early to her meeting with her social worker. "I'm too old to be dealing with all this," she says to herself as she shuffles through the mess of papers in her lap. Social security, Medicare Part D, the eviction notice that was on her door, the letter from her doctor saying that unless she pays them six hundred dollars they will be unable to provide her with further care. Six hundred dollars?! That's how much she has to live on each month. The good news is she is eligible to receive some services, but there will need to be some cuts to her budget before that can happen. "Sixty dollars a month to your church?" her social worker asks, one eyebrow raised. "Oh yes," she explains. "In order to be considered a full member of my church, my pastor says I have to give ten percent of my income. It's non-negotiable." "I'm sorry," replies her social worker, "but most places won't give you assistance for medication or groceries with that expense in your budget."

The truth is they won't miss her at church that much. They've been waiting for her and her generation to get out of the way–to clear the stage so a new generation can step up and move beyond their outdated ideas. They speak of doing evangelism, but by that they mean they want young families to attend the church. They parade their babies up and down the aisles but scarcely mention those who are lonely and homebound. After all, they want the face of their congregation to send a message. They want to look vivacious, full of potential, and prepared to move into God's future.

Luke might test our sensibilities by placing Simeon and Anna–two aged pillars of the faith–in a story so focused on God's future, so charged with an air of eschatological hope. After all, it is a practice of our time to set aside the aging–to keep them in the background. But I want us to hold up Anna and Simeon this morning because Luke has invited us to be converted to another way of thinking. He has invited us into a narrative that challenges our cultural valuation of older adults. In Luke's narrative, when the reign of God comes breaking into the world as a lowly child, judgment is pronounced on whatever devalues human life. As the refrain of one of my favorite Christmas hymns puts it, "When God is a child, there's joy in our song. The last shall be first and the weak shall be strong, and none shall be afraid."[1]

But the truth is that often when we retell the stories of Jesus' birth, Simeon and Anna get neglected. Perhaps we succumb to cultural wisdom when we set them aside to make room for the newborn child. To my knowledge they're not mentioned in any of our Christmas hymns. None of the Christmas cards hanging in my kitchen featured Anna or Simeon; I checked. Friends, one of the Christmas cards I got featured a dog, a cat, and a mouse staring at a Christmas tree, but Anna and Simeon did not make the cut! They are never present, even in the biggest, baddest, most deluxe nativity sets. Granted, they were not present at the time of Jesus' birth. But neither were the Magi, and they always grace the manger scene in their silly hats–standing, kneeling in reverence, or mounted on

[1]Brian Wren, "When God Is a Child" in *The Chalice Hymnal* (St. Louis, MO: Chalice Press, 1995), 132.

their camels. The fact of the matter is that Anna and Simeon get overlooked at Christmas.

But you see, Luke has a different way about him. He introduces Simeon to us as a righteous and devout man. And to that he also adds, "the Holy Spirit was upon him" and "he was looking for the consolation of Israel" (Luke 2:25). Simeon is looking and searching, not waiting in the passive sense. He is engaged and attuned to the movement of God in the world. Therefore, he is positioned to see that Jesus–who was circumcised and named in ordinary fashion–is in fact no ordinary child. Rather, Simeon says he is "the Lord's Christ"–God's anointed one.

Under the guidance of the Holy Spirit, Luke has Simeon discern the significance of Jesus with greater depth and clarity. Maybe the most striking of Simeon's claims comes as he holds the infant Jesus and echoes the words of Isaiah saying, "my eyes have seen your salvation, which you have prepared in the presence of all peoples, a light for revelation to the Gentiles and for glory to your people Israel" (Luke 2:29-32). In these words Luke has Simeon "predict" the unveiling of universal salvation to the people of Israel and the Gentiles alike. Both aspects of Simeon's prediction are realized in Luke's two-part writing. The identity of Jesus as Israel's long-awaited Messiah is made clear in the Third Gospel, and the book of Acts tells the story of the gospel breaking into the gentile world. Thus Luke presents Simeon to us not as an artifact of bygone days, but as a sign that God's promised salvation is upon us and that a hopeful future awaits us. He is not slow and disengaged, but rather, he is a paradigm of spiritual and intellectual awareness. Simeon is not a helpless, non-contributing burden upon his community. Rather, he is an authoritative, discerning interpreter of Israel's scriptures. And he is not stuck in his ways, but rather, he recognizes that God is doing something new through the child he holds.

When Simeon has finished speaking, we are immediately introduced to his female counterpart Anna, who Luke tells us is a prophetess of great age. Luke is not entirely clear about how to calculate her age, but she is either 84 or 105. Whatever the case may be, Anna joins Zechariah, Elizabeth, and Simeon as yet another older character in Luke's narrative who is devoted to God and plays a decisive role in the events surrounding Jesus' birth. We learn that Anna, like Zechariah and Simeon, is associated with the Temple. As proof of her faithfulness, Luke informs us that "she did not depart from the Temple, worshiping with fasting and prayer night and day"

(Luke 2:37). Anna is not only depicted as a dedicated servant of God and a paradigm of faithfulness. Luke also makes clear that this older woman is revered as a teacher in her own community. She is not only prepared to recognize what God is doing in the world, she is also qualified and motivated to proclaim it to others. I have little doubt that the wisdom that can accompany old age is part of what makes Anna so well suited for her task.

Perhaps it goes without saying that Luke's understanding of the importance of older adults is not always shared by people in our society. And for that matter, it is not always shared by people–young and old–who occupy church pews on Sunday mornings. It is not uncommon for me, and probably for you, to hear people talk about waiting for an older generation of church members to die off and clear the way for progress. I have even heard a minister or two say things like that. But the idea that older adults are somehow less capable of recognizing and contributing to the mission of God in the world is entirely foreign to Luke. Furthermore, I would suggest that if we allow Luke's narrative voice to shape us, the idea that older adults are not vital participants in the life of the church will be entirely foreign to us as well.

I think that Richard and Judith Hays capture an important lesson of our text when they write, "The advanced age of Simeon and Anna signifies their time-tested wisdom, while at the same time symbolizing Israel's long-suffering expectation of deliverance. These two aged figures also suggest that radical openness to the redeeming power of God may be found among older adults–perhaps particularly there."[2]

In my congregation, and I would bet in yours as well, we have a few Annas and Simeons–the kind of people who point us to the ways God is at work in the world. Perhaps there are a few in this room today. We are thankful for you Simeons and you Annas because the church needs your wisdom. You are a reminder to us of God's promise of restoration and new life. And should we all be fortunate enough to celebrate your 84th or even your 105th birthday–should you join the ranks of Anna and Simeon and the many aged pillars of the faith–we will expect to find God at work through you even, or perhaps especially then.

---

[2]Richard B. Hays and Judith Hays, "The Christian Practice of Growing Old: The Witness of Scripture" in *Growing Old in Christ* (Grand Rapids: Eerdmans, 2003), 7.

3

"THE LITTLE GREEN SHOOT"
Isaiah 11:1-9

C. J. Childs

Peace. It's an interesting word and a very interesting concept. We hear it written about, spoken of, and sung about, especially this time of year. The hymn we just sang, "I Heard the Bells on Christmas Day," was written by Henry W. Longfellow in 1864 during the American Civil War. We can clearly see this setting in the hymn:

I heard the bells on Christmas day
their old familiar carols play,
and wild and sweet the words repeat
of peace on earth, good will to men.

And thought how, as the day had come,
the belfries of all Christendom
had rolled along the unbroken song
of peace on earth, good will to men.

Till ringing, singing on its way
the world revolved from night to day,
a voice, a chime, a chant sublime
of peace on earth, good will to men.

and in despair I bowed my head
"There is no peace on earth," I said,
"For hate is strong and mocks the song
of peace on earth, good will to men."

As Longfellow points out, it is very hard to find peace on earth. There are actually two more stanzas to this song that are usually omitted from hymnals that reflected the period of war in which it was written:

Then from each black, accursed mouth
the cannon thundered in the South,
and with the sound the carols drowned
of peace on earth, good will to men.

It was as if an earthquake rent
the hearth-stones of a continent,
and made forlorn, the households born
of peace on earth, good will to men.

No one here lived during the Civil War, but can't we relate to these words? Do we even need to name off the list of nasty effects that the absence of peace, that brokenness has created in our world?

War
Crime
Violence
Oppression
Persecution
Racism
Sexism
Abuse of Power
Genocide
Hate
Homelessness
Murder

And on and on and on and on!

We see this brokenness played out in our daily lives. Just at my university, Trevecca Nazarene, I see brokenness in the family when a daughter doesn't know whether she can go home for Christmas break because her father is marrying the lady with whom he had an affair. I see brokenness in the home when a child can't shake the emotional trauma caused by an adult who decided to take advantage of them for years. I see brokenness in the economy when hardworking people are fired and given no other chance to work to provide for their basic necessities.

We live in a broken world. A world so bound up in its brokenness that we literally cannot imagine it any other way. This sort of broken world, one that does not seem to have peace anywhere, is the same sort of world in which the prophet Isaiah preached!

Israel was broken. Israel did not have true peace. Israel needed something to change and quick. And like us, Israel had a whole list of ailments too:

1. They had just been through a whole line of bad kings who did not follow the commands of God;

2. Much of the nation of Israel did not worship the true God as their ancestors had passed down to them;
3. Israel had been invaded by Assyria and only a remnant of the original nation was left;
4. There was much injustice in their judicial system like we have today.

Isaiah is addressing the remnant that survived the Assyrian invasion. They had been through some really hard times. The end of chapter 10 in Isaiah paints the picture for us. This great forest has just been demolished by the LORD Almighty. All that is left is mere burnt stumps. Only death remains.

Yet, in chapter 11, our passage shows us that somehow out of the death, decay, and hopelessness of the previous chapter, God tells Isaiah that a shoot will come out of a stump! Life will come out of death! A tiny green piece of life will spring forth in a barren wasteland of stumps. It almost makes me want to say, "So what?" I mean, what is one single green stem going to do when this huge forest of strong, sturdy trees has just been decimated? If the trees couldn't survive, how could a little green stem? What is this stem going to do?

In the setting of this text, the shoot is referring to a new king from the line of David. A good king. The shoot will spring from the stem of Jesse. A branch from Jesse's roots will bear fruit, and the spirit of the LORD will rest on him.

Isaiah then describes three different attributes that this shoot, this new king, will have. They are traits that will allow him to be a king that follows God's heart–gifts of counsel and strength, wisdom and understanding, and knowledge and fear of the LORD. And to top off this list of God-pleasing characteristics, he will also delight in the fear of the LORD and will judge with righteousness and fairness.

So what will this little shoot do? This little stem will change history forever! This is Isaiah's message to this downtrodden, brokenhearted, walled-up, bound-up people. God is sending someone to bring true PEACE! The scene here is beautiful! Close your eyes and picture it with me:

> The wolf shall live with the lamb,
> the leopard shall lie down with the kid,
> the calf and the lion and the fatling together,
> and a little child shall lead them.

The cow and the bear shall graze,
their young shall lie down together;
and the lion shall eat straw like the ox.
The nursing child shall play over
the hole of the asp,
and the weaned child shall put
it's hand in the adder's den.
They will not hurt or destroy
on all my holy mountain (Isaiah 11:6-9*a*).

This is a crystal clear statement from the God of hope. God is saying that He is not going to leave things as they are! He is not going to let the brokenness continue! He is going to help creation regain the peace it had at the very beginning! Hallelujah!

Let's picture ourselves in this situation. How would you react to the news of this prophecy? This would have been some exciting news if you lived in that time period. You can just imagine how the people felt because the fulfillment of this prophecy would raise them up from the brokenness and troubles they experienced on a daily basis. They couldn't wait!

It's kind of like a kid at Christmas time, right? The child has watched that huge wrapped gift that has been under the Christmas tree for the past week or so. She can't wait to open it, to know what exciting treasure it contains. Her parents have told her she must wait to open it, but the excitement is unbearable!

This passage tells Israel that they will be restored through God's man, this king to come, this gift from God, and they will experience the peace that they never had! A new age is at hand. God is going to do something for Israel yet again! But they can't open it yet because the shoot has not come. Israel, along with every other nation, existed without this "shoot…from the stem of Jesse." They heard him prophesied and lived in expectation and hope for what the future would hold.

This is somewhat different from our world because we have seen the stem of Jesse. We have seen the little green shoot spring up from death. We have seen this prophecy fulfilled in part because we have seen Jesus! Hallelujah! We know now that God did send this person of whom Isaiah prophesied. God followed through on his promise and sent a king from the line of David. God sent true peace through the birth of a baby in the little town of Bethlehem.

Ultimate peace can only come by way of Jesse's roots. We can pursue peace all we want. We can work for peace in our communities and our world, but we cannot bring about the true peace we need. Only the little green shoot can!

Yet, there is tension here. If what I'm saying is true, and Jesus is the Prince of Peace, why is our world still just as broken as the world in which Isaiah preached?

Because God's work is not finished!

We live in expectation of that day just like the Israelites did in Isaiah's time. Just like the child waiting earnestly for Christmas to arrive, we wait with eager longing. We live in a gap–a constant tension between the day that God began to restore creation through the life and work of Jesus Christ and the day to come when God will complete his restoration. A day when our enemies will become our friends. A day when the predator will lay down with the prey. A day when all of creation will be at peace.

Like the Israelites of old, we await the appearance of the Messiah! The One from God, the One who brings peace! The hymn which I referenced earlier–"I Heard the Bells on Christmas Day"–has a final verse that we didn't sing. After all of the despair contained in the previous verses, hear these words of grace and hope!

> Then pealed the bells more loud and deep:
> "God is not dead, nor doth He sleep;
> The wrong shall fail, the right prevail
> with peace on earth, good will to men."

This passage in Isaiah gives us the hope that one day there will be peace on earth and good will to all. One day. In the meantime, look for the little green shoot where you are. Imagine your world. Imagine in the barrenness and brokenness of your own life one tiny little sprig of greenery...then another, then another, then another. Little green shoots everywhere! Can you see them?

4

"RE-PLACING THE GOSPEL"
Luke 2:1-20

Andrew Fiser

Week by week, preaching involves placing the gospel. By placing, I mean identifying *where* the gospel comes to us. Some Saturday evenings come upon us and we cannot find good news for the people. It may be that we have lost track of *where* the gospel came to us, *where* we felt and heard God's call. We might call it "preacher's block." Somehow the gospel gets misplaced. Somewhere between the visit to the shut-in, the committee meetings, and letting the heating and air person in the building, we misplace the gospel on our appointment calendar. Somewhere between the open bible, the electric bill, and the sorrowful statement from the finance team, the good news turns up missing. Somewhere between the political talking heads, less than true theologians on television or in bookstores, and the need to keep our job security, the gospel becomes difficult to hear.

Luke's account of the nativity of Jesus carefully places the good news. The artistry of Luke's writing begs us to pay attention to the place of the gospel. It is easy to miss the setting of the nativity story when Christmas trees, shopping commercials, and the general busyness of the season gain our full attention. We can miss the tension between Caesar and an infant birthed into poverty, the awkwardness of a pregnancy out of wedlock, the fields where the good news comes first to the those who work the jobs no one else wants. Sentimentality can easily hide the importance of carefully reading the gospels, especially this one.

With great imagination, Luke recalls the witness of the early Church about the beginning of the good news in Jesus Christ. The angel places the "good news of great joy" in a particular place. It happened in a barn among the poor and the marginalized. It occurred amid the machinations of a powerful empire. It took place in the middle of the ordinary movements of human birth, life, and death. It arose in the city where Ruth became an emblem of love and where David learned how to shepherd before he became king.

The nativity of Christ sets the stage for the ministry, the death, and the resurrection of Christ.

Part of being a disciple of the Christ witnessed in Luke is paying careful attention to place, to the setting of ministry, to the context of one's theology, to the surrounding or backdrop of our life together. We experience the good news in a place. Kingston United Methodist Church near my home in Arkansas is a place where good news is at work. If I told you that Kingston started a weekly supper and music fellowship, it would be good news. But, if I told you that the church started this supper because the nearest grocery store is forty miles away and there are few jobs in the county, it would add a different dimension to the good news. If I told you that Kingston is the birthplace of Johnny Cash and that the first time the congregants heard "Folsom Prison Blues" was when Johnny played in church, it would bring a different voice to the gospel music they make at Kingston. When we come alongside Luke in the placing of the gospel, it begins to come alive and to move once again.

Discerning the place of the gospel is a conflicted job. Whether we are in college, seminary, or in a church, preaching forces us to make decisions. The place of our ministry should be the place where good news is spoken, but how realistic is that? We are talking about the church, and we know that the main thing that's wrong with the church is that it is full of people. So when the sermon needs to be written, we face choices about what to say in a broken community. There are personality conflicts, theological differences, and political identities besides Christian to consider. And on top of that, a preacher has to navigate this broken community using its scripture, tradition, reason, and experience to craft a sermon coherent enough to let the good news be heard.

However, we have a friend in Luke. Luke places the gospel of Jesus Christ right in the middle of tension and conflict. Luke sets the gospel of peace in the midst of an empire that thought it defined peace. Emperor Augustus was hailed as the "Son of God," the Savior, and the bringer of good news because he ended the long Roman civil war at the battle of Actium in 31 BCE.[1] Luke subversively sets the gospel of Jesus Christ in tension with the imperial theology of Rome. It is a child born into poverty and whose birth in a barn is witnessed by the most marginal persons of society which a heavenly

[1]Marcus J. Borg and John Dominic Crossan, *The First Christmas: What the Gospels Really Teach About Jesus' Birth* (New York: HarperOne, 2007), 61.

army praises as the bringer of peace: "Glory to God in the highest heaven, and on earth peace among those whom God favors!" It is this child who grows up to be a preacher whose first sermon is about "bringing good news to the poor" (Luke 4:18).

Luke's portrayal of Christmas places the gospel in such a way that it re-orients how we understand the gospel. Luke's Christmas gospel is a manger-shattered gospel. Karl Rahner said in a different time, "All God concepts must be crucified."[2] Here, Luke might also suggest that all our God concepts must be bedded down in a manger.

The bringer of true peace comes in the vulnerability of the manger. Our vulnerable good news comes into the ordinary places where truth is crafted by politicians, where peace is made through violence, where the people on the margins are told it's just the way things are, a way out of no way is born.

The Church in North America is struggling to find its place as mainline Protestantism declines, secularism becomes more widespread, and the newer incarnations of the church lose themselves in consumerism and cheap grace. But, some are just out of step enough to make sure their good news is good news for the poor.

Among them are Shane Claiborne and others involved in the New Monasticism movement who have placed themselves in situations of poverty and systemic violence on the margins of our society. These intentional communities have found that the gospel can be heard more clearly where the gospel has its beginning. These Christians (Evangelicals, mainliners, Catholics, and others) have placed the gospel where it can find its voice again; where the grace of God intersects with a broken and imperfect world. They live as intentional Christian communities–praying, studying, eating, and living together in dilapidated houses they renovate. But, because they recognize God dwells among us they help transform their neighborhoods into places where all God's people survive the day.

For we who feel called to preach the good news, Luke's preaching brings us some help. When we think of those late Saturday night sermons, the phrase "only by the grace of God" comes to mind. But from week to week, Luke offers us a lesson in sermon development. It is the practice of placing the gospel, of allowing the fullness of the place of our ministry to shape the voice of our preaching. Our gospel is on the move, transforming the commonplace into a holy place.

[2]Karl Rahner, *Sacrementum Mundi II,* Burns and Oates, 1969, 207f. cited by Jurgen Moltmann, *The Crucified God: The Cross of Christ as the Foundation and Criticism of Christian Theology* (New York, Harper & Row, 1974), 279.

The vocation of preaching is to place the good news again and again, to identify in life the grace of Jesus Christ at work today. Preaching is, among other things, bearing witness to the presence of a way of redemption for humanity which begins in the mundane.

In Luke's nativity story, the angel points toward the ordinary event of the birth of a child into poverty as the place where the good news for "all the people" will begin. And the shepherds decide to go to the place where this great event has happened. Sure, the good news is announced where they are ...but they go and see. If the good news does come in an infant born to an unwed mother, in a barn of all places, and in the heart of a place where peace seems to come only through violent power and coercion, then that changes everything. That is the reason the nonviolent heavenly army and the shepherds in their fields praise and glorify God. Everything has changed.

The Christmas story shapes a whole new reality. The Empire no longer defines human existence. Political, economic, and religious systems which bring peace to some but oppression to others no longer have the last word. The freedom of the gospel is on the move, bringing together a nonviolent movement beginning with Mary, Joseph, and lowly shepherds. This movement will continue in Jesus' ministry and gathering of disciples, be defined by Jesus' nonviolent death on the cross, and continue in the work of the church constituted as the Body of Christ by the power of the Holy Spirit.

The prophetic preaching of Luke's gospel account challenges Christian discipleship and preaching. The gospel, when we allow it to be placed by Luke, provokes a prophetic imagination even in preachers. This imagination enables us to witness in the seemingly routine movements of the church at Christmas the good news beginning anew, even in something as simple as singing of a Christmas carol:

> "He came down to earth from heaven who is God and
> Lord of all,
> and his shelter was a stable, and his cradle was a stall.
> With the poor, the scorned the lowly lived on earth our
> Savior holy."[3]
> Amen.

---

[3]Alexander, Cecil Francis & Henry J. Gauntlett, "Once in Royal David's City," *The United Methodist Hymnal* (Nashville: The United Methodist Publishing House, 2003), 250.

5

"SON OF A ZEALOUS GOD"
Isaiah 9:1-7

Ryan Gilbert

Brothers and sisters, it is with joy that I stand before you today. What we have gathered to celebrate is very close to my heart, as I know it is for each of you. For it was after a powerful experience of preaching my first sermon at my home church (during an informal youth service) that I spoke with a mentor at college who forced me to listen to my heart. I listened until I knew I did not want to be free of this calling, this set of passions that undeniably includes preaching. In the years since, I have praised God more times than I can count for revealing this vocation to me while I was still in college and before I had even chosen a career.

Today I feel called to go back to the book of Isaiah, to those first stirrings of hope for the arrival of a Messiah who would unite not only a divided Israel, but all the peoples of the world who would turn towards his ways.

Sure–the arrival of a Savior who has added our names to the covenant between the Jewish people and God, making us part of the chosen people–that's pretty exciting! And with world peace at the end of time thrown in to sweeten the deal–I think we can all get behind that!

But if that is our attitude, we might just be missing the point. That is, what does the arrival of the Christ child suggest about the character of God–the writer, director, and producer behind all the marvels we have witnessed this Christmas season? For this God is still in our midst, reshaping our lives on a daily basis so that we might more perfectly serve as instruments of God's peace.

Perhaps the most troubling thing about this God is that even after we have given up on ourselves, God refuses to do the same. God is absolutely relentless in pursuing what is truly best for us. And even when we say "No" to the light that God offers us, even when we say, "I'll just stay here in the shade," God immediately switches to plan "B," or plan "C" or even plan "Z," patiently awaiting the next opportunity to offer us God's hand yet again. This is why, at the conclusion of today's reading from Isaiah, the prophet tells us that the arrival of the Messiah, his restoration of the United Kingdom of Israel and his establishment of perfect peace upon the earth–that each of these earth-shaking events will have but one cause: "The zeal of the Lord of Hosts will do this" (Isaiah 9:7*b*).

We often think of "zeal" in terms of the willingness of terrorists to kill in the name of God. From the Bible, we instantly think of Jesus' disciple, Simon the Zealot, who was a terrorist if you asked a Roman, a rebel if you asked a Jew. This is unfortunate. But another way of translating the word for "zeal," is to speak of God's passion for humankind, the kind of passion that we only catch glimpses of amongst human beings themselves. Throughout the Christmas story this zeal that burns in the heart of God for each and every one of us becomes so visible that we cannot deny its power. In fact, there is so much light that we often have to shield our eyes.

The heavenly chorus sings "Hallelujah" in all their glory and majesty, and we are absolutely overwhelmed. However, as the season ends, we find that our souls are grateful to return to the shade. We breathe a sigh of relief, and deep down we tell ourselves, "Whew! Now I can finally relax." I can slip off my shoes and rest knowing that I am truly loved by God.

However, God's unconditional love is only one dimension of God's holy covenant with us through Jesus Christ. There is that other dimension–of God's tremendous zeal and passion–which can be far more disturbing. For if the Son of God comes to us as a "Mighty Counselor," always making himself available and forever encouraging us to no longer deny that we are utterly broken and in need of care, then we have no choice but to constantly turn to him to pick up the pieces and to put us back together.

And if the Son of God comes to us as a "Mighty God" in his own right, not only inviting the little children to sit on his lap, but commanding every power on heaven and earth to create a world where every child is loved and truly cared for, then we, my friends, should be ready to serve.

And if Jesus is truly our "Everlasting Father"–the one who is forever waiting to provide for our every need and to guide our every step–then we have no right to continue our foolish struggle to prove to ourselves, the world, and God that we can take care of ourselves.

Finally, if Jesus is the "Prince of Peace," then we have little choice but to creatively confront the violence that rages not only in our world, our nation, and our communities, but in our hearts, erupting into angry words and deeds that damage those we love most.

In our scripture reading, King Ahaz of Judea has already chosen to ignore God's advice–and on no small matter. Isaiah had pleaded with him to put his trust in God alone, and to ignore their threatening neighbors to the north who were trying to pressure him into an alliance against Assyria. Nor should the king turn to the "protection" offered to Judea by the Assyrian Empire– the "Evil Empire" of its day. But King Ahaz did not need a Ph.D. in Political Science to figure this out–all he needed to do was to remember his Torah–the five books of Moses: Genesis, Exodus, Leviticus, Numbers, and Deuteronomy. For if he had remembered what his parents had taught him, he would have remembered that the Jewish people were always outnumbered, and that they never lost a battle whenever they allowed God to fight the battle for them, leaning neither on their own strength, nor on their own understanding.

King Ahab, of course, made the wrong decision, as we humans are prone to do. He chose the protection of the Assyrian Empire over the protection of God, and for that mistake he lost not only the region of Galilee to the Assyrians, but eventually the Temple in Jerusalem was destroyed and the leaders of his people were exiled. This is the cycle that the Jewish people kept falling into, time after time. There would be a time of faith in God. Then either the people would lose faith, their leaders would lose faith, or, usually, both would, and in their hearts they would convince themselves that the God who had freed them from slavery was no longer in the business of saving them from all the nations who plotted their downfall. They would play with the big boys. And when you are small and you play with the big boys–or the big girls–you always lose big!

There was once a mayor of a fairly large city that had a fairly large amount of debt. A nearby power company offered them a deal that would pay off a good chunk of the city's debt in exchange for the acquisition of the city-owned power company. The young mayor, who was only 31 at the time, let the public know that he was considering turning down the offer. The bank immediately made it known, in turn, that all of the city's loans would be considered in "default" if the power company deal did not go through. They said that turning it down would be considered a sign that the city might never choose to pay back its considerable debt.

People of all political persuasions came out against the mayor's proposal. For if they became the first American city to default on its loans since the Great Depression, imagine what that would do to their already tarnished reputation. The political factions showed a united front and promised to defeat him soundly in the next election. Isn't it wonderful how politics can bring people together? But as the young mayor sat at the negotiating table with the bank and the power company, do you know what he felt? He said he was tempted to sell the municipal power company, but he could not shake from his mind the sound of the pennies that his parents used to count at the kitchen table because they could barely make ends meet. He thought back to his Christian upbringing, to the values of fairness and hard work that he was raised on. He thought of all those families who could scarcely afford to pay more for their power.

The young mayor said "no," and all his enemies delivered on their promises. The city's loans went into default and the young mayor was kicked out of office in a landslide defeat. His political career was considered over. He couldn't even find a job in another city in another state. He was heckled every time he came back to town. Decades later his career recovered and he now serves in Congress. And in 1992 the mayor of that city estimated that this man's courage saved the city 195 million dollars over the course of ten years. In that moment of deciding between going with business-as-usual and going with his heart, the young mayor decided correctly. He chose to act courageously, whatever the consequences might be.

You may have faced decisions like that yourself, decisions that may have cost you jobs, decisions that may have cost you friendships, or even marriages. Yet in that moment the dawn broke in from on high, piercing the darkness that surrounded you. And from that moment on you knew you could not live any other way. The zeal of God, the passion of God, had come bursting through your frail mortal frame and into the world. And for a moment you felt what it was like to have Christ speak and act through you, even as many of the faces in the room looked at you like you had lost your mind.

Certainly, we can't expect to have such moments on a daily or even on a monthly basis.

The zeal of the Lord made known to us in Jesus Christ can also work in quieter, more subtle ways that are far less damaging to our mental health. But as the holidays conclude and as we return to our everyday lives (and as some of us go back to school), these moments of pure zeal are important for us to remember, for they clarify for us the values of justice and righteousness that God has incarnated in us–through the life, sacrifice, and resurrection of Jesus Christ–to guide our lives.

I once believed that it is one heroic action or one heroic speech that really gets people's attention. Now, however, the people who provide the most powerful witness to me are those who let the passion of God shine through the most mundane of activities.

Cooking a dinner for your church family.

Picking up a piece of trash on the side of the road.

Managing a sincere smile whenever the world tells you that your life is hopeless and that you should just give up.

Amen.

6

"ISAIAH'S INFOMERCIAL"

Isaiah 9:2-7

Adam F. Graham

At some point in life, the following scenario occurs. You sleep peacefully upon your pillow unaware of the world around you. Suddenly, your mind starts spinning round and round over what did not get accomplished yesterday and all the work ahead today. Anxiety takes over and your eyes pop open reading the alarm clock, 2:30 a.m. Unable to fall asleep again, you do what most other people do when insomnia strikes, turn on the television.

The problem with this plan is that there is nothing worth watching. Instead, the guide channel lists most stations as offering "paid programming." We all know what that word really means. Paid programming refers to that delightful invention known as the infomercial. These segments offer products such as knives that cut through cinder blocks, kitchen gadgets that replace seven others, and towels that absorb 99% more moisture than your average towel. All of these destined to be the greatest invention since the development of the infomercial. Every infomercial uses the familiar catchphrases to lull numb, sleepless folk into buying nearly any product for six easy payments of $19.95.

Yet, these infomercials work to bring a person back to sleep. They provide some sense of comfort that all is well with the world since crazy inventions still exist. The comfortable words arrive at a time when a person can use them.

Suffering insomnia spans the generations. Many people went sleepless during the time of the prophets. Wars and famine abounded. Yet, the prophets, whom the people thought should bring comfort, offer more words of doom to add to the sleeplessness. King Ahaz of Judah, on the brink of impending war with a cousin neighbor to the north, wrestles with an important strategic decision. Will he join Israel and Syria (Aram) in resisting the new superpower Assyria? Will he play Assyria against the other two? Political leaders do suffer insomnia sometimes.

One prophet offers Ahaz words to provoke his restlessness. Cities will become the place where cattle and sheep graze. God intends an army to invade the land. The worst news Ahaz hears is that if he does stand firm in faith he will not stand firm at all. These words seem equal to road repair outside during the night. All it does is continue to keep you awake. Yet, the prophet Isaiah does not give him all gloom. He offers these words of comfort, hope, and consolation:

> The people who walked in darkness
> have seen a great light;
> those who lived in a land of deep darkness–
> on them light has shined.
>
> You have multiplied the nation,
> you have increased its joy;
> they rejoice before you
> as with joy at the harvest,
> as people exult when dividing plunder…
>
> For a child has been born for us,
> a son given to us;
> authority rests upon his shoulders;
> and he is named
> Wonderful Counselor, Mighty God,
> Everlasting Father, Prince of Peace (Isaiah 9:2*b*-3, 6).

A sign of promise provides for a restful night's sleep. The appearance of this child marks not only a return to normal life, but life better than ever. Ahaz looked for that child; perhaps he thought his son Hezekiah would fulfill that role of a king as mighty as God and whose reign would be characterized by peace. It was not to be, for many other sleepless nights came to the people of God. During the exile, anxious minds wondered how their God who led them out of Egypt and crushed their enemies could let them dwell in a foreign land. Was Yahweh not as powerful anymore? Was Yahweh even their God while they captors demanded of them a song? Their very existence as a people caused them to sit up in the night staring at the ceiling. Still, someone must have remembered this oracle from Isaiah. Where is that light from the son, that child who bears authority on his shoulders? Who will be the son who will treat our oppressors like firewood? This glimmer of light prods the people as they walk in darkness toward another sleepless night with yet another oppressor.

It seemed like every other night. Shepherds kept watch over their flocks by night all seated on the ground. I guess they were a preindustrial third shift. Astrologers in the east spent time gazing at stars and noticed one hovering before them. Somewhere, a mother brings a new life into existence. She definitely is sleepless. The anxieties collide when the heavenly hosts burst forth on the scene singing, "Glory to God in the highest, good will and peace to his people on earth!"

The shepherds leave their flocks to see the oracle. The Magi go to Herod asking, "Where is he who is born King of the Jews?" They walked in the darkness to see a great light. Mary and Joseph bask while prophets declare their son to be a light that will lighten the Gentiles. This babe in the manger would grow to bring joy back to this sleepless people who had grown weary and glossy-eyed.

One more sleepless night happens a little while later. The disciples sit in disbelief. That child grew to establish David's kingdom. Instead of receiving it with joy, most people ignored it preferring the yokes on their necks despite the fact that these yokes were the very things keeping them awake. They would rather wait for another cure for their insomnia. The people who did listen and followed witnessed the death of that son. Now, the night after his crucifixion, they lay awake in fear. As they kept hearing this oracle, this infomercial, about the one who would bear authority on his shoulders, they kept looking at this man who said, "Blessed are the peacemakers." They thought he was the Prince of Peace. He taught as one with authority, perhaps a wonderful counselor. Other people called him the son of David. They wondered what would happen next. Is this not the Emmaus complaint? The stranger appears and asks why the travelers are forlorn. One almost scoffs, "Are you the only stranger in Jerusalem who does not know the things that have taken place there in these days?" He asked them, "What things?" They replied, "The things about Jesus of Nazareth, who was a prophet mighty in deed and word before God and all the people, and how our chief priests and leaders handed him over to be condemned to death and crucified him. But we had hoped that he was the one to redeem Israel." The followers thought it was the one in Isaiah's message.

Then the women went to anoint the body with proper funerary spices. They walked through the darkness to get to the tomb, but when they reached the sepulcher, they beheld a great light. The one who had died broke the rod of the greatest oppressor and all oppressors. Midian was no more. The son claimed his right for the increase of his government and for a peace that would not and does not know an end. The kingdom was established. Moreover, that zeal did accomplish it, for it was zeal that healed the sick. That zeal fed thousands. That zeal caused the powers that be to despise and kill him. Yet, it was that zeal that raised him from the dead. It multiplied to include all nations and it increased the joy of all those who heard the words and allowed the rod of their oppressor to be broken. No longer did the disciples have to use Isaiah's oracle as a look toward the future, but they received it as present reality.

Perhaps you don't suffer from insomnia like I do. You might not worry over food policy, school schedules, unemployment, hunger, economics, politics, and relationships. These might not bother you at all. You can sleep blissfully unaware of what's around you. If, however, you lie awake wondering, "What am I going to do?" "Why does this happen?" I urge you not to continue with bleary eyes, aching heads, and stumbling throughout life. Insomnia causes a dullness in our senses that limits us. Instead, watch an infomercial with me. This infomercial does not have a talking head barking prices for a food dehydrator or a hair treatment. Instead, watch the infomercial with the prophet showing us the Son given to us, caring for us both as Almighty God and Everlasting Father. Then we can rest and refresh our eyes that we might see the light shining upon us.

7

"A LIGHT FOR OUR DARKNESS"
John 1:1-18

Allison Hicks

Night lights were a good invention; simple, yet useful. They've withstood the test of time. Did you have a night light as a child or maybe you still have one? No judgment here. A night light is a good thing; in the darkness of night, it's a reminder that the darkness is not endless; there's a light nearby. I appreciate a good night light, especially in an unfamiliar place, don't you?

No, it's not what you think, I'm not scared of the dark per se; I'm just not a big fan of darkness. Darkness is unsettling; it's uncomfortable. I don't like the feeling of losing orientation to my surroundings, which perhaps says more about my personality than darkness itself. The teenagers I work with discovered my aversion to darkness fairly quickly. A few months ago, after our Sunday night youth gathering, we started down the stairs from the gym. Daylight Savings Time had just ended, so it was especially dark as I turned off the lights leaving the gym. I navigated myself through the hallway carefully by the light shining from the stairwell door. Once I crossed the threshold of the door, there was light, and so I began making my way down at ease. I was the last one coming down. There were a few girls in front of me, but some of the boys had already made it down to the bottom of the stairs. And then, suddenly, there was darkness. Pitch black darkness. I could no longer see the girls in front of me or the steps below me or the wall beside me. Just darkness–uncomfortable, unsettling darkness.

Darkness has always existed. In Genesis we read the story of God speaking light into the dark beginning. Darkness has always existed, covering the earth at the beginning of time and remaining with us to this very day. Darkness has always existed. In the Bible we read stories of lives enduring darkness, and lives endure darkness even now. Uncomfortable, unsettling darkness.

In her book *Eat, Pray, Love*, Elizabeth Gilbert shares her journey to wholeness after she finds her life unexpectedly falling down around her. In the midst of her deep depression, she finds herself lost in darkness. She writes, "For the longest time, you can convince yourself you've just wandered a few feet off the path, that you'll find your way back to the trailhead any moment now. Then night falls again and again, and you still have no idea where you are...you don't even know from what direction the sun rises anymore."[1]

My first year of seminary was a time I can only describe as resembling the darkness of night. It wasn't all dark all the time, but the intensity of seminary growing pains were upon me. Sometimes I could see what seemed like a light of dawn breaking over the horizon; other times it was like that stairwell and my night vision wasn't so good. As a Religious Studies minor in college, I had already been exposed to biblical scholarship and theological debate, but the first year of seminary was different.

I started seminary and suddenly I had to unpack everything I'd carried for so long. I had to take each piece out of my suitcase and give it a quick glance over before going into more systematic study of each part. I was starting to notice some of the ideas I'd traveled with were jagged and worn, there were edges I'd never seen before, and some of what I was carrying just didn't work anymore. I was frustrated with the political perspectives I also found rooted within me. They were no longer satisfying, and so, unpacking my suitcase wasn't easy. I was having trouble reconciling the darkness I was seeing in my world with the light I knew. It left me feeling hopeless, helpless and confused. The old, simple answers weren't working anymore.

In the midst of exploring my "embedded theology," I was also sorting through my notion of calling, trying to understand God's call upon my life. It was changing and developing within me, challenging me beyond where I was when I first arrived, and calling me to voice something new. I was also settling into life in Atlanta that first year. I moved into my one bedroom apartment and found myself enjoying life in seminary, but also battling moments of loneliness and enduring times when inner confidence seemed to be far from me. While living alone, I was left to my thoughts a lot of the time–thoughts of trying to sort out my theology and questions and my calling, trying to find answers to my questions, trying to keep myself oriented to some sense of light when all I could see, most of the time, was a dim darkness.

---

[1]Gilbert, Elizabeth, *Eat, Pray, Love* (New York: Penguin Books, 2006), 48.

Out of the darkness, the first chapter of the Gospel of John proclaims to us the good news of true light. It's the message of Christmas, yet there is no manger in Bethlehem, nor are there angels, shepherds, or wise men from afar. The writer includes none of the traditional elements of the Christmas story, but instead tells us the story of the eternal Word of God and what difference his light makes in the midst of our own darkness.[2] This first chapter describes the major themes of John's account of the Gospel story–Jesus is light and life; and it sets up all the stories in John's Gospel that will follow. It's the prologue to the miracles Jesus will perform and the teachings he will proclaim. But before John can tell these stories, he's got to talk about the Light. His discussion of the Light in God's eternal Word is the beginning, middle and end of the story. The true light which gives light to everyone has come into the world, and the darkness did not, cannot, and will not overcome it.

And what is the nature of this light? How exactly do we experience this light? John's beautiful climax of the first chapter comes in verse 14: "And the Word became flesh and lived among us" (John 1:14). God's eternal Word became flesh. The light of God coming to be with us in the person of Jesus Christ, coming to dwell among us, coming to be a part of who we are, coming into the "everydayness" of humanity. Not just entering into the joy and happiness of human life, but also the pain, sorrow, confusion and difficulty we encounter. And it's not just a story about Jesus, it's God's story. It's the story of God among us; God comes to be in the "everydayness" of what it means to be human. The good news of light shining through darkness we encounter.

True Light has indeed come among us, the light which we celebrate at Christmas. But the reality of our world today is this: even though we've seen the light, we still live in a world with darkness. Though we have been given the light of Christ, we still carry darkness with us and we still live in a world with dark corners. The Light of Christ come to us doesn't mean much if we aren't carrying this light to the dark corners of our world, and more importantly, if we aren't using this light to shine into the shadowy places of our lives. It's not just about the far off darkness; it's about the shadowy places in our own lives. We have a habit of thinking the darkness is only out

---

[2]Gail R. O'Day, "John 1:1-18, The Prologue," in *The New Interpreter's Bible: A Commentary in Twelve Volumes,* vol. IX, ed. Leander Keck, (Nashville: Abingdon Press, 1996), 526.

there, far from where we are, but we live with darkness here too. The darkness around us today is in the hopelessness of unemployment, the tragedy of war, the pain of loneliness and depression. We see its shadows in the suffering of disease, the restlessness of cancer, the stronghold of addiction. Its murky bottoms find us in the disgrace of low self-esteem, the anguish of grief, the confusion of uncertainty, and the complacency of purpose.

If we're honest, we know we find ourselves in darkness sometimes. There are places and times of darkness in our lives. The good news, the Gospel story: the darkness does not, cannot, and will not overcome this light we know. We find ourselves in darkness, but the candle continues to burn, giving light to our path and warmth to our journey. "The true light, which enlightens everyone, was coming into the world" (John 1:9). Sometimes the light to guide us only shines a couple of feet ahead. We continue to walk trusting the light to guide us, trusting the light for each new step, trusting the light will continue to brighten our path as we go even if all we can see otherwise is darkness.

Elizabeth Gilbert's journey takes her to three places, and in each place she learns a powerful lesson about how to live again. Somewhere along her journey, as she is learning how to pray again, she rediscovers God in a powerful way. In the midst of her dark situation, she begins to reconnect with the light of God. Liz confesses she doesn't know it all and she never will. But even if she did understand God fully and completely, faith would no longer have a place in her life. She writes, "Faith is walking face-first and full-speed in the dark."[3] Liz realizes faith is accepting God when you can't know it all or understand it all, when you can't see it all. It's a new understanding of faith for Liz apart from trying to rationalize the reality of God in her life, when all she sees is a dim dark night. Her conclusion–"I'm tired of being a skeptic, I'm irritated by spiritual prudence and I feel bored and parched by empirical debate...I just want God. I want God inside me. I want God to play in my bloodstream the way sunlight amuses itself on water. I just want God."[4]

These words were especially meaningful to me during that first year of seminary. During the first few months I was beginning to

---

[3]Gilbert, 175.
[4]Ibid., 176.

think there must be something wrong with me; my faith must be weak and dry and stale if all I can see is darkness. Though I found myself struggling through a dark night I did not expect, the breaking light of dawn allowed me to keep walking. The light of dawn allowed me to see my path–to see the value in my struggle, to see the person I was becoming, to see the importance in all my questions. It was a process that started then and continues now–a process of reconciling the darkness I see around me with the light I know within me. It's a way of working through life's journey in times of light, as well as darkness.

Darkness has always existed. Uncomfortable, unsettling darkness. But, the darkness we see will never overcome the light we know. May we journey in the knowledge that God is among us even in times and places of deep darkness. May we be surrounded by the light of Christ even though in darkness we may sometimes tread. May we find our hope in the breaking light of dawn, for true light has indeed come among us. Amen.

8

"THE DANGER OF SELFISH PIETY"

Isaiah 40:1-5

Jeffrey Hood

Brothers and sisters, this afternoon we gather in the midst of great turmoil. We are a people bewildered and afraid. We look around and see nothing but tragedy. Wars rage on every horizon. The United States is currently involved in conflicts in Iraq and Afghanistan–regularly killing and regularly being killed. Pain is inflicted on the families of those who hold the guns and on those being senselessly massacred in the name of an elusive peace. Economic recession has broken our stride. People all over the world are being tossed out in the street as greedy banks foreclose on their homes. Millions of people all over the world live without the essential means to survive. This phenomenon is usually coupled with no hope of securing such means. Violence in many different forms rule over our lands and evil rules in the human heart.

Yet in the midst of such troubling times, brothers and sisters, we still gather here at the Festival of Young Preachers to celebrate an art form that seeks to give people the great weapons of truth and hope to rise above such madness and seek a newer world. Indeed, it is in this spirit of a newer world that I proclaim the greatest event in all of human history–the resurrection of Jesus Christ.

The Christian community has always looked to the empty tomb for direction in the midst of great peril. Today is no different. We look to that tomb because it is at the center of all that we know as Christians. Yet today I arise not unfamiliar with the previous Friday. This day was a day of intense desolation and destruction. It was a time in which the very Son of God cried out "My God, My God why have you forsaken me" (Mark 15:34*b*). Disciples ran in every direction not sure how to carry on. There was a spirit of defeat among the followers of Jesus Christ. Today we sit here aware that such defeat would not last for long.

This was an important day and we must never forget that this was the day that the atonement for the sins of humanity was secured. But, brothers and sisters, we must also not forget that ours is a tale of two days. Far too often we speak of the atonement and we fail to speak of the restoration that is the resurrection.

I am very familiar with this phenomenon. I was raised like any good modern evangelical to be a "Good Friday" Christian. I was taught to stay there at the cross on Friday mining the nether regions of my soul. I was taught to follow the rules or the aforementioned atonement would not be for me. I was taught, "to know that I know that I know that I know" that I believe that Jesus died for my sins. This has been a common thread woven through everything I have been taught as an evangelical, from youth ministry to the highest reaches of evangelical education. Indeed, like any other modern evangelical, I was taught that Christianity was all about me. Brothers and sisters, there is grave danger in only being a "Good Friday" Christian.

When one is taught only to be a "Good Friday" Christian, they are unfortunately not educated as to the restoration that accompanies the resurrection of Jesus Christ. In the resurrection there is a conquering of death that is complete. In the resurrection there is conquering of all that holds us down in torment here on this earth. In the resurrection there is a promise of a new world that we have a duty to work toward. In the resurrection is an end to all that afflicts us, and yet mine is a community that has completely failed to be a resurrection and restoration people.

The evangelical community has neglected the greatest social, moral and political issues of our time as we all huddle around the cross participating in a selfish piety that does not give a damn about the restoration of a planet. I have cried many a night when I hear my people screaming about political issues drowning out the cries of the hungry in our streets. I have wept over the fact that the evangelical community is more concerned with "knowing that we know that we know that we know" to the neglect of healing a broken world. A resurrection and restoration people do not live like this. Indeed a restoration people should care more about others than they do about their own power and influence.

And so on this day, I rise to apologize for my people, the evangelical community. We have been seduced by our own piety. We have been seduced by our newfound power and influence. We have been seduced by our leaders to place ourselves far before anyone else. We have not cared at all about deep injustices that are taking place all over the world and for that we are deeply sorry.

Today I bring this confession on behalf of a new generation of evangelicals that is absolutely fed up with the selfishness of a communion that has failed to be a resurrection and restoration people. We have often proven through our actions that we would just as soon leave humanity dead in the grave of sin and destruction than take any focus off of our own piety and power. Ours is a communion that has spoken often of a Jesus that is mine, but failed miserably in speaking of a God that absolutely loves the world and wants to see it put right. We have cheered on blatant sins, whether that be in the form of war, racism, poverty, healthcare, or immigration. And in the very same breath, we call it God's will.

It is a stinging indictment that the evangelical community is known for everything it is against and very little it is for. We have placed our political candidates before you long before we ever get around to placing our Savior in your midst. Indeed, Jesus seems quite often to be noticeably absent from most of our efforts. We have so often kept our views fresh on our lips while God and God's people are far from our hearts. And in this, our selfishness, we have failed billions.

As a child, I spent much time in an evangelical church that exhibited this selfish piety very well. The church was a church that found itself in an increasingly uncomfortable situation in the community. Everyone in the church was upper middle class and everyone outside the church was dying in his or her respective fights against the various systems of oppression that fill our lands. Crime and creeping poverty surrounded the church on all sides. During worship services it was absolutely impossible not to hear the sounds of gunshots and sirens as the pianist played. After some time, the people realized that the church could not just sit there and do nothing any longer. They decided to act swiftly, and act they did. The next business meeting the church decided by unanimous vote that it should move to the suburbs. Jesus said that we would find him among the least of these. Well at this church, and in many evangelical churches just like it, when Jesus moved into the neighborhood the church quickly moved out.

My generation of evangelicals seeks churches that change the world, not churches that leave when the world changes. Today I confess our actions on behalf of the evangelical community. Jesus, we have failed you and your people over and over and over again. We confess our sin and seek redemption knowing that you rose from the dead to convert us not from life to something more than life, but from something less than life to the reality of a world made fully alive.

Brothers and sisters of the broader Christian world, we, like you, seek the promise of the restoration. We seek it not just for ourselves, but also for the entire world. The death and resurrection of Jesus Christ represent a demand as well as a promise. The demand is that we bind ourselves to the crucified Christ, and the promise is that through pledging our loyalty to the risen Christ we will bring about a new world. This means that all loyalties to systems and institutions of injustice that perpetuate the destruction of this world must cease.

Today, brothers and sisters, we declare that we will be loyal to such systems and institutions no more. We seek to join the broader Christian community in seeking the new world promise of the resurrection. We stand united with you.

We stand united with you against the destruction of life.
We stand united with you against war and violence.
We stand united with you against systems of economic oppression that rule our lands.
We stand united with you against the evils of prejudice and racism in all forms.
We hurt. We are filled with pain. We long to see this new world promise of the resurrection.
We stand united with you against all forms of oppression and injustice so that we will no longer be part of the problem, but part of the solution.
We promise to never turn our backs on God's people again.

This day we stand with you. We stand united with you to clear a way for the Lord in the wilderness, to "make straight in the desert a highway for our God. Every valley shall be lifted up, and every mountain and hill be made low… Then the glory of the LORD shall be revealed, and all people shall see it togethe…" (Isaiah 40:3*b*-4*a*, 5*a*).

Can it begin today brother and sisters? Can such unity begin today? Will this be the day that we Christians finally begin to seek a new world together? I am tired of this dark tomb!

9

"BUILDING THE PEACABLE KINGDOM"
Isaiah 11:1-10

Roger Jasper

I'm an associate minister. That means I'm a slightly better paid youth minister that gets to preach more often. Some of you know about that. So, I do a lot with the youth at our church, and one thing I try to do is get into the community and do things. I serve a fairly affluent church, and we went to the Lexington Rescue Mission one afternoon to help serve lunch to the homeless of Lexington. It is a nice program. The homeless come in and are seated. A tray is brought to them. The silverware is wrapped up with a napkin. When you bring the tray to them, you ask them if they want something to drink: lemonade, water, coffee. It is a little more dignified in some ways.

We served for about an hour doing that. Folks were coming in tired. Some of them boisterous and outgoing. Some withdrawn. Some knew each other. Some knew the staff. All the while our youth were doing their job, serving the food. About an hour into our work, the staff came to me and said, "Well okay, it is your all's turn. Come on in here and get you a plate. Then go on and sit down with the folks." I thought that was a nice gesture; you don't think about getting anything out of doing something like this.

I go in to get my youth and they're all sitting in the hallway, cell phones out, talking to folks at home. They've got their Blackberries and their iPhones, texting and playing games. I said, "Put those away! Who do you think you are?" I told them, "Come on in here, get some food, sit down and eat." And they said, "Oh, uh, no, oh no, we couldn't do that." And I said, "What do you mean you couldn't do that?" "Oh, umm, I'm not hungry. We're not hungry. We already ate." Well, this was at an overnight retreat, so I knew they hadn't eaten since breakfast because I fed them.

I don't believe they consciously thought that they were better than the people at the mission. They felt that they didn't want to take away from those people. They didn't want to give of themselves. They could give away their food, their time, their energy but they needed to retain a wall of separation whereby they were in control of the relationship. It's about control.

The people of Judah knew about control. They had known the pride of having strong monarchs like David and Solomon. They had suffered under the control of the Egyptian empire. They were afraid, in this text, that the Assyrian empire would sweep in and control their land. Later, the Babylonians would control. The Greeks would control. The Romans would control. These empires would come and for hundreds of years they were under the control of foreigners. Isaiah speaks a word of hope that one day the anointed of God would liberate his people.

However, for the people of Judah, it's not that they had a problem with empire. It's that they had a problem with someone else's empire. They wanted a piece of the empire pie. They wanted to be in control. And so, they were waiting for the anointed of God. They were waiting for the messiah, the prince that would make peace in their name and on their behalf. A king who would establish a kingdom like David and Solomon.

Well, they never saw that kind of king. There were good kings. Hezekiah was a good king, but he did not fulfill this passage. Instead, the Christian tradition tells us that this passage is ultimately fulfilled in a child born in a manger, in one whom lived the life of a homeless man.

Yesterday was Epiphany; we finished the Christmas season. Now we start to look forward to Lent and to Easter. We celebrate the life, the death, and the resurrection of a man that had no status in this world, yet he preached about a kingdom.

Well God, where is this kingdom? You know, I was told as a child that this kingdom, this peaceable kingdom that we read about in Isaiah, is a kingdom for which we have to wait. That's what I was told as a child. Just wait! I believed in this kingdom to come, but Jesus said the kingdom is at hand. This is the conflict that we feel inside. This is the world that we, as the Church of Jesus Christ, live in–a world between two advents. We live in a kingdom that has been inaugurated but has not yet been consummated. We believe that we are leading a revolution, in a battle that has already been won, waiting for out liberator. We can't control the establishment of this kingdom. We can't pass a law that brings about this kingdom. We can't gain a political office and build this kingdom. But we can establish a relationship and start the revolution.

Can you look at the image here? The wolf shall dwell with the lamb. The calf and the young lion will feed together. The cow and the bear shall graze together on the grass. It's an image of reconciliation that reaches beyond the need to control and seeks relationship. A lot of times we approach a text like this and we see ourselves as the victims. We think, "Well, the poor little lamb that I am. If only the wolves weren't picking on me so often we could be reconciled."

But we've got to reflect for a moment and think how often we are the wolves in the simplest of things.

I went into my senior pastor's office the other day, and he had a big bowl of Hershey's chocolate. I ate half the bowl. Then I said to him, "You really shouldn't buy this blood chocolate that was made using slave labor." We fill up our Christmas stockings with this stuff. Slaves, child slaves in the Ivory Coast harvest these chocolate beans. How often are we the wolves?

I spoke to a woman at my church the other day about this passage, and she said to me "Boy, that got me to thinking. I'm a sales person. When someone walks into my place of business, do I see them as simply the next meal? Am I a wolf on the prowl?" We've got to reflect on these things and consider how they meet us where we are.

The kingdom of God has got to affect every area of our lives as Christians. We've got to think about how we view each other as brothers and sisters in Christ. Are we really brothers and sisters, or do we objectify each other in our minds and hearts? Do we make one another into objects to fulfill our own personal desires?

How often is our mission simply charity. Something that allows us to stand up here and keep those that we serve down there. We can pat them on the head and leave unaffected because we've given to them. Of course, there is nothing we could receive from them. We've got to move to a place where we can eat together…not dine on one another but dine with one another. Look at the image here of the cow and the bear. For the bear it takes more than just eating the grass. It involves stooping down to the ground and grazing next to the bear. We have to humbling ourselves, not to lift others up, but to join them where they are.

Reconciliation, I think, is most of all about forgiveness. We can talk a lot about how we should forgive others, and it is a beautiful thing to forgive others. But, often it is much more difficult to be forgiven. In forgiving you retain control, but if I go to you in repentance and accept your forgiveness, I have lost control of the relationship. Then I have really given it up to God. We meet each other at a level of intimacy that is terribly uncomfortable.

The curious thing about this is that it doesn't make any since at all. It doesn't work. It's not expedient. It's not efficient. The lie that we've bought is that we need to do what's pragmatic. At church, at home, at work we need to do what is pragmatic, what works, what's efficient, what's expedient. But it doesn't work! Our Lord practiced this and he was crucified. It didn't work. It wasn't expedient. By the measures of this world it did not work, but Jesus turned the world upside down. He conquered death and hell. And what we have in the resurrection is liberation from the consequences of this world.

You see, we can practice this kingdom of God, this peaceable kingdom, without fear, not because the world does not have consequences for us, but because those consequences dissolve in the light of resurrection. There is nothing this world can take away from you–your pride, your home, your life–which cannot be restored in the resurrection of Jesus Christ. He is the first fruits, and in him we will find true life.

I really believe this is how we build his kingdom, his peaceable kingdom. The text says of this king that his delight is in the fear of the Lord and that the earth shall be full of the knowledge of the Lord as the waters cover the sea. We reach a lost world by just being this kingdom and seeking reconciliation with our God and with our neighbor. We do this not on our own terms, but on the terms of the kingdom constituted by Christ in Galilee and consummated in a day to come. Let us hope, pray, and look forward to that day. Amen.

10

"ORDINARY STUFF"
John 1:1-14

Matthew Kelley

A few years ago you couldn't turn on CNN without hearing the story of Ashley Smith and Brian Nichols. Brian Nichols was on trial in Atlanta for rape and assault. As a security guard was escorting him to trial, Nichols grabbed the guard's gun, killed her, a judge, and several other people as he made his escape. A massive manhunt was on, every moment of it broadcast live. When he was finally caught, we found out that he had taken a woman named Ashley Smith hostage in her home. Nichols was threatening to kill her, but Smith was kind to him. She made him breakfast and shared passages from the Bible and *The Purpose Driven Life* with him. Eventually Nichols let her go and he was captured by the police.

The media immediately focused on the role *The Purpose Driven Life* played in this story. Its author, Rick Warren, was on all the cable news shows and the book shot back to the top of the bestseller list. That was all they could talk about for a few days. This was all well and good, but perhaps we should ask ourselves if in our collective amazement over this story we missed something. What if God had been at work in ways we hadn't yet considered?

Brian Nichols was obviously a very different man after his encounter with Ashley Smith. From all the stuff we heard on the cable news shows we might think that Brian Nichols was inspired to change because of some great power in this book. But it might be that he was not so much swayed by a rational argument in a book, but rather, to quote John Wesley, his heart was strangely warmed. So what did it? What could have broken through all of the rage and fear and actually warmed this man's heart? While the passages from the Bible and *The Purpose Driven Life* were important, what if the biggest difference she made for this man was that she cooked him breakfast? This could be significant because during the manhunt we kept seeing a snippet of an interview with an FBI agent. The agent said that they didn't expect to take Brian Nichols alive, and he said it with kind of a smirk on his face. The police already knew the outcome: they were going to kill this man. To them, Nichols was less than a person. He was more like an animal that needed to be put down.

Ashley Smith, on the other hand, didn't see him that way. Even though he was holding her hostage in her own home, even though this man was threatening to kill her and leave her daughter without a parent, she looked at him and said, "You look hungry. Let me make you something to eat." That's not something a hostage held at gunpoint does. It's something a mother does. While the rest of the world looked at Brian Nichols as something less than human, Ashley Smith saw a man who was scared, tired, and hungry. Because she treated him like a fellow human being, and not like a criminal, his heart was strangely warmed. A miracle happened through something as simple as pancakes. In the midst of the common things of ordinary, everyday life, God showed up and healed the intense brokenness in this man's heart.

"In the beginning was the Word, and the Word was with God, and the Word was God. He was in the beginning with God. All things came into being through him, and without him not one thing came into being" (John 1:1-3). In the very beginning of John's gospel we have this powerful, poetic image of the interconnectedness of all creation: you, me, our families, our friends, complete strangers on the other side of the planet we'll never meet; all of us are fundamentally connected with one another because we are created by God. But somewhere along the way we all got lost to one degree or another. We became isolated. We became estranged. God didn't leave us because of any deficiency on our part. God didn't leave us at all: we left God. We just somehow forgot about the God who created us and remains with us no matter what.

So we began to lose our way. We began to forget about the Light, and the way became darker. We couldn't perceive this fundamental interconnectedness with everything and everyone else. We could only see ourselves and what was right in front of us. So we began to act selfishly. We only looked out for number one. Some of us became so lost in the darkness that we began to physically assault and abuse others. We so lost sight of God's image in others that we saw them as only a means to an end, a way to fulfill a desire. Not everyone was that far gone, of course, but regardless of whether we're guilty of rape and murder or whether we're just a lost, lonely person who's been disappointed by life, we're all estranged from God and from one another. We've all lost sight of the Light, but the Light never lost sight of us. The Word, the one who was present and active with God in the creation of all things, came to remind us of the Light, of the one who created us and draws us all together.

"And the Word became flesh and lived among us..." (John 1:14*a*). That's not exactly what we'd expect God to do. If I were writing the story I'd have the God of the universe come and break through the darkness in such an obviously powerful way that no one would miss it. I'd have it be like in *Monty Python and the Holy Grail* where the clouds part and there's God with the long white beard and big golden crown. I'd have it be big and obvious, but that's not how God wrote the story. Instead of a big, grandiose in-breaking into history, the Word became flesh. Not some fancy, gilded vessel we'd put up on a pedestal so we'd know for sure that it's holy, but in the flesh. Flesh is ordinary, not extraordinary. It's not remarkable, but that's where God chooses to encounter us: in the fleshy, earthy, ordinary stuff of everyday life.

God works in all kinds of ways, and sometimes it is in the things we'd expect. God can speak in the pages of Holy Scripture. God can speak through a religious bestseller. But more often than not, the ways that God speaks are through the small, everyday things that we often take for granted. In the simple gesture of making a meal for somebody who is tired and hungry. In the simple touch, a hand on the shoulder that says you care that you empathize. We're so busy looking for God to show up in the sky with trumpets blasting that we miss the simple, everyday, fleshy realities where God speaks to us. It's the simple stuff that makes the hairs on the back of our neck stand up and our heart feel that strange, warm sensation. It's not big and obvious, but it is powerful.

The Word became flesh. The Word became pancakes. The Word became bread. The Word became wine. Two simple elements, bread and wine, somehow become a means of grace that we can share together, celebrating how God is incarnate in ordinary, everyday stuff. We gather around a simple table, we share simple bread and wine, and all of the sudden we realize that the very body and blood of Christ, the Word that is present and active in all creation, is among us.

When I got married, near the end of the ceremony we celebrated Holy Communion. Bishop Pennel was performing the liturgy, and as he spoke the words of institution he lifted up the brass chalice signifying that we are all one in Jesus Christ. And as he lifted it up, Jessica and I looked at the cup and saw the most amazing thing. We could see our reflection, and all of our friends and family behind us, as well as the stone walls of the church and the soft blue light coming through the stained-glass windows. In a simple cup made of curved, polished brass we could see what it was that this cup symbolized: a fundamental connection that we all share by virtue of having been created by God and an awareness that the incarnate Christ restores us. The wine inside the cup symbolized the connection that we could see reflected on the outside of the cup. All of us, together, because of what God has done.

It's in the simple, ordinary stuff of everyday life that we see most profoundly how God is present with us. And by God's grace we, too, can become more aware of the divine which dwells in the everyday, ordinary things. May we have eyes to see in simple gestures of kindness, in passing words of hope, in pancakes, in bread, in wine, in each other's eyes, that we are never far from God. The Word became simple, ordinary flesh, and saw fit to make its dwelling among us. Thanks be to God. Amen.

11

"JUST GIVE ME THE WORD"
John 1:1-18

James Kinnard

The Gospel of John differs in many ways from the other three gospels found in the New Testament, and for this reason John is not categorized as a synoptic Gospel like Matthew, Mark, and Luke. A distinguishable aspect of this Gospel is the vast reduction that is applied to the things listed in the other gospels as this author chooses to focus on the person and identity of Jesus as the Christ, the Son of God, and faith in his name.

Our scripture today is located in the portion of the text known as "the prologue" of John's gospel. It contains the longest introduction of any gospel, and it emphasizes that Jesus is not only a human being but a social being, the incarnation of God. The author wants us to know that Jesus is both fully human and fully divine. Immediately in the opening of the gospel, the author explains the way in which he understands the life of Jesus. Jesus is the Word that was present in the beginning with God.

Many scholars have raised the question of why John made Jesus the main concern of this his gospel while subordinating many other major issues? One answer is that as Christianity grew every discussion ended with one question, "Who is Jesus?" In 2010 the same question is being asked, and I have come to be the chief defense attorney to present the case for Jesus. What's all the fuss about? Why are you building multi-million dollar facilities in the name of Jesus? Who is this man you get excited about and want others to meet? Who is this Jesus of Nazareth who was born of a virgin birth and is in the bloodline of King David? Who is this man who was born in a manger, walked the earth for a little over thirty years, and turned this world upside down and inside out? Who is this Jesus?

Let us walk through the text and find out just who this Jesus is. John simply calls him the Word. Now wait a minute! I am not crazy, nor is John crazy! Jesus is the Word! The Word John is talking about in his first chapter is the Greek word "logos." "Logos" is more than just speech; it is God's preeminent agent in the world. It is what God uses to create, to destroy, and to redeem. It was with "logos" that God stepped out into nothing and created the universe. I'm walking on "logos." You're sitting on "logos." This isn't just any word. This is the Word of God.

With just one Word, God speaks things into being. With just one Word, God can make things go away. So when God saw that things were going horribly awry with his beautiful creation, God did what God has always done and sent his Word to make the difference. You see, that's all you need today. The Word! Those of us who understand the power of this Word don't mind getting a bad report from the doctor because we can let the doctor know that "He was wounded for our transgressions, crushed for our iniquities; upon him was the punishment that made us whole, and by his bruises we are healed" (Isaiah 53:5).

Brothers and sisters, I've come to a place where I don't need money, and I don't need fame. Just give me the Word, because when I have the word everything else falls into its place. Somebody knows what I'm talking about. It was late in the midnight hour. Momma wasn't around and daddy couldn't be found, so all you had was the Word and as you spoke that Word things had to change. Isaiah says, "so shall my word be that goes out from my mouth; it shall not return to me empty, but it shall accomplish that which I purpose, and succeed in the thing for which I sent it" (Isaiah 55:11).

That's why somebody ought to help me praise God because the Word works! It cannot fail! But I can't get stuck there, let us move further in presenting this case for the Christ.

Looking at verse one of our text, John declares that in the beginning was the Word. That's enough for me to shout right there! Before your problem or your situation there was the Word. What does this mean preacher? That means that there is nothing under the sun that the Word cannot fix. Before there was a beginning there was the Word.

Since we talking so much about the beginning, let's look at the book of beginnings. In the book of Genesis, chapter one verse 26, there is something quite interesting: "Let us make humankind in our image, according to our likeness." In this great verse, God shows us that the Son (the Word) is already present; because the Father and the Son are one and the same. You see, when the author says that the Word was with God, he is saying that the Word is personal. It suggests a face-to-face relationship. In the ancient world, it was important for people of equal standing to sit face-to-face when communicating. Thus, the Word which is representing Jesus the Christ, is personal and still equally divine with God. That's why the next phrase says that the Word was God. I get excited when the preacher gets up and the man or woman of God begins to bring forth the Word of God, because you are not just giving me a word, you are giving me Jesus!

The Bible declares in this same pericope of scripture that "in him was life, and the life was the light of all people" (John 1:4). This is why I can stand before you today and say that there is no real life until you know Jesus. Those living without Christ think they are living, but they have no idea what real living is. John continues, "The light shines in the darkness, and the darkness did not overcome it" (John 1:5). Let me pause right here to remind the believer who is getting weary–the darkness/the world does not comprehend the light. So don't expect them to appreciate you. I don't know who that was for, but stop getting mad when they don't pat you on your back at work. The darkness simply cannot comprehend the light.

John goes on to say that "He was in the world, and the world came into being through him; yet the world did not know him...But to all who received him, who believed in his name, he gave power to become children of God..." (John 1:10, 12). Now, I'm going to try not to get stuck here, but there is something about that name! You see, demons tremble at that name! Cancer dries up at that name!

At the name of Jesus, those things that were dead must come to life!
At the name of Jesus, those family members you have been praying for must shake themselves from the world and run to the Savior!
At the name of Jesus, those plans that the enemy had made are diverted and aborted.
At the name of Jesus!

We are not talking about Mohammed. We are not talking about the Buddha. We are not talking about Confucius. We are talking about the all powerful, one true and living King Jesus! And I declare that there is power in that name! I can't help but I get excited every time I hear that name. It does something to me on the inside.

Finally, John says, "And the Word became flesh and lived among us, and we have seen his glory, the glory as of a father's only son, full of grace and truth" (John 1:14). Ladies and gentlemen of the jury, the Bible declares that this Word put on a flesh suit and began to walk with us. And when he put on that flesh suit, he understood our predicament. He understood what it was like to battle thoughts of fornication and sexual sin. He understood what it was like to battle drugs and alcohol. He understood what it was like to get that text message in the middle of the night inviting you over. Jesus had to be born in the flesh to show us how the flesh can be defeated. That's why we don't have to give in every time our flesh craves something. I get excited every time I get a chance to hear the Word!

I know the Word gets me up every morning. The Word starts me on my way. The Word keeps me in my right mind. When there is no food on my table, I have the Word. When there is no gas in my car, I have the Word. When there is no money in my pocket, I have the Word. You can have all the fame you want and all the attention you want. Take all the money, houses, and land. Take it all. Just give me the Word!

12

"A GIFT FIT FOR A KING"
Matthew 2:1-12

Sarah Lewis

January 6th is the celebration of Epiphany. For those of you who are not in the liturgical loop, Epiphany or Three Kings Day is the celebration of the visit of the Magi to the baby Jesus. Rather than celebrate Christmas, many cultures around the world celebrate this night instead.

Why is this significant? What does the visit of the Magi really have to do with the birth of Jesus? A lot of people will argue that the Magi weren't even present on the night Jesus was born, therefore making them a superfluous part of the nativity display. I even know some people who won't put their Magi figurines in their nativity sets because there can be no mingling of donkeys, sweet baby Jesus, and some mystical fellows from the East. However, I believe that those who remember Epiphany have a better grasp on the significance of the birth story than those who only utilize the shepherds, the angels, and the hay. The significance is found in Matthew 2:1-12.

Verses one and two give us the background: where, when, and who. Where? Jesus was born in Bethlehem, a religiously important but politically insignificant city in Israel. It was the hometown of King David and would be meaningful to those adept readers of the Old Testament.

When? Jesus was born during the reign of King Herod. He was king in Judea from about 42 BCE to 4 BCE. Many scholars have determined the birth of Jesus to be somewhere between 6 and 5 BCE. Who? We should all know who Jesus is. If you don't, please find me after the sermon and I'll be more than happy to explain. King Herod gave us the timestamp. Now we meet some characters called "Magi."

Magi have been called all sorts of names throughout history–astrologers, sorcerers, advisors, viziers, wise men, kings. Some early Christians even gave them names in an attempt to identify three of them. However, Matthew gives us no such indication. All we know is that they are plural, as in more than one, and that they are from the "east." From where I live, Kentucky is to the east, but so is Idaho. That leaves a lot of ground to cover, and Matthew doesn't seem to take pains to help us out. It would be assumed that east of Israel would be somewhere on the Asian continent, but again–that's a lot of east to think about. Many scholars have many opinions as to their origins, but for Matthew these Magi arise as mysteriously as they disappear. It's not necessary to get bogged down in the "who" and the "what." The most important facet here is the "why." These mysterious chaps saw something that captured their attention. Since it's highly plausible that they were astronomers or astrologers, it is safe to say they were probably watching the heavens and waiting for something to appear.

August 12th is one of my favorite nights of the year. For some reason unknown to me, every year there is a huge meteor shower that peaks on the night of August 12th. On clear nights and in unobtrusive places, up to eighty meteors an hour can be seen with the naked eye. It's ridiculous! Unfortunately, I live in a state of perpetual rain and clouds, so I don't often get to see too many. But when I do, it's awesome.

I'm no scientist, but the Magi perhaps were. At the very least they were extremely familiar with the heavens and would know the patterns. If they saw something out of the ordinary, it would catch their eye. A new star? Oh yeah, they might wonder about that. But somehow they knew that it pointed to the King of the Jews. That's what boggles my mind. I may just be really dense, but I don't know that I would automatically put two and two together. "Oh cool! A new star!!" That would probably be as far as I would get. However, these guys were smart (hence, the "wise-men" thing). They knew what it meant. Scholars speculate that these wise men may have been learned in the Jewish religion and may have even been God-fearers. They understood the significance of the star; they knew that it pointed to the King of the Jews.

Another question is raised then. If they knew this king was the King of the Jews, why would these Eastern, Gentile astronomers come to worship him? They have no relation, no investment in Jewish history or religion. Why? When you hear a tornado siren, what do you do? If you're me, you get your tornado flashlight and go cry in the bathtub. What do you do when you hear the "Star-Spangled Banner?" You stand up and place your hand over your heart, right? What about when someone sneezes? You say "Bless you," I assume. There are events and conditions within our world and culture that require a specific response. The tornado, sneezing, the national anthem–the responses associated with them are ingrained and automatic. That's what these wise men were doing. They saw the star; they went to Jerusalem and inquired where to find this King. Such news requires a specific response. Their response was traveling a great distance. Ah, but it can't be that easy, can it? No... enter Herod.

To say that Herod was troubled would be like saying Billy Graham likes evangelizing. Herod was EXTREMELY troubled. Imagine you are Herod. You've had to fight your way to the top of the government tower, killing off anyone who comes in your way. No one likes or respects you. If you heard that there was a King of the Jews recently born, wouldn't you wonder if he would usurp your throne and everything you've worked for? Herod was no fool. He was part Jew himself, so he'd heard the prophecies about the King of the Jews to come. He knew that if that person came, Jerusalem and Israel would rally under him and Herod would be out of a job. To say that Herod was troubled is quite an understatement.

However, before he gets all riled up, Herod wants to get his facts straight. For someone with a "shoot first...ask questions later" mentality, he shows a remarkable desire for accuracy.

He may have been crazy, but he was no dummy. He didn't just call anyone to give some answer; he called the people he knew would give him the most accurate answer. These chief priests and scribes were to the Jewish people what N. T. Wright and Bruce Metzger are to seminary students–they know where to find the answer. The answer to the question was a prophecy from Micah. The scribes and priests answer Herod's query with scripture. Several decades before the birth of Jesus, the prophet Micah predicted that one day, out of Bethlehem, a Messiah would be born and he would shepherd the people of Israel. The Old Testament Hebrew text of Micah says "O Bethlehem of Ephrathah" (Micah 5:2*a*), but when Matthew quotes Micah here he says, "Bethlehem, in the land of Judah" (Matthew 2:6*a*). This is no mistake on the part of Matthew, nor is it improper prophecy. Rather, Matthew is clarifying the birthplace of the Messiah from the prophet Micah. It is indeed in Bethlehem, in the land of Judah, which is a small town but an important and significant town, where the Messiah will be born.

However, this knowledge did not make Herod's outlook any brighter. He now knows that the prophecy is true, and it's come true in his backyard. So what does he do? He does what any crazy king would do who is in jeopardy of losing his empire; he twirls his sinister mustache and schemes. I picture Herod here as a little kooky, but also with a Boris and Natashaesque flavor. Like I said earlier, Herod is no fool. He knows what the proper response is to the news of the Messiah's birth. He knows that this event calls for a response of worship. But since he doesn't want to lose his kingdom, he has to find the baby King under the guise of worship. He can't simply say, "A Messiah has been born. Nice. Send my congrats to the parents." The entire nation of Israel knows that this birth calls forth worship. So he summons those mystical magi and tells them to find this baby Messiah with the pretense that he wants to worship also. Yet like Boris and Natasha, he has another plot brewing, and the Magi know nothing of Herod's plan.

These Eastern, non-Jewish wise men do what they know is expected of them. They go on to Bethlehem to find Jesus in order to worship him. The text says that they followed the star in order to find the place where the Messiah was. For many of you scientific people out there, this might come as a difficult text to read. How can they follow a star? Can a star practically land over the very house where Jesus was? I can't answer for you how this works scientifically. I can't even answer how it works logically. The Bible has some weird stuff in it. Joshua made the sun stand still. Noah had an ark full of every creature that moved on land. Almighty God came to earth in the form of a baby. This feat of nature doesn't stress me out anymore than other non-sensical, non-logical miracles in the Bible. Matthew, like many other biblical authors, doesn't seem to find it strange or out of character for God to move in creation to help bring about his plan, and his plan here is to have the Magi find the baby Jesus.

So they don't hesitate. They go into the house and Jesus and Mary are there. Without waiting for an introduction or anything, they drop like rocks and worship the King of Kings, this little baby, Jesus. We've already seen how Herod's response to the news of the Messiah was the wrong one, but why is theirs the right one? Why is it important that these wise men, sages, magi, worship this random child born out in the backwater of Judah? It's important because it's the only response that's appropriate for the news of the Messiah.

The news that the Messiah had come, the realization that heaven had come onto earth, demanded worship. That is the only response appropriate for such news, and these Eastern, Gentile Magi were the ones who understood. Not the semi-Jewish king, not the scribes or the priests or anyone else in Jerusalem rightly responded to this news. Herod knew that the news of the birth of Jesus demanded an act of worship, but all he could muster was a disguise.

Does anyone else wonder what Mary was thinking during this moment? These Gentiles have come into her home and start bowing down to her son. Now she knew the prophecy. She heard the angels. She welcomed the shepherds. But all of that falls into the realm of Jewish history and religion. Where do these Eastern Gentiles come into the picture? Their presence indicates that Jesus was not only the King of the Jews; this King was the King of the world. Jesus came to earth as a Jewish baby, the answer to the prayers of thousands across the decades; however, his life was given for the world. Our friends, the mysterious Magi from the East, recognized that immediately. God could have come to only Jewish shepherds, to the priests in the Temple, to the Jewish families, but he didn't. He came for everyone. He came for you and me.

The realization that Almighty God came to earth in the form of a human baby, as the Messiah and Savior, demands our attention, demands our action, and demands our worship. There is no other response that is appropriate, worthy or justified. We must worship!

For a lot of us, it's easy to get caught up in the chaos of the holiday season. And I know that technically, it's over now. The New Year has started; new events are on the horizon and people won't start looking towards Christmas until at least August. Nevertheless, when we consider what it meant for Christ to come to the earth, to come as the Messiah, bringing heaven to earth, what is our response? Not only that, but are we helping others respond in worship as well? Are we coming to Jesus, bowing before him and giving our gifts as the wise men did so many centuries ago? Or is our response merely the semblance, the charade of worship?

Our Magi friends gave gifts of frankincense, gold, and myrrh. I doubt you have possession of any of those things; if you do, way to go! But you have things to give to God. You have ways to worship him that are unique to you. Allow God to guide you to the place where you can worship Him and offer your gifts in acknowledgment of the great message of his birth, life, death and resurrection.

Thus concludes the tale of the Magi. You may be asking yourself, "Why did I just suffer through one more sermon about Christmas? Now I'm going to be singing 'We Three Kings' for the next eight hours!" Perhaps, but I hope that through this time together you also had an "Epiphany" about your response to the news that the Messiah has come.

13

"THAT LIBERATING WORD"
John 1:1-18

Cody Maynus

The Word became flesh. What a fantastic notion! Savor it! The Word became flesh. Think about it. The Word–Jesus the Christ–became flesh–a human being. Internalize it. The Word–Jesus the Christ, the savior of humanity and the son of God the Creator–became flesh–a human being who experienced hunger and desire. The notion that an omnipotent God–the Creator of the Heavens and the Earth–would come down to this dirty, hell-hole of a world, assume humanity and become one of many of God's creation is either radical or ridiculous.

This definitely radical and perhaps ridiculous notion, my friends, is the central element of Christianity. Two thousand years of ecclesiastical history can be traced back to one event: the Incarnation, the moment when the Creator became the created.

If we were to look at the Incarnation from a non-Christian perspective, we would see something very strange. We would see a potter becoming one of his or her pots. We would see a painter becoming one of his or her paintings, a child becoming one of his or her sandcastles. Why would a Creator God become one of said Creator God's creations? It doesn't make sense, does it? In the person of Jesus Christ, God took on humanity so that God could liberate humanity.

The writer of the Gospel according to John tells us several things about Jesus. Of the many things we are told, we are told that Jesus is life and that this life was humanity's light. Can you imagine the world that Jesus was born into? Jesus was a Jew. He was born into poverty. He was born into a people living under imperial oppression. He was born into a people who had been waiting for a savior–for a light–for hundreds and hundreds of years. Jesus the Christ is the Anointed One, the Messiah, the Savior of these people. He is their light and he comes to set them free from their own darkness.

For those of you who may not celebrate the liturgical calendar in your faith traditions, Christmas comes after the season of Advent–four weeks of waiting, hoping, and praying that the Messiah–the Anointed One, the Savior–would one day come. During Advent, those of us in the liturgical traditions light candles that represent the Light of the World–Jesus the Christ, the Word of God who was made flesh. At the College of St. Benedict, where I'm a Minister of Spirituality and Social Justice, we celebrated Advent with the community of 200 or so Benedictine nuns, professors, and students. Our chapel is absolutely gorgeous with wonderful neo-gothic architecture which leaves the chapel quite dark unless lit by electric lights.

During an evening worship service toward the end of Advent, we turned off all the electric lights in the chapel, leaving only the four pillar candles surrounding the altar lit and providing illumination for the crowd of students, professors, and sisters. As the scripture was read for the evening–this very scripture that I'm preaching on now–a group of nuns and students took small candles, lit them on the altar candles, and moved throughout the congregation sharing light with each person. By the time the lector got to the part in the reading where it says, "A light that shines in the darkness, a light that the darkness has never understood," all of our candles were lit.

The group assembled that evening were very much representative of humanity. We were men and women. We were young and old. We were students and professors. We were of European, Asian, African, and Native descent. We were Christian, we were Jewish, we were Buddhist, we were Agnostic, we were Wiccan. We were rich and we were poor. We were wise and we were foolish. We were future theologians, scientists, authors, teachers, politicians, lawyers, doctors, nuns, criminals. We were future mothers and future fathers. We were the people who will be sitting in your pews one day. We were representative of all facets of humanity, and it was for us that God became a human in the person of Jesus the Christ. The scripture does not say, "the life was the light of Catholics" or "the life was the light of white people." No, the Gospel says that the "life"–Jesus Christ–"was the light of humanity"–of all of humanity. Again, this is a radical notion! It is really radical to think that a magnificent and awe-inspiring God would enter into humanity to save humanity–even the humanity who may not be getting it just right or may not be pretty or may not smell nice or may not be able to recite the Creeds and quote scriptures and solve algorithms or tie shoes or even possess shoes to tie.

It is important for us to examine the conditions of the Incarnation. The Incarnation happens in a specific way during a specific time and place. Logically, the Incarnation could have happened ten or fifteen years ago, in the fanciest of hospitals, with the wealthiest of parents and the salvific results would have been the same. Humanity would have been reconciled to its Creator. Salvation would have occurred. Heaven's gates would have been opened wide. Jesus would still have been the Son of God, the Messiah, the Anointed One, the Savior. Bu it didn't happen ten or fifteen years ago, in a fancy hospital, to two wealthy parents. In fact, it happened 2,000 years ago, in a stinky barn, to a teenage woman and her fiancée. Why? What is the importance of the Incarnation happening under those circumstances?

The early church historian, St. Iranaeus, explains the Incarnation by saying, "The Word of God, Jesus Christ, out of his boundless love, became what we are, that he might make us what he is." Jesus became what we are so that we could become what he is! Ahah! Therein resides the reasoning behind the Incarnation happening in a specific time and place in human history.

If one reads this section of the Gospel with a copy of the Magnificat of Mary–the song that Mary sang after Gabriel announced that she would be pregnant with Jesus–one can see the distinct social message that the Gospel is trying to present. In her song, Mary sings of God lifting up the poor and throwing down the rich. She sings of the oppressed being liberated. Jesus is the example of the oppressed being raised and liberated. It is evident, given the Magnficat and the life of Jesus as shown throughout the Gospels, that God was very purposeful in scheduling and working the events leading to the Incarnation. God selected a poor, unmarried woman to bear the Savior of the World, the Light of the World. God selected a people living on the fringes of society–a people whom the Romans looked upon as weird for their dress, their cuisine, and their religious practices. Jesus connects with those who reside on the fringes of our society. Christ is the immigrant man who works three shifts at the factory in order to put food on the table. Christ is the young woman who is told that she may not preach because of her gender. Christ is the gay man who is told that he may not marry his committed partner merely because of his sexual orientation. Christ is the black seamstress who is told that she may not sit down on a bus merely because of her skin color. Christ is the Buddhist who is trying to make sense of life in a Christian world. Christ is the pacifist who seeks to proclaim a Gospel of nonviolence. This is who Christ is. By the Incarnation, we are made to be like these people. We are made to be the people, the churches, and the communities of Christ. In doing so, we are liberated from the bondages of human darkness. Jesus Christ is the candle that brings light to our dark, cold chapel. Jesus Christ is our Savior. Amen.

14

"WE MUST CLAIM IT FOR OURSELVES"

John 1:1-18

J. Barrett Owen

I pastor a church south of Atlanta. This past Christmas Eve was my first ever Christmas Eve Communion Service. It was quite the memorable service. Our piano player decided not to show up and we ran out of wine during communion. During the service I retold the Christmas story to the children. One of the children had a newborn baby brother. I used the baby brother as an illustration of the size of Jesus and said, "Just as God holds baby Jesus in the palm of God's hand, so too does God hold you and me." The birth of Jesus allows you and me to also be God's babies.

This is one of many reasons why John's prologue is so unique. The narrator doesn't give us the birth account. Instead, the narrator comes right out and tells the reader this Jesus is more than you can imagine. This Jesus is God incarnate walking this earth, wrapping himself in our dust, eating our food, and redeeming us at all times. This Jesus born baby is far more than a baby. He is divinity intersecting with humanity and changing everything.

John's prologue is quite intricate. It's written in an ancient word scramble. If you take thought for thought starting at the beginning and the end and you work your way to the middle then you will see that the prologue carries an impressive consistency. When you do, you arrive at the hinge on which the gospel turns. The central message of the prologue and all of John's gospel is this verse: "But to all who received him, who believed in his name, he gave power to become children of God" (John 1:12). This is the most important message for you to receive and to give others. We are God's children. God enters our world, lives among us to give us love, hope, power, and an opportunity to become God's babies.

As fun as this is to say, the truth of the matter is that we have trouble accepting our identity as children of God. To be a child of God would be to mimic the life of Jesus–right?

When I look out at Christians, especially in the Baptist world, we don't love and serve as well as we would like. We fight denominational wars and cast people away for being different. We draw lines in the sand and vote people in and out. Our churches decide who should be forgiven and who should be damned. We become tribal and introspective and build a callus over anything outside of our worldview. This is not Jesus' gift to us in the prologue. John says that all who call upon the name of the Lord are given power to become children of God. So why do we do it? Why do we fail to acknowledge the holiness of others? Why do we not see everyone as God's beloved?

When I was in college, I was a youth minister at a church outside of Nashville, TN. When I got there they had a pretty routine calendar and a lot of expectations. I quickly learned they had people behind the scenes that got things done; they just needed a face and a communicator. But I was 21 years old and just cocky enough to think I didn't need anyone's help. By the time a year was over, I had successfully ostracized myself from any sort of lay member support. When I look back on it, this memory is truly the biggest learning lesson of my life. The church body loved me, and the youth group actually grew a little in numbers, but I neglected to care for the six adults who poured their heart and soul and time into the youth group. When I left the church to go to seminary, I had one of the adults write me a letter. In that letter she said, "This was supposed to be the happiest year of my life. My daughter was as senior and about to graduate, but your inability to include me made me feel useless and unwelcome. You are a good guy, but you did not do a good job."

I tell you this story because what drove me apart from my adult workers was my inability to care for their belovedness. I neglected to see them as children of God. Even the best of intentions can cause division and hurt. I didn't hate them; I just didn't use them. I excluded and therefore hurt them. I thought I was a big shot, but truthfully I was scared, timid, uncertain, and in desperate need of compliments. I wanted to do it all myself, and I didn't want their help.

I reflected on this memory for some time after I left. I realize now that what you can't see in yourself, you will never be able to see in others. My inability to see myself as a child of God made it too difficult to recognize the belovedness of my youth workers.

In his book, *The Inner Voice of Love*, Henri Nouwen says, "Your true identity is as a child of God. This is the identity you have to accept. Once you have claimed it and settled in it, you can live in a world that gives you much joy as well as pain. The temptation to disconnect from that deep place in you where God dwells and to let yourself be drowned in the praise or blame of the world always remains. Gradually, though, you will begin feeling more connected and become more fully who you truly are–a child of God. There lies your real freedom."[1]

Being a child of God is what allows you to take love, peace, justice, righteousness and forgiveness to all people that you meet. It allows you not to judge. Your identity is now in Christ. But on an individual level we experience too much hurt and sorrow to be any different than who we have always been. The struggles of life create a callus. Never feeling like we have enough and always feeling inferior to those around us doesn't make us want to love and forgive. People's pain, sorrow and despair are too great to just cast it aside and say, "You're forgiven." We have our own pain and our own baggage. We have our own sensual and sexual need to be loved and to be served. So as long as we can't see ourselves as a child of God, we will fail to recognize these gifts in others. The real truth is that people are angry. They are angry at God and angry at the church. Why should we forgive others when no one forgives us? Why should I continue to love when every time I do my heart is broken?

I almost got married once. It was back in college. Well, we talked about getting married once. We built our lives around one another to where every decision and action included the other person. Oh, we were in love. She was my world. Well, we thought we were. But as the relationship continued she fell further and further out of love with me. I tried to salvage the relationship but to no avail. I wasn't the strong white knight that she thought I would be. And the day we broke up, she looked at me and said, "I just thought you were the one." Let me tell you, that is hard to hear.

I quickly learned that when we meet people who touch our inner selves, the inner part of who we are, they carry a deep and impactful power over us, so much so that when they decide to leave us high

---

[1]Henri Nouwen, *The Inner Voice of Love: A Journey through Anguish to Freedom* (New York: Doubleday, 1996), 70-71.

and dry it leaves an overwhelmingly sharp anguish. But this pain of losing someone so dear actually served as helpful reminder to me that I was trying to let someone fill a very sacred role, a role that belongs to God. At the core of who we are, the inner most part of ourselves, we must claim to be children of God.

Only God can dwell in your most sacred space and offer you a sense of safety. Only God can cradle you in God's arms to make you feel safe. Only God can safely hold you in God's hands and whisper in your soul that you are a true blessing and beautiful child of God. Because God's love tills the soil of your broken heart and nurtures it back to health.

Why is this important? Because in this very room sit current and future preachers and future leaders for the Kingdom of God; because it is as a child of God that you are sent out into this world. In this room are revolutionaries, pastors in the truest sense of the word, prophets, movers and shakers, and priests. If you do not claim your identity as a child of God how will anyone see it in themselves through you? You are the mouthpieces of God and you must carry love not anguish in your heart. People are going to see hope through you. People are going to want to grow because of your willingness to grow. People are going to be willing to forgive because of your leadership to do so. People are going to see their true selves as children of God because you do too.

However, what you don't see in yourself, you won't see in others. You must claim your identity as a child of God so others can too. You have been called out by God to lead. You must accept the challenge to love yourself and the God who calls you blessed. It's what God is calling you to do.

15

"WE STILL PREPARE THE WAY"
Mark 1:1-8

Steve Rhodes

When I was in college, I worked as a McDonald's manager. I worked full time and went to school full time. The McDonald's I managed was a franchise, and a couple of times a year we would have a corporate audit. There was a specific person who worked for corporate who would come in and spend two days auditing our store. They would check the paper work, but mostly they would check us for cleanliness and service times. They would time us at the drive through, the grill, the front counter and everywhere else. Looking bad on this audit would mean more audits and other consequences for the franchise. These audits had scheduled dates, and because they were so important we worked extra hard getting ready. The days and weeks prior to the audit were filled with extra hours and extra staff to clean the store and prepare. Many times I came in extra early the day of the audit and the closing crew from the previous night was still at the store cleaning. We cleaned under the counter, under the grill, and under everywhere else. We had to prepare the store for the coming of the corporate people. We had to be ready.

You know, there are biblical parallels to this story. In the passage we are looking at, we see the text talk about John preparing the way for Jesus. I would like to take a few moments and talk about how John prepared the way for Jesus and also how we still prepare for his coming. How do we prepare the way for Jesus' coming today?

We notice that Mark opens his gospel with three Old Testament quotations. The first of these quotations is from Malachi 3:1 and the second is from Isaiah 40:3. There is also a quotation from Exodus 23:20. As you read this you may notice that Mark says, "Isaiah the prophet" and then quotes Malachi. It would be very easy to make a big deal about this, but it really is not a big deal. This was common. The New Testament writers knew the Old Testament so well that many times they would mention several quotations at once.

They often expected their readers or listeners to also know the Old Testament well.

I find the quotation in Isaiah 40:3 particularly interesting. In the context it says: "make straight in the desert a Highway for our God." It makes it sound like this messenger will symbolically be clearing a highway. This messenger will be getting rid of the trees and stumps and making a type of highway for a king. I think that is what John the Baptist did in a symbolic way. He prepared the way of the Lord in people's hearts. He did this by what follows in the rest of the text. An example of this in our time is when the President of the United States comes to a town and the Secret Service come beforehand to make sure the location is safe. They prepare the way for the President. We also prepared the way for corporate to come and audit McDonald's. John the Baptist did this symbolically in the people's hearts.

In verse four, following these quotations, Mark starts talking about John the Baptist. We, the readers, don't yet know anything about John the Baptist. But now Mark introduces him. I think it is very interesting that Mark introduces him in this way. John follows the Old Testament quotations about this messenger who will prepare the way of the Lord. I think that Mark is trying to tell the reader that John was that messenger. John was sent to prepare the way of the Lord. Mark gave those two Old Testament quotations to give a little more credibility to John. Isaiah was known as the greatest Old Testament prophet. Inserting his name probably helped build the case for John the Baptist as this messenger. If John is the messenger, that means the messenger has come. If the messenger has come, that means Mark can establish that the Messiah can come.

Then verse four gives some more ideas of how John prepared the way of the Lord. John prepared the way of the Lord by baptizing. But John was not baptizing in the Temple or another religious place. Mark tells us he was baptizing in the wilderness. Furthermore, John did not only baptize, he proclaimed repentance for the forgiveness of sins. John's baptism was a baptism of repentance.

That leads us into verse five which talks more about this baptism. It notes that all the country of Judea and Jerusalem were being baptized. I think this is a little hyperbole at work. I really don't believe that all the country was being baptized. But I do think that a lot of the people were. Even those not getting baptized were probably coming out to see what was going on. Matthew tells us the Pharisees were coming out. John was making quite an impact and rightfully so, because John was preparing the way for the Lord.

Verse five continues to clue us in to how John prepared the way of the Lord. He prepared the way by baptizing them in the Jordan River. They were also confessing their sins. That struck me. John was not simply baptizing for its own sake. John was calling the people to repentance and confession. We also must do this. We cannot take sin out of the message of the Gospel. In Acts 2:38 Peter had just gotten finished with his Pentecost sermon and they asked how they could be saved. He said, "Repent and be baptized in the name of Jesus." We must also call people to repentance and confession.

Then we come to verse six. I think it might be easy to come to this verse and think, "Why does it matter? Why does it matter how John was dressed?" Well it does matter. It matters because I think Mark was trying to establish John as a prophet. Jesus said that John was among the greatest of the prophets. For Mark's Jewish readers, they may have recognized this type of dress as comparable to that worn by Elijah. But verse seven continues to tell us how John prepared the way of the Lord. John was preaching, and his words pointed to Jesus. He said that someone is coming after him. Furthermore, John said that the one who comes after him is mightier than him. Isn't that humble? I find this very humble. Here John has all these people coming out to him yet he acknowledges that Jesus will be mightier than him. John could have stolen the thunder. He didn't have to point to Jesus, yet he did. John said that he is not worthy to unstrap this person's sandals. Only slaves would wash feet and unstrap sandals. So John is saying that he is not worthy to be Jesus' slave. Very humble! This reminds me of John 3:30 in which the gospel writer said that Christ must increase and he must decrease. John recognized his place in God's plan.

Finally, in verse eight, John contrasts the way he is baptizing and the way Jesus will baptize. Jesus will baptize with the Holy Spirit. In the Old Testament, only God could give the Holy Spirit. So John is ascribing divinity to Jesus! Also, Mark strategically places this as the eighth verse in his gospel. In the very beginning of Mark's gospel, he is saying that Jesus is Lord! John prepared the way for Jesus' first coming.

We must preach the Gospel as John did. We must do this in humility. There is no other way to introduce Jesus but in humility.

He is God! That means we preach the gospel of Jesus, not the gospel of Steve, the gospel of self, or the gospel of prosperity and success. We must preach the gospel of Jesus Christ. We must recognize that Jesus is greater than us. We must lead people to Jesus. That means we must recognize our place in God's plan.

Remember the Secret service preparing the way for the President? It is quite easy to figure out that the person or people preparing the way for the President are not the important people. However, they do have an important purpose. We prepared the way for the corporate representative at McDonald's, but none of us were that important person. Our salaries made it quite clear that we were not the important person. They were. Plus they had company cars. We need to remember the distinction between the person or people preparing the way and the important person. John did.

I once heard a preacher talk about a time when he was an associate pastor. This preacher was just starting out in the ministry. He said that his job as associate pastor was to support the senior pastor's vision. His job was to make the senior pastor look better. Likewise, we must support Jesus' vision as John did. We must point to Jesus. We must preach that people confess their sins and be baptized into Jesus. We must do this because we still prepare the way for Jesus' coming.

I told you about those corporate audits. In five years as a manager, I worked many of those audits. But after a few years corporate changed the rules of the audits. They made it clear that they would come for a two day announced visit. The first two days they came, we knew they were coming. Then after that corporate visit, they would come within a month and do an audit that would be unannounced. We had very little idea when they were coming. This was more difficult because we had to be ready all the time.

John the Baptist prepared the way for Jesus' first coming. We must prepare the way for his second coming. Like the unannounced visit of corporate to McDonald's, Jesus will come unannounced. He will come like a thief in the night, so we must prepare the way. We do this by preaching the gospel. We still prepare the way for Jesus' coming!

16

"THE POWER OF ONE"
Isaiah 9:1-5

Nicholas Richards

We find ourselves at the end of a war. Now this is not the war you might be thinking about. This is not the war within your marriage or over your mortgage. It is not the war over your faith or your finances. No, we stand on the heels of a battle between Israel and Assyria. Israel, the fledging nation-state of the Near East and Assyria, the dominant colonial empire. The preceding chapter said Israel would suffer under Assyria because of their own sins of idolatry. We know Israel often struggled with the issue of idolatry, always wanting to serve two deities. Yes, Israel wanted to serve the God of their liberation, but they also wanted to serve the Gods of Sinai, those they worshipped when everything seemed to be going alright.

Before you are too critical of Israel, isn't it true that many of us do the same thing? We have the same problem. We want to serve two gods. There is a God we serve when we need something and our midnights won't seem to end. There is a God we serve when the doctor gives us bad news or when we need a job. Yet when the dust settles, when God has answered our prayers, we then make all sorts of new Gods. We make Gods out of our leaders, our pride, our money, and our minds. Like Israel we suffer because the Gods we have made cannot stand up against the God who made us.

So Israel is suffering defeat after defeat, and the northern territory of Judah is almost fully occupied by Assyria. The mood has shifted, and the people have fallen into what the text describes as distress. The tolls of war have destroyed both their physical and spiritual foundations. This normalcy of pain and destruction affected Israel greatly; the people could see only gloom and despair. How sad that we can be so influenced by the frequency and persistence of trouble.

This is the context of our text, dealing with a people distraught and devastated, hopeless and unhopeful. Yet in the midst of all of this, there is still a word from God. God says there shall be no more gloom for those in distress. How strange that our scenery is not one of glistening skies or chirping birds, not one of prosperity or wealth, but one of pain and suffering and despair. If the truth be told, many of us are in some wars right now. Many of us are being attacked on all fronts, and it seems like we are about to lose. Yet like Israel, God wants you to know there is a word for you in the midst of your suffering.

The strangeness of this text is not limited to the scenery, but also includes the one who comes to the scene. The prophet Isaiah, son of Amoz, a trained and educated aristocrat, is called to speak out against a war. Despite his pedigree, God calls him in the context of war. Isaiah is wealthy and secure. He did not suffer in the same way the others suffered, yet he is called to speak out against a war that did not directly affect him. The truth is when you are a prophet, you will have to speak out against some wars that don't directly affect you. You will have to speak out against wants of racism and homophobia, against wars of injustice and poverty, against wars in Iraq and Kentucky. But it seems like so many of those who should be speaking are silent. Could it be we are more concerned about preserving our pedigree than being prophets who preach?

So Isaiah begins this word by saying there will be no more gloom for those who are in distress. We know Isaiah is not ignorant to the reality of war, yet he seems to almost dismiss its influence with an ease only God could assure. Isaiah dismisses the gloom. He does not say the war will end, nor does he say the Assyrians will flee. He says the gloom will cease. Notice the word of God doesn't remove the condition, rather it changes the perspective. There are many people who are looking for God to change their condition without changing their perspective. How you think controls what you do, and what you do controls how you live. Therefore, before God can change your life, he needs to change your mind, and too many of us are asking for things our perspectives can't handle.

So God uses one person to change the perspective of a nation. Isn't it interesting that no matter how congested our worlds may be, change is often started by just one person? The mood is shifted by one, gloom is brightened by one, and hope is restored by one. Sometimes before there can be a communal revolution, there must be an individual revolution. It's like the first time you fall in love and that one person has complete control of you. You start doing things and going places all because of this one person. So my brothers and sisters, we ought never to forget the power of one.

I'm sure as Isaiah began to speak, a whole bunch of people thought he was crazy. What's he talking about? No more gloom? Doesn't he know Judah has been captured? Doesn't he know we are the laughing stock of the region, that we've lost battle after battle? The people of Israel were used to prophets who described the scenery, but Isaiah was sent to provide an alternative. As preachers, we have to learn to do more than just describe the scenery, we have to learn to be like prophets and provide an alternative. As you do this, you may be the only one who is saying anything different, but continue to speak, remembering the lyrics of the great hymn, "a charge to keep I have, a God to glorify…to serve this present age, my calling to fulfill."

Our world is filled with people who are afraid of being themselves. In our thirst for recognition and acceptance, we try to be like everyone else, yet the text reminds us that God is still interested in using just one. No matter who you are or where you find yourself, God wants to use you just as you are. God wants to use one just like you to preach about the One. God wants to use one to tell about the One who is the rose of Sharon and the fairest of ten thousand. Today God wants to know, will you be the one? Through Jesus Christ our Lord. Amen

17

"THE CONTINUATION OF THE GOOD NEWS"

Mark 1:1-8

Adam Quine

Good news everyone!

This is the greeting Professor Hubert J. Farnsworth, "mad scientist," uses to greet his staff in the cartoon show *Futurama.* Farnsworth, a frail, 160 year old man, is the founder of the futuristic package delivery company Planet Express. They ship basically anything and everything all across the galaxy around the year 3000. In each episode, we see the staff set sail on adventures which get them into quite a bit of trouble and plenty of predicaments, usually leaving one of their employees in a tight spot. Nonetheless, each episode the staff is greeted by the professor with, "Good news everyone!" He then tells them which wacky planet or dangerous delivery they are off too next. I guess it is his ironic greeting that makes this sister show of *The Simpsons* so funny.

I love this show, and it is no wonder I connected Professor Farnsworth's greeting to the one made by the writer of Mark–"The beginning of the good news of Jesus Christ, the Son of God" (Mark 1:1). If that phrase didn't make the connection for me, then it would be the odd character who ushers in this good news, the man who is out in the wilderness with his frizzy hair, his outdated camel skin parka, his tired leather belt, and his hands which are covered in dirt.

Compared to the other Gospels, Mark leaves little room for things to get in the way. No stories about how John and Jesus came to be, how they are related, and how John leaped and Jesus cried. Instead, Mark welcomes the reader with, "Good news everyone!" and immediately we are thrown into the good and the bad that come with Christ's ministry.

Just as quickly as the Planet Express space ship takes off, Mark launches quickly and we meet John in the wilderness crying out about how one who is greater than he is soon to come. John goes on to say, "I am not worthy to stoop down and untie the thong of his sandals. I have baptized you with water; but he will baptize you with the Holy Spirit" (Mark 1:7*b*-8). Here John leaves it up in the air for us to discover just who this Jesus is and what he will do. A secret epiphany if you will.

Then it happens. Jesus comes, ready to make his identity known in the waters where God claims him as God's beloved. Jesus' baptism states how his identity lies not in Rome's kingdom or under Caesar, but to God's kingdom which is not of this world. Each of these radical statements occurs in the prologue of Mark's gospel.

This good news is interesting and, to be honest, nothing like what they or we expected The good news Jesus offers comes with an urgency to take note of our lives and rearrange them in the hope we will become good news to others. It happens to different people Jesus encounters in his ministry. There are those Jesus heals and encourages to stop sinning. There is Jesus' immediate family whom he denounces and explains how those who do the will of God are his family. On the surface this looks nothing like good news; however, in order for something to be good there has to be something bad, right?

What then is this bad news? There isn't much bad news that came with Jesus, is there?

To understand this irony of good news, let's consider the disciples. It starts at the beginning with the choices they had to make: leave everything, follow him, risk your life, give up your job, give up your comfortable lifestyle, and maybe be put to death. If that wasn't bad enough, they're told to take very little on their journeys and to not expect warm welcomes and open arms. The disciples rarely "got it." They got upset when they saw someone else doing things in Jesus' name? They argued over who was the greatest among them. However, in spite of their failings, they set us up to see and receive the good news.

How easy it is for us to get caught up on how bad things are. It seems as if we are always surrounded by bad, violent, greedy, uncertain, and questionable news. We say that any news is good news, yet we don't really want bad news. But regardless of what we want, news will always find its way to us, and sometimes it is the worst of news. War over here...hate crime over there...violence here... natural disaster there. Or what about the false news we believe about ourselves. Bad news.

However, God in Christ offers us good news–news that proclaims we are loved, cherished, forgiven, and not alone. This is what is extraordinary about the Gospel. We may have lived a scandalous life, yet somehow we come out made new.

All of us carry around baggage, things that bring us down and are heavy and burdensome. Some of those things linger, that death, that affair, that binge, that depression. All too often, the bad news drowns out the good news that with God all things are possible. This news of how we are loved comes to us in our baptism which calls us into public ministry. Through Jesus' baptism we are reminded of our identity as God's children.

Friends, the annual observance of the liturgical seasons of Advent, Christmas and Epiphany invites us to begin expecting the good news of God. It was in Christ's baptism that God's faithfulness was displayed and God's love made known and available to us. Whether it happens early in life or later on, good news comes to us in the water of God's grace, the water that calls us to newness of life. Good news has come to us. In turn, we must preach good news to the world.

St. Francis of Assisi once said, "There is no use walking anywhere to preach unless our walking is our preaching." Gandhi expressed a similar sentiment when he said, "Be the change you wish to see in the world." The good news is that we are included in God's grace and love, but the good news does not stop only with us as individuals. Indeed, it overflows onto all people, uniting us in Christ through the saving waters of baptism. In Christ there are no barriers of race, gender, status, or age. We are sealed in God's inclusive love.

May we, in our baptismal identities, find the good news in our lives and hold on to it. In the midst of chaos, may we look for the good news coming to us in a form of a small break, some much needed rest, or an unexpected sense of peace. In our attempts to filter out bad news, let us remember good news has come, good news is here, and good news will come to us again. May we join with the hopes of the prophets and bring justice and peace to those who do not have it. As we reprioritize our lives and set course down the Jesus way, may we demonstrate good news by practicing radical hospitality and extravagant generosity, for the kingdom of God is at hand. Continue to preach the love of God through Jesus Christ, and in this season of Epiphany may your life declare…

Good news everyone!

Life & Ministry

18

"A TALE OF TWO SISTERS"
Luke 10:38-42

Katie Anderson

This is a tale of two sisters. In their story we see very distinct ways of attending to the work of God. This is the story of Martha, the "busy bee," and Mary, who some would label, "the lazy bum." Throughout the course of my life, this has been one of my very favorite Bible stories. In this story I have always identified more with Martha. I'm a doer. Part of the reason I found my place, the reason many of us find our place, in service to God's church is because I like "doing" God's work.

I'm a full-time minister. I'm a full-time student. I'm a wife and a mother of two adorable little girls, Georgia (4) and Shelby (2). My entire life I have been one of those people who runs through everything, going from this to that, racing from here to there. I love the rush of getting things done. I love hearing "job well done" when someone smiles at me; the thrill of getting it done well. I like to see all that I can accomplish within a day's time. At the end of the day, I plop myself down into my bed, lay my aching neck across my favorite pillow, the tension from the day's journey pulsating through my shoulders, and I say to myself, "I made it. Thank you, God. I made it through one more day."

So you see how I can relate to Martha in this story of two sisters. She is running around trying to prepare the most wonderful, delicious, warm meal for Jesus. She knows him. We know that Jesus breathes life into her brother after he has died in order to answer the need of her broken heart and to reveal God's glory. We know that she trusts him to be a hopeful answer to her need. She knows him as Savior and friend. And Martha, of course, wants everything to be wonderful for his meal there. She is checking the fire and turning the bread. She is where women of this time were supposed to be. Martha is fulfilling the expected actions that would offer her home most graciously to a guest, especially an honored guest. She is serving, with all the strength and energy she has in her. Troubles arise when she looks at her sister, the one who is also expected and socially mandated to help welcome this guest.

Where is her sister? She is sitting at the feet of Jesus, a place usually reserved only for the disciples. It was almost unheard of for a woman to be the student of a rabbi. It was unimaginable that Mary chose to be present alongside the chosen disciples of the Son of God. Is this what bothered Martha so much? Or was it that she felt abandoned by the only person she counted on to offer support in her life's work?

We can relate to this feeling. Most of us here are ministers, ministers in training, or active leaders in our churches. We are not members of the congregation who have yet to announce Jesus Christ as Lord. We know the responsibility that comes with our profession, and we do what we can to participate with the gifts we have been given. We have been called to his service, and we know what it is to be a "doer" in the midst of church life.

Each of us has lived in those moments of being frazzled in our doing. We have experienced those moments at the end of the day when we're still there after the lights throughout the building have been turned out. We're still there when everyone else has said they are tired and have gathered their things and made their way home. We're still on call when someone becomes gravely ill in the middle of our vacation, when a crisis arises with a member of the church. We know what it is to cut a family outing short when a member of our congregation dies. We can understand the frustration because all who do the work of God experience it sometime or another. We are meeting the expectations set for us. We took on this yolk in faithfulness to our God who made us to do this work. We knew it would be difficult. We knew it would be tiresome and sometimes heartbreaking, but we answered our call. We answered the call because it is our means of glorifying the God we love. We work just as Martha worked to perform the duties of the hostess when a crowd of believers and Jesus came into her home. This was the good and faithful service that was required of her. It was a good thing, a beautiful offering.

When Martha asks Jesus, "Lord, do you not care that my sister has left me to do all the work by myself?" (Luke 10:40*b*), we see that here service has lost its center! We hear resentment in her question. We see that she feels burdened by caring for the guests alone. It's too much to bear, making a hospitable meal for all of these guests, serving and preparing for everyone. Who would want to do this alone? Sometimes it can seem overwhelming to those of us who have chosen to do the work of God in this world.

This world carries within it a lot of darkness; we all know this truth. We know that despite our best efforts and our endless sacrifices of time, resources, and strength, the need is never going to be fully met until the day of Christ Jesus. It is easy to become lost in the hard work that comes with serving a congregation or community. It is easy to look at others around us and become frustrated because we think they are being lazy. It is easy to get angry because we don't feel they make half the difference they could. It is easy to feel frustrated as we see people cycle in and out of crisis and dysfunction. We should know that the easy way is not the best way. It is when this type of resentment wells up in me that I realize I have missed something very important in God's message. It is when I judge others so harshly that I realize I haven't judged the woman in the mirror very well. When we allow our fatigue and our weary souls to be overwhelmed by the world's darkness, we lose the center of our Christian identity.

We serve because God calls us to serve. We minister because God calls us to minister. We preach because God calls us to proclaim. When we find ourselves taking on anger or frustration that would distance us from God's people, we know that the service in which we are engaging is no longer of God. It may have begun that way, but somewhere the entanglement of our identity and the world's expectations have clouded our vision. When we condemn brothers and sisters, even if only in our thoughts, we place ourselves on a pedestal of judgment that belongs only to God. We need to be careful of pedestals. My daddy always told me to be wary of them because it is hard to balance on one for too long time.

When Martha says to Jesus, "Make her get up and help me," she speaks volumes about her concept of who Jesus has come to be in her mind. She was working and working, but did she want to make everything nice because of her love for Jesus or because of her feeling of obligation to meet the expectation of this guest in her home? She has this idea of what it should be like to welcome and feed the Son of God. She has a preconceived expectation of what Jesus deserves, and she doesn't want to be solely responsible for that. Who would?

Jesus is not condemning her person, but he is offering a holy breath of wisdom. "Martha, Martha..." I see him shaking his head with loving knowledge of her need in his eyes. "You are worried and distracted by many things; there is need of only one thing" (Luke 10:41-42*a*). She had worked so diligently to make everything the way she thought it should be that she didn't slow down to hear what Jesus was teaching. She didn't remember who he was. In this type of desperate, hurried action, the peace of God is seldom found. When we are feverishly running through each moment of the day doing all we can do, we don't have time to reflect on our place in the journey of our life. We don't take time to be the precious child of God. We don't claim the time intended to maintain a deep relationship of love. We cannot commune with the Spirit if all we can find within us is one 'to do list' after another. We get so caught up in the activity of answering our call that we cease to hear his whisper in our ears.

Please don't hear me wrongly. I believe that faith without works is dead. I believe that our love and honor of God should invoke an active, passionate response. It is necessary to keep in careful balance the amount of attention we give to the care of others and the care we give to ourselves. Jesus says "there is need of only one thing" (Luke 10:42*a*). That "one thing" is left for us to define. We each name it in our own lives and our faith.

Jesus says, "Mary has chosen the better part, which will not be taken away from her" (Luke 10:42*b*). On this occasion, Mary chose to sit and absorb the words that Jesus had to offer. She chose to sit alongside the disciples where some would say she didn't belong. Mary didn't choose to sit there because she didn't respect Jesus. She didn't choose to leave Martha to do all of the work because she didn't care for her. Mary simply chose to allow herself to be in awe of this man, this incarnation of God. She sought what she needed, what her faith needed. Adoration held her in the grips of every word Jesus was speaking.

In the story of these two women we see a contrast and quandary that still exist in communities of faith today. The worker, Martha, is tired. She is a righteous, devout woman, answering the call of hospitality. She is anxious. She is doing all she knows to do for Jesus. She is working with all the strength she has to offer, but in her hurry and her effort she becomes a little lost. She becomes lost just as we do when we lose sight of why we work. It is ironic to think that in answering a call of God there may be moments in which that service hinders us from our walk in the Holy Spirit. God does not intend for us to be blind slaves that work and work until we have nothing left to offer. God does not expect that the righteous should sacrifice time to receive peace, tranquility, and strength granted through prayer and rest.

Last week, a very hectic one for me, I was working feverishly on my laptop at the kitchen table. I was distracted from my seminary, paper-writing, hermeneutic-dissecting trance by the giggles of tiny voices. I took a minute to sit and watch my husband playing with our girls. They were laughing and having a great time. They were consumed not by the world around them or the work yet to be done, but by their love and adoration for one another. I had to smile with a slight sting of tears in my eyes. I had taken for granted all that God had given me. I had taken for granted my place in the rolling laughter. I had taken for granted my part in this circle of adoration. What's more, I had done the same thing in my relationship with God. I was lost in the demands of my work, my hunger for success, and my education.

In the midst of the shuffle, when you can't hear past the "to do" lists and the needs of those to whom you minister, take a moment and breathe in the breath of life. Close your eyes. Focus in on the face of Jesus. On your knees, even when the world is calling, find yourself at the feet of Jesus and seek the better part, your place in the intentional, reciprocal love of God. A love that will never be taken from you.

19

"WHO DO YOU SAY I AM?"
Mark 8:27-38

Katie Beachy

Now me preaching, people would just say, "Wow, why are you preaching?" Because if you know me, my whole life I have been struggling with faith and who is Jesus. I figured that it was just going to church and sitting in pews and giving money. If you do that then you'll be eternal; Jesus will be in your life and you will have eternal life and be happy. But that's not what it is. For me, my whole life, I didn't believe in Jesus. I thought church was the stupidest idea. Of course my parents would make me go to church in the morning and at night. Every single year, year after year, I would say "Youth group? I'm not going to youth group next year mom and dad! I hate it! It's so stupid!" Yet I would always go because my youth minister, Dave Seely, would want me there. I'm seen as a leader. Everybody knows me, blah blah blah. So I always went. But then about three or four years ago, during the "We Believe" sermon series at my church, I actually questioned my faith. I was getting in trouble at home, I didn't have the best of grades, and I was a very troubled kid. And it's because I never had faith. Faith in my family is a great thing, but during the "We Believe" series, I finally listened to the sermon and finally tried to believe what I needed to believe. So I met with my pastor, David, and told him, "I don't believe in Jesus. How am I supposed to know who he is? Where do I find him? How am I supposed to see?" So over the next couple of years, I listened to the sermons, I became more involved in the church, and I actually looked for God and for Jesus. And that happened for me during the summer when I participated in going on all the youth mission trips. We just went on our sixth one this year. Mission trips to me mean everything. We go to Appalachia and stay there for a week to help out the community. This year we built three porches from scratch, and we still didn't have anything to do at the end of the week because we accomplished it within two days.

For me, the main question is who is Jesus? Who is he? Everyone asks that question. Everybody, no matter who you are. Now there are two examples I can think of that relate to this. In Mark 4 there's a story about Jesus going out onto the sea with some of his followers, and while on the sea there's a huge storm that comes and the water floods the boat. All of the followers are scared to death, but Jesus being a chill guy, is sleeping in the stern while his followers are freaking out. They all go to Jesus and wake him up asking him, "Are you not scared? Are you not scared of perishing?" Jesus looks at them and he says, "Do you not have faith?" So he calls out to the wind and to the storm and rebukes them. He calms the sea and the storm goes away. His followers are puzzled, and they look at each other and ask, "Who is this guy? Who is this man that calms the sea? Who is he?"

The other story I like is about four friends who have a friend that's paralyzed. Jesus is teaching in a house and everyone crowds inside to see him. These four friends want to take their paralyzed friend to him but they can't. So they go up to the roof, and they make a hole in the roof. Then they take their paralyzed friend and lower him down into the hole to where Jesus is. Jesus reaches out to him and heals him. Everyone is so amazed and puzzled, "Who is this guy? Who is he that heals?" That's my question! Who is he? How do we know who he is?

In this passage that same question is answered. But who asks it? Jesus! Jesus asks the same question, who am I? So Peter answers him, "You are the Messiah." The Messiah! Now to me that doesn't mean much, just another Bible word for Jesus. But Jesus explains how he is the Messiah. He's going to go suffer, he's going to die, die for us. Peter automatically rejects that and says to Jesus "No, no, no! You're not going to go do this! You don't have to do this!" But Jesus is a servant. He does not want the riches and power. He does not want the fame of being the one who heals. He wants to be like me. He wants to be like you. He wants to be a servant. He then starts teaching his followers about being a servant. In verse 34 he says, "If any want to become my followers, let them deny themselves and take up their cross and follow me." Deny self? What does that mean? Well to deny self means that you throw away all your humanly possessions. You don't need a cell phone, you don't need a computer, you don't need your car. Instead, what you need is a heart; you need the mind and the soul. You need that to go out and to serve the community. Denying self, you don't need the fame and the glory. You need to be Jesus' servant. Jesus is exactly that, Jesus is a servant.

Now my mission trips have shown me that. Mission trips are one of those great things; you go out and serve the Appalachian people. You see the suffering; you feel the pain that they're going through. They don't have the money, they don't have the nice house, and they don't have any of that stuff. But they're still happy, they still have hope, and they go to work every day. To many that doesn't mean anything, but to me that means a lot. See them suffer like that, and I'm not suffering like that? Mission trips make you appreciate the things you have. The Appalachian people, they don't have the things we have. But we don't need those things to be happy.

Deny yourself is something that we all need to learn. It's not something that we just have. You have to learn to give away your life. Giving away life means so much to people, and it's something we should do, we're called to do. Now taking up a cross is hard to do. Jesus takes up the cross; he takes it up for me, for you, for the people who are suffering. He goes and dies for us. Now we teenagers don't want to take up the cross. We don't want to die for people. It's all about us, me, I don't want to go die. I don't want to go suffer. I want the money, I want that car, I want to go live the college life and go party every day. I don't want to do any of that "godly" stuff, but that's what we're taught to do. That's what we have to do in order to have Jesus in our life. Taking up the cross is something we can each do; it's just a matter of us putting it into action. It's a matter of me going on mission trip. It's a matter of you going and seeing someone in the hospital. It's a matter of you going to church and helping out. It's not just about giving money to the church. That's great, but it's not enough. It will never be enough. Your purpose is to be a servant. Your purpose is to follow Jesus. In order to follow Jesus you have to be a servant. You have to be able to give up your life and go help somebody shovel the snow out of their driveway. You have to be able to take somebody hot chocolate. You have to be able to give up your soul.

Jesus is finally in my life now. Even though I still don't know exactly who he is, he's still there. I have grown up so much the past couple of years. I have grown into loving Jesus. Now my friends who I hang out with, they're not so much. They say, "You're crazy for doing this. Why do you help out at church? Church is stupid." It's not. My life has gotten so much better now that I have accepted Jesus. And I have become a servant for him. We all need to become servants, servants to the Lord.

The big surprise is when Jesus says, "You give your life away, you get it back." If you go out and serve, you get satisfaction. You get the satisfaction of seeing other people happy; you get the satisfaction of knowing that you're making the world a better place. It's not about what you have in life. It's not about the clothes, and it's not about the labels. It's all about Jesus.

20

"THE GOSPEL OF APARTMENT #22C"

Micah 6:6-8

Mary Alice Birdwhistell

As the Children's Minister at Calvary Baptist Church in Waco, Texas, I had spent the entire morning at our church's Children's Christmas Party in a room full of excited children who were all on sugar-highs from the Christmas cookies and sweets they had all eaten. We played games, made crafts, sang songs, and even read the Christmas story from the Gospel of Luke. It was such a fun morning; nothing like the laughter and singing of little children puts me in the Christmas spirit!

After the party, I took two children home, Sam and Devon. Well, actually we went to McDonald's first, because I didn't know if these two boys would have any food at home. They stuffed their faces with French fries and cheeseburgers and played games in the kids' play center until they were completed exhausted. Sam and Devon live in a public housing unit just a few blocks away from our church, the Brookside Apartment Complex. As we were driving back to their apartment, I asked the boys what they were asking Santa Claus to bring them for Christmas. They said, "Miss Mary Alice, do you believe in Santa?" I paused. "We've never gotten anything from Santa, so we don't know if he's real...but what we really want are bicycles!" I asked if they had Christmas tree, but they said no. I asked if they had any Christmas decorations at their house, and they said, "No, Miss Mary Alice...we don't have anything like that."

When I walked back with Sam and Devon to their apartment, #22C, their dispositions completely changed. Two little boys who had been so excited all morning were now quiet with empty expressions on their faces. Their mom was nowhere to be found when they got back to their apartment. She didn't know who I was, that I had taken her children to church that morning, or that I was bringing them home. And the one room I saw of their apartment was completely empty: dirty tile floor, white walls, and only a small book shelf in the corner of the room. I told the boys I'd had such a great day with them and that I would look forward to seeing them again at church the next day, and they gave me tight hugs goodbye.

I spent the rest of the day literally sick to my stomach over what I had seen. My Christmases as a child involved making Christmas cookies, decorating the Christmas tree, not sleeping a wink on Christmas Eve, and waking up with a gush of excitement on Christmas morning to open presents with my family. Somehow, I knew that Sam and Devon wouldn't get much of that. How was I supposed to enjoy Christmas when I knew that Sam and Devon probably wouldn't? I questioned how God could let these little boys live in such an environment. I thought to myself, doesn't God care about them at all?

Then I realized, perhaps this is exactly how God wants me to feel. God wants me to be disgusted with injustice. God wants my stomach to turn when I think about children living in poverty. Perhaps what would make God even angrier would be if I were completely apathetic toward children like Sam and Devon, if I'd left their apartment that day indifferent toward their circumstances, or if I didn't feel compelled to do something to help. That led me to wonder if God is ever disgusted with us, his church, over our lack of involvement in situations like these. Sam and Devon live in Waco in one of the poorest zip codes in Texas. However, they also live in a city that claims to have more churches per capita than almost any other city in the United States. Doesn't that seem like an oxymoron, for a city with so many churches to also have such a high poverty rate?

A recent poll released by the *New York Times* revealed the most religious states in America.[1] Mississippi was found to have the most religious population of all. Ninety-one percent of Mississippians said they believed in God with absolute certainty, and seventy-seven percent of Mississippians said they prayed at least once a day. Sadly, Mississippi is also known as the state with the lowest per capita income in the United States.

Do you think God is heartbroken by these statistics? Are we as the church truly being the hands and feet of Jesus to those who are

[1]Catherine Rampell, "The Godless States of America," *The New York Times,* 23 Dec. 2009.

in need? Are we loving and serving people who are so precious to God? It's not that we are intentionally ignoring what God has called us to do. Instead, Christians today are simply out of focus. Instead of being focused on others, we are much too focused on ourselves. Society teaches us to look out for number one, to push our way to the top of the ladder, to do whatever it takes to be the best. And this way of thinking has slowly etched its presence into the way in which we view our relationship with God. The question we often ask ourselves in Christianity today is, "What can I do to gain personal approval from God? What can I do to get God to bless me?" Don't get me wrong. The inner desire to please God is an inherently good thing. It's a holy ambition for us to want to please God, but perhaps our focus in this pursuit is what needs to be sharpened. By asking how God can bless us, we are completely focused on ourselves.

Our text today begins with a series of questions by a prophet who is thinking in the same way: "With what shall I come before the LORD, and bow myself before God on high? Shall I come before him with burnt offerings, with calves a year old? Will the LORD be pleased with thousands of rams, with ten thousands of rivers of oil?" (Micah 6:6-7*a*). These first three suggestions of the speaker are inwardly focused. Can I gain the Lord's approval with all of these signs of my success and achievement? What can I do to get God to bless me?

However, the prophet continues to push the idea even further. "Shall I give my firstborn for my transgression, the fruit of my body for the sin of my soul?" (Mic. 6:7*b*). Doesn't it seem a bit absurd to offer to kill your firstborn child in order to win God's approval? Perhaps the idea isn't as uncommon as we would think. Archaeologists actually find the remains of sacrificed children all the time! What we view today as murder was seen by them as something that might win them honor or favor from God. Now, you and I can recognize that none of these options are going to win favor from God because our physical possessions and our earthly achievements aren't what satisfy God. You and I probably never make such absurd offers to God in order to win his approval, or do we?

What if these verses were rewritten in today's Christian culture? With what shall I come before the LORD? Shall I earn His blessing if I go to church this week? If I sing in the choir? Will the LORD be pleased if I read my Bible today? If I put some money in the church offering plate? Perhaps you and I actually make similar proposals to God all the time. Again, it's not that any of these actions are wrong in any way. Of course God wants us to attend worship and to fellowship with other believers. Of course God wants us to read the scriptures and give of ourselves to the church. However, these are not items on a check list that we can simply check off in order to feel like a "good Christian" for the week. We do not go to church or read our Bible to get God to bless us. Hopefully, these actions are the response of a heart that seeks to be obedient to God and not actions that are seeking a specific response from God.

We have asked for far too long, what can I do to get God to bless me? Perhaps the real question of our faith should be, how can God use me to bless others? Isn't a life that seeks to bless others precisely the example that Jesus lived? Isn't a life that seeks to bless others precisely what God requires of us? Our text continues to say, "He has told you, O mortal, what is good; and what does the LORD require of you but to do justice, and to love kindness, and to walk humbly with your God?" (Micah 6:8).

This verse tells us that God has shown us what is good. He is saying, contrary to these ideas that you have tried in order to win my favor, I am showing you a better alternative and a better way to live. These are the three things that the Lord requires of us: One, to act justly–to act with integrity and to treat others fairly. This is an action on behalf of others. Two, to love mercy–to show loyalty and kindness to others. This is a disposition or a frame of mind. And three, to walk humbly with God. This is a lifelong vocation, an orientation of ourselves toward God.

Now, we could spend hours talking about what it means to act justly, to love mercy, and to walk humbly with God, because these three items sum up the meaning of the Christian life. My goal today in preaching is not to share with you examples of how to act justly or to love mercy–that's your job and mine. Instead, my goal is simply to help us sharpen our focus.

When we live a life that constantly asks the question, "What can I do to get God to bless me?" we may never be focused enough to even notice the opportunities God is giving us to act justly and to love mercy. However, when we wake up each day and ask the question, "God, how can you use me to bless others today?" we will be astounded by the opportunities we have to be the hands and feet of Jesus because we have the proper focus. We will see the world around us not with a self-focused frame of mind but with an others-focused mentality. Perhaps we will begin to see the world through the eyes of Jesus.

When we ask God to use us to bless others, we will notice that places like the Brookside Apartment Complex #22C are all around us. After all, aren't places like apartment #22C the exact places where Jesus himself would have ministered? He calls us to do the same. He shares with us in the Gospel of Matthew: "I was hungry and you gave me food, I was thirsty and you gave me something to drink, I was a stranger and you welcomed me, I was naked and you gave me clothing, I was sick and you took care of me, I was in prison and you visited me" (Matthew 25:35-36). The people respond, "Lord, when was it that we saw you hungry and gave you food, or thirsty and gave you something to drink?" (Matthew 25:37). And Jesus replies, "Truly I tell you, just as you did it to one of the least of these who are members of my family, you did it to me" (Matthew 25:40). But to those who did not have their eyes sharpened with the proper focus to even notice these opportunities, Jesus says, "Truly I tell you, just as you did not do it to one of the least of these, you did not do it to me" (Matthew 25:45).

When we focus on getting God to bless us, we might not even notice Jesus in the faces of those who are in need. But when we ask, "How can God use me to bless others?" we will begin to notice Jesus in the faces of people all around us.

On the Sundays when we celebrate the Lord's Supper at Calvary Baptist Church, there are stations all around the sanctuary where people can come to receive communion. At the same time, the children who have not yet professed faith in Christ are invited to the front of the sanctuary to receive a "reminder of God's love for them," usually a sticker, a bookmark, or some small toy that says "Jesus Loves You." One Sunday, I was sitting on the steps at the front of the sanctuary, and Devon came running down the aisle as fast as he could to get to me. I smiled, handed him a small prize and said, "Devon, this is a reminder that God loves you!" His eyes lit up and he looked at me with such an innocent expression of pure excitement. I saw Jesus in Devon's face more clearly than I'd ever seen it before. Then he said, with such honest enthusiasm, "You mean God wants me to have this? I love God!" Yes, God wants Devon to have this…and so much more.

God wanted Devon and his brother to have a good Christmas, which is why their church family was able to provide financially in order for Sam and Devon to wake up on Christmas morning to find clothing, presents, and two brand new bicycles under a Christmas tree in apartment #22C. But God wants Sam and Devon to have much more than that. God wants Sam and Devon to have a safe place to live and food on the table. God wants Sam and Devon to have a solid education and good healthcare. I realize that we're not solving all of Sam and Devon's problems by giving them a joyful experience at church or some presents on Christmas Day. But we are opening a door. We are taking the necessary first step.

Imagine what could happen if we began each day with a simple, yet powerful prayer: "God, use me to be a blessing to others today." Will this be your prayer? Will it be mine?

Because I hope that at the end our lives, people can look at us and say, "Look how God used Brandon to be a blessing to others. Look how God used Cody to be a blessing to others. Look how God used Dr. Moody to be such a blessing to others!"

Perhaps one that day, when we come face to face with God, we will finally look around and see that there is no more poverty. There is no more injustice. There is no more hunger or pain. Instead of an empty room in apartment #22C, everyone from the Brookside Apartment Complex will live in mansions. And we will even see Sam and Devon riding their bicycles down streets of gold. And we will finally look around at the Kingdom of God and in the words of little Devon say, "You mean God wants me to have this? I love God!"

21

"BURNING BUSH ENCOUNTER, TAKE TWO"
John 4:1-42

Paul Booth

In the film industry, the art of cinematography is the discipline of making lighting and camera choices in order to properly record images. The cinematographer or director is the chief person responsible for analyzing the script, plot, and characters in the production scheme of the motion picture. The lighting, lens choice, composition, exposure, filtration, and film selection are critical elements that the cinematographer must consider in order to determine the angle or schematic slant of the motion picture.

In addition to these preproduction duties, there are some practical research and design functions that the cinematographer conducts in order to ensure that the quality, integrity, and legitimacy of the film's thematic message is not compromised or corrupted. More intentionally, if a scene is being filmed outside, the cinematographer will check the local weather forecast and plot sun locations in order to ensure that the production is shot in the most optimal conditions possible.

As we consider the context of this text, John–the divinely inspired cinematographer–carefully sets the scene by positioning the lights to reveal and reaffirm to the audience that Jesus is the Messiah. He remixes Matthew's Christological account of Jesus which portrays him as the promised Messiah, the King of the Jews. He revises Mark's portrayal which shows Jesus as a suffering servant of God. John also amends the script of Luke by persuading us to believe that Jesus is the Son of Man.

In spite of the critics who claim that John's on screen presentation of Jesus represents his divinity but not his historicity, he refutes this in the opening scene of the Johannine account by declaring the complete deity and chronological inception of Christ to demonstrate that Jesus is the Word made flesh. John's depiction of the incarnation reveals the salvific yet paradoxical nature of God. God put on the work suit of the flesh in order to demonstrate eternal dominion over the finite and the celestial. Jesus was not a hybrid model, manufactured prototype, instant oatmeal in a box, prepackaged or a blending of God and man. He was both man and God simultaneously.

He was man enough to weep, yet God enough to encourage.
He was man enough to die, yet God enough to get up from the grave.
He was man enough to be persecuted, yet God enough to pray for his persecutors.
He was man enough to experience pain, yet God enough to heal the sick.
He was man enough to thirst, yet God enough to be the living water.
He was man enough to be humble, yet God enough to be exalted!

As we further examine and engage John's on screen production, we attain greater insight into why Jesus' meeting with the Samaritan women signifies and symbolizes a "Burning Bush Encounter, Take Two."

A burning bush experience is when God unapologetically and unequivocally reveals the essence of Godself in order to communicate a message of sovereignty and salvation. A burning bush meeting is when we see God face to face. A burning bush revelation is when we engage in a transformative teleconference with the Holy. A burning bush summit is where we acknowledge the glory and dominion of God. When Jesus engages the women at the well, it is indeed a burning bush moment. It causes us to ask the critical and poignant questions, "What does it mean for our personal liberty and spiritual deliverance to hear God for ourselves? What is the existential significance of the Godly encounter?"

Take two denotes that God is revealing Godself once more in the life of humanity. Take two simply means the scene of interaction between divinity and humanity is happening once again! The Pharisees began to hate on Jesus because his ministry was crazy successful. Jesus encounter with the Samaritan woman was not an unannounced visit or an unlikely circumstance. The text said Jesus had to go through Samaria. In other words, this route was a divine appointment.

As John focuses the lens closer on this meeting between Jesus and the Samaritan woman, there are some characteristics of a burning bush encounter that are revealed. First, we see that God meets us in our routine. In the Biblical text, we first encounter the burning bush in Exodus 3 while Moses is tending his father-in-law Jethro's sheep. Exodus 3:2 records, "There the angel of the Lord appeared to him." In John 4:7 we learn that when the Samaritan woman showed up at the well, Jesus was already there!

The route that Jesus traveled through Samaria took an extra three days. He didn't meet her on Wall Street. He didn't find her in the board room of Apple or Microsoft. He didn't kick it with her at Nordstrom's or Neiman Marcus. No, Jesus met her where she was! And the good news is that Jesus meets us where we are! It doesn't matter what our predicament or circumstance, God will show up! In spite of Moses' criminal past as a murder and the Samaritan woman's adulterous lifestyle, God meets them at their station and vocation. Jesus wasn't concerned about the socio-political tension between Jews and Samaritans or the gender conflict that would ensue because he was publicly speaking to a person who was considered "unclean."

I'm reminded of a story about a native of China who wanted to become a Christian but couldn't understand how Christianity differed from Confucianism or Buddhism. One morning he came to the missionary in a gleeful mood saying, "I had a dream last night and now I understand. I dreamed I had fallen into a deep pit where I lay helpless and despairing. Confucius came and said, 'Let me give you advice, my friend; if you get out of your trouble, never get in it again.' Buddha came and said, 'If you climb up to where I can reach you, I will help you.' Then Christ came, climbed down into the pit, and carried me out."

The second characteristic of a burning bush encounter is that God speaks through signs and symbols. God revealed himself to Moses in a burning bush to demonstrate God's judgment, grace, and protection for Israel. Fire is often used in scripture as a symbol of God's holiness. In verse 13 of our text, Jesus declares that he is the "living water." The women at the well had experienced the brokenness of failed relationships, the misfortune of vain love, the void of identity, the perils of a bad reputation, and the injustice of discrimination. But when Jesus offered her living water that couldn't be tapped from the well, Jesus wasn't talking about Dasani, Dannon, or even Sobe Life Water. Jesus was offering her the opportunity to unite with the spirit of God, step out of her life of death, and enter into eternal life.

The third characteristic of a burning bush encounter is that there's always an "I AM" statement. Just as God told Moses, "I AM that I AM," in verse 26 of tour text Jesus tells the woman "I who speak to you am he." It was a take-two moment because God was revealing himself once again in the life of humanity. When Jesus said, "I AM," he was affirming that he was the one; he was denouncing her past of brokenness and shame. If we take a moment and pause the DVD of spiritual experience, we'll encounter some moments where God says "I AM!" If we use our Holy Ghost imagination, we can see the credits of eternity announcing the historical imprint of the Great "I AM."

In chemistry, he turned water into wine.
In biology, he was born without the normal conception.
In physics, he disproved the law of gravity when he ascended into heaven.
In economics, he disproved the law of diminishing returns by feeding 5,000 people with two fishes and five loaves of bread.
In medicine, he cured the sick and the blind without administering a single dose of drugs.
In history, he is the beginning and the end.
In government, he said that he shall be called Wonderful Counselor and Prince of Peace.
In religion, he said no one comes to the Father except through him.

Jesus had no servants, yet they called him Master. He had no degree, yet they called him teacher. He had no medicines, yet they called him healer. He had no armies, yet rulers feared Him. He won no military battles, yet he conquered the world. He committed no crime, yet they crucified him. He was buried in a tomb, yet he lives today!

Let the church say Alleluia! Let the church say Amen!

22

"PORTRAITS OF THE OPPRESSED"
Matthew 5:38-41

Neal Brooks

My dad is a good man. He's a harsh man, but a good man. If there is any sort of problem, he will not hesitate to tell you that your attitude needs an adjustment or that something needs to change. I've got to tell you, brothers and sisters, we've got a problem. It's all of us. It's you and it's me. The problem is when we look at the life and teachings of Jesus Christ, for some reason our minds jump to the conclusion that he was one of us, a twenty-first century American Christian. In doing so, we do a great disservice to Jesus Christ. He wasn't talking to us when he spoke. I hate to break it to you, but his words were not initially intended for us. They were spoken to a specific people, his contemporaries, in a context that they would understand. If we are unwilling to figure out what Jesus was actually trying to say to those people in their situation, it will be impossible to figure out what Jesus Christ would actually want for our lives today. So as we look at the Sermon on the Mount, I hope that you will be open to the idea that even though the interpretation I present may not have been the one you grew up with, it is based on what the people heard and what Jesus likely meant.

When Jesus begins in verse 38 he says, "You have heard that it was said, 'An eye for an eye and tooth for a tooth.' But I say to you, Do not resist an evildoer" (Matthew 4:38-39*a*). Jesus is correcting a preconceived notion, one that is not unfounded, but is stated plainly in Old Testament law. In Leviticus 24:19-20 the law states, "Anyone who maims another shall suffer the same injury in return: fracture for fracture, eye for eye, tooth for tooth; the injury inflicted is the injury to be suffered." To our ears this sounds harsh, but God's purpose is good. This law protects people from over punishment. Many ancient cultures believed in a revenge-based system that allowed for double punishments. God's law was not so. It only allowed for restitution, not revenge.

However, Jesus says that's not good enough; the old law is insufficient. Instead Jesus says, "You have heart that it was said, 'An eye for an eye and a tooth for a tooth.' But I say to you, Do not resist an evildoer." Our English translations have butchered the real interpretation of the word "resist." We see that word appear in Ephesians when it talks about "standing against" evil. It implies a specific military context, when two armies of the ancient world would come at each other on the battle field, the moment just before their ranks would collide. This word means "standing against," or "opposing" of another. In reality, Jesus is going to paint three portraits of people who are living amid violence and oppression. But rather than resorting to violence and oppression, they instead resort to a third way.

The first one is this, "But if anyone strikes you on the right cheek, turn the other also..." (Matthew 4:39*b*). Now if I am going to strike you on the right cheek, I will likely either slap you or punch you, correct? Either hand is at my disposal depending on which I choose. However, when we realize that in the time of Jesus the left hand was out of the question, it begins to narrow down a person's options. You see, the left hand was reserved for the most unclean of duties. Being touched by it would make a Jew unclean for a period of several days. So the only option is that the right cheek is being struck by the right hand, which in turns makes only a backhand possible. In the time of Jesus Christ the backhand was reserved for specific times. A younger Jew caught in heresy could be backhanded, as well as a slave by his master and a Jew by a Roman. These specific times all illustrate that a person has acted out of social status; they have upset the status quo. In essence, the backhand is the world's way of putting these people back in line.

Jesus then tells them to, "turn the other also." If this is done, the only type of striking still possible is either an open palm slap or a punch. We quickly realize that an open handed slap seems unlikely for that is the strike of a woman. Nothing against women, but in the time of Christ no man would strike another like that for it would bring insult to him. Instead, he must resort to punching the man, which means more than we might think. In fact, it is speculated in ancient writings that if a master punched his slave, he could incite a revolt. Why? Because you only punched a man who was your equal. The decisive action that this oppressed person is taking basically asserts that, "I will not back down. What you intended to put me in my place will do you no good, for I know in the eyes of the Lord we are equal, and I dare you to make the fool out of yourself!" Jesus has provided for us our first portrait, in which a man dares his "master" to either make a fool of himself or assert himself as an equal to the one he was attempting to ridicule.

In our second illustration, Jesus says, "and if anyone wants to sue you and take your coat, give your cloak as well" (Matthew 4:40*b*). In this time, a person only wore two pieces of clothing, a tunic and a cloak. Interest rates had gotten so high in the time of Christ that a scene like this would not have been so unusual. However, Deuteronomy 24 stipulated that if you were sued for your clothes, you could only be sued for your cloak, not your tunic. We see here an infraction of the law of God in which the cloak had to be returned every night. I think it's likely that this man was not going to get his cloak back, and Jesus tells him to give him his tunic as well! Now I know you all are smart people. I bet you can figure out what this leaves this poor guy…Nothing! He stands there in his birthday suit, in court, which was likely outside near the city gates! To the people of Jesus' time nudity was an extreme taboo! To us even the situation sounds ridiculous, but can you imagine the implications of a man who basically says to the man he owes money, "You can take everything I own! But you can never take away my dignity!" Surely the man who is owed money has to see how ridiculous it looks like to sue a man for the very shirt off his back.

In our third portrait of the oppressed, we read, "if someone forces you to go one mile, go with him two miles." We see once again, that that word forces implies a specific military context. When we consider the historical context, we can easily assume that Jesus is talking about what would happen to the Jews when the Roman army would come through town. You know that the Romans forced the Jews to carry their packs, for one mile outside of the Jewish cities. The Jews hated this! It was Rome's way of further asserting their dominance over the Jew's. How would you like it if a bunch of strangers made you carry all their heavy stuff around? It's like asking some random guy on the street if he wants to help you move! Likewise, the Jews hated this! They hated it so much that they marked out one mile outside of the city with rocks, so they could tell exactly how far they had to go. However in this situation Jesus tells them to go two miles, which seems like overwhelming kindness, especially in light of the previous two examples, until we realize that forcing someone into two miles of service was an infraction of military code. It made the soldier subject to a beating or punishment dictated by his commanding officer. Now by no means should we assume that Jesus is telling his followers to get soldiers beat up, on the contrary, it is also well known that often the Roman army had little respect for its codes. So likely this wouldn't be an issue, but we can certainly imagine a situation in which it would. What if a Jew tried this and the guy whose pack he is carrying is in a little "hot water" with his commanding officer. Maybe he stumbled in late from the tavern the night before, or has been caught in some lewd behavior. He finds himself walking and looks back only to realize that the rock marking one mile is well past, but the Jewish man is still carrying his things. When he tries to take them back the Jewish man tells him he wants to keep going. Maybe the soldier panics and even tries to forcefully take the pack back, how amusing! Even the other officers might notice what's happening and laugh, or say something like, "Look at this guy! He's lost his marbles!" It's funny to our ears, but a little humor can quickly change a persons' mind about what they are doing, our third portrait.

What all these portraits illustrate is that to God we are not to be set apart from each other in inequality of worth, but instead in total equality. When God looks at us he sees us as equal to those next to us, not less than or greater, simply equal. Unfortunately we have a hard time coming to terms with this; we instead have a tendency to live the exact opposite. I know I'm gonna step on some toes, but is it possible we let gender get in the way of feeling equal, is it possible we let race get in the way of feeling equal, is it possible that we let denominations divide us? Why do we search so hard for something to assert ourselves as superior to others? We will try and find anything to separate ourselves! We will look at non-Christians and say they are inferior to us because we have Jesus Christ. It's disgraceful that we compare sins in order to determine if we are "more sinful" than our neighbor. We compare the tiniest things that should never separate us from each other.

Maybe today this is hitting home, that you need to stop treating people like an unequal to you. Maybe you find yourself feeling like the people around you look down on you, and if it finds you there, realize that you are worth so much more than the world can make you seem. There are always ways to react to situations without resorting to anger and violence. Please as you leave today remember that as you scan faces and houses and even other churches, that these are all God's people, and they are all equal in his sight! Amen.

23

"MORE THAN THE MINIMUM REQUIREMENTS"
Micah 6:6-8

David Depoister

What would you do to absolutely appease God and know that you are found righteous in His sight? This scripture was written in the day of animal sacrifices. God laid out regulations and laws for His people to follow so that they could claim righteousness and be found "not guilty" in the sight of God. It was like a recipe given for righteousness and it had to be followed. A thousand rams and thousands of rivers of oil would be the equivalent of being at the Temple every hour it was open throughout the year. This would be like a car salesman totaling up his car sales for a year and then giving that same amount of cars to the Lord or to the church. Then, God would accept his sacrifice, and he would be justified by God despite whatever kind of life he may live. It was righteousness by works. In many ways we still try to obtain a right relationship with God by doing works. We may say to ourselves: if only I pray enough, or go to church enough, or volunteer to ring the bell for Salvation Army, then I can find favor with God. These things seem to take the place of the animal sacrifices of old.

The old system of justification doesn't work. In fact, it never did work. All the animal sacrifices in the world couldn't pay the debt that we owe due to sin. The Mosaic sacrifices serve as a foreshadow to His better sacrifice. Luckily our debt has been paid by Jesus. When he died on that cross he was the ultimate sacrifice for our sins. No longer is there a need for us to make offerings by sacrifice. The car salesmen can keep his cars, the farmers can keep their crops, and people can keep their paychecks because our salvation doesn't depend on the things we can offer to God. That is not what saves you. Salvation depends on our faith in Jesus as our Savior. If you accept that, your debt has been erased.

So, in light of this, how do we live our lives? Do we go on living however we want knowing that our faith in Jesus ensures us a place in heaven? Do we sit on our hands and do nothing because faith is all we need? No. Indeed, God still requires things from people. In the text we see what God would have us do in order to please Him. "And what does the Lord require of you? To act justly and to love mercy and to walk humbly with your God." These three things are more precious to God than any animal sacrifice that could be offered.

First, we are to act justly. I have to admit that I have a movie screen idea about justice and what it means. The first thing that comes to my mind in thinking about justice is when a person gets what is coming to him or her. An example is when a murderer gets life in prison or lethal injection. It happens when the bad guy in the movie gets a taste of his own medicine. This is a faulty idea though. In actuality, justice is so much more than that. The first thing that must be present in understanding justice is recognition that God sets our standards and values. This standard applies to all people. Justice involves a standard of fairness and equality. Justice involves a standard of values and the value of creation. The world tells us one way to see, judge, and treat people according to their social status, race, gender, and age. But we are to hold to the standard by which only God can give. Injustice takes place when action is taken or denied that would deny the standard or values God has set for all. We are to know that everyone is special and precious in the eyes of our Creator and God the Father and that we are to act accordingly.

Sadly, it just so happens that we live in a world full of injustices and many people are content in turning their heads and pretending that they don't happen. Let us consider a few instances. It is common knowledge that the Holocaust claimed the lives of 6 million human beings, although it is being taught in some places that such a thing never took place. In 1994 an estimated 800,000 to almost 1 million people were killed in the Rwanda genocide.[1] But let's talk about some going on right now.

The conflict in Darfur is another one. An army formed in Africa and accused the government of oppressing black Africans in favor of Arabs. Going village to village the army has kidnapped children and trained them for combat. They have raped and killed all others in an estimated 300,000 deaths being reported.[2]

---

[1]Frontline, "Timeline," PBS, http://www.pbs.org/wgbh/pages/frontline/shows/ghosts/etc/crontext.html (accessed November 21, 2009.

[2]BBC News, "Darfur deaths could be 300,000," http://news.bbc.co.uk/2/hi/7361979.stm.

World hunger is and has always been an injustice. Every 3.6 seconds someone dies of hunger in the world.[3] By the time it takes me to give a 15 minute sermon, 250 people have died in the world due to starvation. World hunger really is exposed as an injustice when you think of it in another way. For the price of one regular old missile, a school full of hungry children could eat lunch every day for five years.[4]

People think slavery is a thing of the past, but an estimated 27 million people are caught up in human trafficking today. Most of them will be sold as slaves or sex objects. All these things happen so far away though. It is so easy to not focus our mind or waste our time thinking about what goes on in another part of the world. If this is your attitude, I will bring it a little closer to home, and we will look at some injustices taking place in our communities.

We will start with domestic violence. Approximately 1.3 million women and 835,000 men are physically assaulted by an intimate partner annually in the United States.[5] The people affected by domestic violence are not just people in some other country or part of the world. They are men and women with which you work. Your neighbors and peers get caught up in spousal abuse.

Child abuse is another injustice running wild in our communities. In 2007, it was reported that five children die every day in the United States due to child abuse. Three out of the five children were under four years old.[6] A report of child abuse is made every 10 seconds.[7] There will be 90 cases of child abuse reported before I give this 15 minute sermon.

It must disappoint God the way some people are treated because of the color of their skin. Even today with the standard of equality that is present in our country, there is racism passed down to generations. This goes many different ways. There are slanderous names and slanderous attitudes toward blacks, whites, Mexicans, and Asian people. It is not often when we are all seen as simple human beings, precious and loved in the sight of God.

---

[3]ThinkQuest Team C002291, "The world hunger problems: Facts, Figures, and Statistics," http://library.thinkquest.org/C002291/high/present/stats.htm (accessed November 20, 2009.

[4]Ibid.

[5]American Bar Association, "Prevalence of Domestic Violence," http://www.abanet.org/domviol/statistics.html (accessed November 21, 2009)

[6]Child Help, "National Child Abuse Statistics," http://www.childhelp.org/resources/learning-center/statistics (accessed November 21, 2009).

[7]Ibid.

Once again, it is easy to shrug these things off and pretend they aren't in our midst. So, once again, we will bring it in a little closer. Many injustices happen right in front of our eyes. They happen in our homes every day and become such a natural part of the day that we may not even recognize them as injustices. They don't even faze us.

One of the best answers I heard when asking friends about injustices here in America was that of the money spent on entertainment in American homes. Just think about it. Some people are willing to spend hundreds and even thousands of dollars each month on activities whose purposes are to provide momentary distractions from life. How much money do you have wrapped up in movies, cable, game systems and games? This becomes a reality for us as an injustice when it is told that 3 billion people in the world today struggle to survive on two and a half American dollars a day.[8]

Another injustice brought to my attention recently is the unfair treatment of children in homes. Parents pick and choose which kids they want to show favor to. A lot of this comes from the rising number of mixed homes where divorce has affected the lives of the family. Some kids are treated harshly while others are the "favorites." Injustices could occur in disciplining children also. Parents do not treat their children justly when they discipline their children too hard. In fact, Ephesians 6 bears a warning for fathers not to exasperate their children. This means to give up any unreasonable treatment of the children. There is also an injustice in not disciplining your kids enough. Great injustice is done to the future of children when parents cannot maintain a consistency in fair treatment of their children.

We have an obligation to be informed of the injustices going on around us and to act justly in our own lives. I am not only talking about breaking the law. Most acts of injustice happen without being against the law. Injustices lie in false attitudes and values in life that are contrary to God's values and God's standard of living for us. Such false attitudes make a mockery of God.

Acting justly means for the younger ones to stand up for the kid that gets picked on all the time at school, or the older ones not to park in the handicapped spot because you're not handicapped. Justice involves our whole lives and a dedication to doing what is right for all people. A dedication to living by the standards that God

---

[8]Anup Shah, "Causes of Poverty," Global Issues. http://www.globalissues.org/issue/2/causes-of-poverty (accessed November 21, 2009).

sets. Living a life of love and integrity is needed. When we act justly, it will show itself in our lives. We are to be salt and light. This means to be as different from the standards of the world as light is different from darkness. Acting justly will also show itself in our lives through mercy. So, as the text says, we are to love mercy.

A mother once approached Napoleon seeking a pardon for her son. The emperor replied that the young man had committed a certain offense twice and justice demanded death.

> "But I don't ask for justice," the mother explained. "I plead for mercy."
>
> "But your son does not deserve mercy," Napoleon replied.
>
> "Sir," the woman cried, "it would not be mercy if he deserved it, and mercy is all I ask for."
>
> "Well, then," the emperor said, "I will have mercy." And he spared the woman's son.[9]

There is a distinction made here between what people deserve and what people actually get when mercy is involved. The truth of the matter is that each and every one of us should be grateful for the mercy extended to us by God our Father. I often hear people say, "Well, they made their bed and now they have to lie in it." If we all had to lie in the beds that we make for ourselves without any mercy, every single one of our lives would be dramatically different. The difference would not be a good one either. God extends his mercy to us through offering us a second chance. God offers us the ultimate do over. Jesus took our sins to the cross and our slates were wiped clean. "All who believe in Him shall not perish but have everlasting life." We deserved death and destruction, and yet we received so much love and mercy. In turn, this mercy shown to us should move us to show mercy to others.

In Mathew 18:23-35 a story is told about a king who wanted to settle his debts. One man owed him ten thousand talents and could not pay it so it was ordered that he, his wife, his children and everything he had be sold in order to repay the debt. The servant fell on his knees and began to beg and ask that the king to be patient with him. The master took pity on him and canceled the debt. That same man went out and found one of his fellow servants that owed

---

[9]Luis Palau, "Experiencing God's Forgiveness," Multnomah Press, Sermon Illustrations, http://www.sermonillustrations.com/a-z/m/mercy.htm (accessed November 22, 2009.

him a hundred denarii and began to choke him and tell him that he must pay back the debt he owed. This was considerably less money than the debt which he owed the king and was canceled. The fellow servant fell to his knees and begged him to be patient with him and that he would pay it back. He refused to be patient with the man and had him thrown in prison until he could pay the debt. The other servants around were distressed and they went off and told the master. Then the master called the servant in, and we find out what took place in verse 32. "You wicked servant," he said. "I cancelled all that debt of yours because you begged me to. Shouldn't you have mercy on your fellow servant just as I had on you?" In anger, his master turned him over to the jailers to be tortured until he paid back all he owed.

We see here the mercy that the master or king had on his servant and how that mercy has been extended to us by our debt being canceled. Mercy is part of the nature of God. If we love mercy like the scripture tells us to, then we are also showing our love for God. How can we not love the mercy we bask in every day? And how can we condemn and judge others when we are so unworthy of the many blessings and mercies extended to us every day. The question presents itself, "Are you known for loving mercy and being merciful?"

In light of the mercy we receive from God, the next point should be easy enough for all of us. It is to walk humbly with God. Philippians 2:3-7 says, "Do nothing out of selfish ambition or vain conceit, but in humility consider others better than yourselves. Each of you should look not only to your own interests, but also to the interests of others. Your attitude should be the same as that of Christ Jesus: Who, being in very nature God, did not consider equality with God something to be grasped, but made himself nothing taking the very nature of a servant, being made in human likeness." Jesus was the ultimate example of making oneself humble and putting other before self. We find ourselves back at the point of recognizing God's standard for all people and the equality that is found there. To take it one step deeper, we are not to put ourselves above others, we are to "consider others better than ourselves." One definition given humbleness and humility alike is freedom from pride. A person cannot be humble if they are self-absorbed and think only of themselves and their own interest. I like that this verse states that we are to walk humbly with God. Sometimes it is in comparison of the great and mighty God that we serve that makes us grasp how small we are in creation.

Louie Giglio explains in one of his videos just how small we are in comparison to our God. There is a huge star called the *Canus Majorus.* He calls it the "big dog" star. This star is massive. If the earth were the size of a golf ball, *Canus Majorus* would be the height of Mount Everest. Seven quadrillion earths can fit inside of this star. It is hard to even fit our head around a number as big as seven quadrillion. Let me say it another way. If the earth were the size of a golf ball, the amount of golf balls it would take to fill *Canus Majorus* would enough golf balls to cover the entire state of Texas 22 inches deep in golf balls.[10]

The humbling part comes when we read what the Bible says in Psalm 33:6. It says, "By the word of the Lord the heavens were made, and all their hosts by the breath of his mouth." Out of God's mouth came this enormous star. By his breath it came into creation. And even though our awesome, powerful, beautiful God made such things, he looks down on us with care. He looks down on us with love. He looks down on us with mercy.

Sometimes I take a look around at people and ask, "Just how high and mighty do they think they are?" Then I must look at myself and ask, "Just how high and mighty do I think I am?" We are all small in this world. We should be humbled simply by the thought of who God is. If any one had the right to act high and mighty, it was Jesus. But instead Jesus "did not consider equality with God something to be grasped, but made himself nothing taking the very nature of a servant, being made in human likeness."

In the world of today we must be careful when thinking about what God requires from his people. It is often found that belief takes the place animal sacrifices once had. Back then people said, "As long as I make the proper sacrifices, I will find favor and righteousness." This type of attitude is not worried about pleasing God with everything we do. Today people say, "As long as I have my faith, church, and volunteer work I will find favor and righteousness." This too lacks the attitude of wanting to please God with every breath we take. God requires more of us. He has charged us to do his work here on earth. He has charged us to be salt and light in the world. He has charged us with doing good in the world. And so, we return to the text. Micah 6:8 says, "He has showed you, O man, what is good. And what does the Lord require of you? To act justly and to love mercy and to walk humbly with your God."

---

[10]Loui Giglio, *Passion Talk Series: How Great is our God,* DVD, 2009.

24

"WHAT THE LORD REQUIRES"
Micah 6:6-8

Christine Coy Fohr

What is being attempted in this place, on this weekend, is remarkable. Brave, really. Bringing together people from various traditions and denominations and telling them "preach!" Preaching–that form of speech that has taught generations, inspired dedication and emboldened movements for justice. Preaching–that form of speech that has caused debate, disagreement, and incited division. It will be all around us this weekend. That form of speech that is both a means of spreading hope and a prophetic call for change. What is being attempted is remarkable and brave, and maybe even a little dangerous.

This weekend, we young preachers approach this place, fully embracing who we are. We will not downplay our differences in order to create a diluted attempt at ecumenism. No, rather, we will approach this place, this pulpit that has borne prophets and pretenders alike and say, "This is who I am." My name is Christine. I am twenty-seven years old. I am a wife, a daughter, a student, a Presbyterian, a wanderer, a doubter, a hopeful believer, a child of God. We are who we are, and we have not been asked to hide it. It is a radical notion–unity amid difference. A radical, vision of reconciled diversity. Radical, much like everything else Christ calls his people to. Such reconciled diversity in the Church is extremely difficult. Ecumenism is not easy. Just growing up in Owensboro, Kentucky taught me that. It was a place where friends of Baptist and Catholic backgrounds often questioned my affiliation with this strange Presbyterian Church.

In Northern Ireland they have a special term for the conflicts that have come from their ecumenical situation, "The Troubles." Unlike our mostly doctrinal disputes, Northern Ireland has seen the wrath that Christian brothers and sisters can bring upon one another, a wrath that comes in the form of hatred, intolerance, violence, and blind fear. During the time I spent in Belfast, Northern Ireland, I witnessed what division looks like: twenty foot high "peace walls" laced with barbed wire that run between alleys to parse the city out. Catholics here, Protestants there. It looks like murals depicting prominent religious figures alongside militant calls to intolerance. These are the markings of a past blemished by hate-filled, unwavering exclusion of "the other," even when "the other" lives down the road from you, prays to the same God as you, and is called by the same God as you to do justice, love kindness and humbly walk this journey of life. Northern Ireland may be extreme, but they are not so different. We in America have our own experiences of ecumenical discord to share. They include stories of frustration and experiences of division.

Yet somehow, miraculously, here we are gathered together by the grace of God to listen for words of hope from our diversity. Here we are, encountering brothers and sisters of different faith traditions, brothers and sisters whose beliefs, theologies, and doctrines may differ greatly from our own. Here we are, people tied to traditions that have shrugged off, resisted, protested and split from one another, traditions that bear not only the marks of great testimony, but the marks of division. Painful marks like disagreement, exclusion, and even violence that compose our history of Christian life together. We might rather forget these marks and hide behind our denominational tapestries of faithful life together, but the marks nonetheless remain. They explain our lives spent apart from one another, in our various chapels and churches, meeting houses and assemblies. Christian lives lived in separation, and often, in disagreement.

Yet, here we are, brothers and sisters of different backgrounds and traditions, gathered together to share a word of grace. What might come of this encounter–of this unique opportunity to listen, to share, and to embody the unity Christ calls us to? I worry. Might our words further divide us? Perhaps someone will hear something they find theologically unsound. Perhaps another will hear words that starkly contrast with their understanding of orthodoxy. Someone may speak of God with feminine imagery. With our words, we may yet again find ourselves divided. In our sermons and testimonies, we may yet again threaten the unity Christ hopes for us when he prays "that they may be one." And yet, is not this act of preaching what God calls us to through the words of the prophet Micah? To speak clearly, to preach earnestly, and deliver the message no matter the consequences?

Speaking, surprisingly, does not seem to be in the top three of what the Lord requires. Doing justice, loving kindness, walking humbly are the offerings we bring when we come before the Lord.

It is not our thinking, but our moving, not our talking about Jesus, but our sincere efforts to embody who Christ calls us to be.

But how do we do it? How can we stop ourselves from wanting to share that which has transformed us, which has moved and provoked us to action? Surely we want to tell. Of course we want to spread the good news of life in Christ, but how can our call to share this good news escape the trappings of the human tongue and the judgment of the human ear? For some, the best approach is to simply to avoid dialogue and to quiet that which so often inspires conflict.

I am reminded of a recent visit I had with one of my professors–one who, herself, is often known for causing conflict through her use of words. This Christmas, she graciously invited a few students to her home to break bread. And on her mantel, I saw a Christmas decoration–perhaps an Advent devotion of sorts–that bore the words, "May the baby Jesus open your heart and shut your mouth." Beautiful, I thought, if a bit simplistic.

Others, however, find hope in digging into that tension, in picking those wounds where words cut deeply into Christian unity, hoping that through the struggle a deeper healing might emerge. In the international Ecumenical Movement, diverse groups have intentionally gathered for this reason: to seek unity through deeper conversation and understanding. It has brought together Baptists and Reformed to talk about baptism; Lutherans and Catholics to hash out justification. These conversations are often a painful, painstaking process, but in many cases they have led toward some semblance of unity, some understanding of that faith which we and our neighbors so boldly attest to.

Yet, what do we achieve as we reify that which we believe, as we create false gods from the scraps of our faith that we gather in this trying world? Is it our own interpretations that we worship? Is it our own convictions that we cling to for guidance, inspiration, and hope? Or can we still acknowledge our confusion, our doubt, and our need to rest our weary heads upon something stronger than our minds can conceive and our mouths convey?

In the prophet Micah's words, we are reminded of our call in this life: to live as humble pilgrims alongside our God. We are not called to distill God and obtain truth. We are not called to debate or vanity. We are called to a humble walk alongside the God whose vision created all facets of this world, who preordained a diverse world of rich textures and colors, ideas and imagination, who can be praised by all she created, followed by all whose marvelous uniqueness he shaped, and understood in a variety of ways. It is from God that all manner of diversity comes. This journey need not be taken alone, but is often best travelled alongside one another.

Shortly before leaving Northern Ireland, I followed through on a New Year's resolution to run in the Belfast marathon. Well, to be honest, to run the relay version of the Belfast marathon. And I called dibs on the shortest leg, the first miles of the race. But my physical fitness aside, I wanted to do this because I wondered how a marathon that wound through all districts of such a divided city could possibly happen. How could runners maneuver peace walls? Would Catholics find threatening glances in Protestant areas and vice versa? Would they run alongside one another for the 26 miles, or would division find its way into this venture?

At the starting line, I found a vision of hope, an embodied embrace of God's call. Thousands of people from all backgrounds, denominations, and politics, gathered together not to talk or debate, but to walk a difficult journey together. They ran the streets of Belfast as witnesses to what might be. Diverse brothers and sisters accompanied one another–faithfully, intentionally, indiscriminately–down the hard road toward the goal. In their humble journeys, the city was, if only momentarily, transformed.

Our ecumenical struggle represents but one example of conflict in this world. But unlike debates of the secular world, where ends are achieved through the eventual separation of "winners" and "losers," we are called as Christians to model the radical example of Christ, who rather than seeking to win debate often incited further conversation in a humble desire to draw people closer to God. In this way, we are called to accompaniment of sorts, to a journey, sometimes with our feet and sometimes through words. In this place, on this weekend, may we grasp this rare opportunity to walk alongside one another, diverse pilgrims humbly seeking to dwell in the presence of God. The end may not yet be known, but the path undoubtedly treads the Way of Christ so long as we seek to do justice, to love kindness, and to walk, humbly, with the Holy One our God.

May that Way of Christ be our path today and forevermore. Amen.

25

"WORTHY WORSHIP"

John 4:5-42

Patrick Garcia

Last summer horrific news scanned across the screen of every television station in America and around the world. People were absolutely devastated with the information the media was communicating that day. Some were sad, some were in shock, and others found themselves in denial. But I'll never forget watching *Fox News* in a hotel room on that June afternoon as the cameras surveyed a crowd of worshipers mourning the death of their idol, Michael Jackson.

One fan recalled her reaction of Jackson's death in an interview with the *Los Angeles Times* by saying, "When I heard the news of Jackson's death I crawled on the floor sobbing."[1] And the more I read the article, the clearer it became that she wasn't just a fan of Jackson, she was a worshiper.

Fans responded to the tragic death of the "King of Pop" in various and interesting ways. In fact, some even went way overboard with it. A group of fans birthed their dream into a reality when they launched "The International Group of The Anointed Michael Followers Fan Page" on Facebook! The members unashamedly worship Michael Jackson and are encouraging the public to participate. But before becoming a member of their "movement," the leaders of the group require all members to acknowledge that Jackson is the Messiah. Heretical nutcases or not, if they ever get enough members to form a church at least the hymns would be great! Right?

Call it honor. Call it respect. Call it what you want. The reality is that a majority of people outside and inside the church have misguided their worship at some point and directed it towards some meaningless thing. For you, rather than Michael Jackson, your object of worship might be a car. Instead of the "King of Pop," perhaps it's the pursuit of success. Rather than the 80's megastar, it could be a

[1]Nicole Santa Cruz and Carla Hall, *Los Angeles Times,* June 27, 2009.

relationship. Because, you see, what people worship is an accurate indication of what is really valuable to them.

Truth be told, we are a culture of misplaced worship. We've gone from a nation that prioritized Sunday morning church to a people who idolize soccer tournaments and football games. Rather than fathers taking their leadership roles seriously in the home, they find themselves working late hours in the office and label it "climbing the ladder of success." Rather than faithfully tithing 10% of our monthly budgets despite an economic crisis, other important things seem to get in the way like paying off credit card debt, making the mortgage payment, buying a nicer car. America's primary enemies are not the radical extremists from the Middle East. More precisely, it's our decision to surrender ourselves to unworthy, misplaced worship.

This is no new dilemma though. In fact, it's been around for quite some time. The Gospel of John tells of a historic encounter Jesus had with a particular woman in the town of Sychar. Christ was by himself as he and the disciples made a little rest stop in the town of Sychar. Now this may have confused Jesus' Jewish followers, because Jews always avoided this town due to its racial prejudices and divisions towards one another. Sychar was a city in Samaria, and its inhabitants were despised as outcasts in the Jewish culture. An upright, first-century Jew would travel from Judea to Galilee and intentionally go around Sychar to avoid contact with the lowly Samaritans.

But Jesus was never one to hold to tradition and scorn those who were undistinguished. Rather, he came to earth to save humanity from our sins and proclaim the truth. And connecting and teaching the truth is exactly what's going on here as Jesus meets this unlikely individual in an improbable place found in John chapter four…the Samaritan woman.

After engaging the woman in conversation during the hottest and least busiest time of day at the city's water well, we see Jesus diving into a deep discussion regarding what authentic and true worship looks like to the Lord. Her religious heritage was one filled with false teaching, pagan gods, and could be characterized as just "missing the point." The Samaritans picked and chose what they wanted to believe, hear, and worship from the Old Testament–so rightfully, the Jews felt as if they "perverted" their worship and religion.

And so in verse 20 the woman strives to understand meaningful worship by asking, "Our ancestors worshiped on this mountain, but you say that the place people must worship is in Jerusalem." Jesus said to her, "Woman, believe me, the hour is coming when you will worship the Father neither on this mountain nor in Jerusalem" (John 4:20-21).

Jesus was gently clarifying the misconception of worship. By this point, the woman perceives that Jesus could be the Messiah. She could have asked many things, but in essence she desires above all to know what worthwhile worship looks like to the Father. For all intents and purposes, she says to Jesus, "Where is the best place to worship? Where can I go in order to give glory to God? At what location is God most likely to accept my sacrifice?"

And the problem with her pursuit to define worship was that she believed it was centered upon external circumstances. So the first principle by which Jesus defines worship is to say that it is a way of life.

In verse 21, Jesus responds to her question by saying, "You're missing the point! Your location, what you wear, and all those other external, outside elements are meaningless to God! It doesn't matter if you worship God in the Temple, or in your home…it is to be a lifestyle, not a location."

You see, worshiping as a way of life isn't so much an outward act as it is an inward disposition before God. That's what Jesus is getting at here with the woman at the well. He uses the Greek word, *proskuneo*. It means, "to have reverence and acknowledge someone in high regard; to kiss towards; to bow yourself low in a posture of humility." It is a word that is used to describe what God's people are to do in His presence 24/7.

A friend of mine said it like this, "[I worship] because I have a relationship with God and I am adoring, admiring and expressing my response to the love Christ has already shown me."

That's *proskuneo*!

Worship is to be voluntarily offered to God as He has offered Himself to us, because what Christ was really getting at in his response to the Samaritan woman was this, "Surrender completely. Worship is surrender. Because in essence, what you surrender to is what's most valuable to you.

Now I know (being in a room full of preachers) the temptation is to write off the challenge of worshiping as a way of life, because that's our profession, that's our calling. We're constantly focused on God and His work and His will. But allow me to speak to you for just a second. Sometimes we can get so wrapped up in the Lord's work that we forget the Lord of the work. Jesus assures us, "On that day many will say to me 'Lord, Lord, did we not prophesy in your name, and cast out demons in your name, and do many deeds of power in your name?' Then I will declare to them, "I never knew you; go away from me, you evildoers" (Matt. 7:22-23).

To be honest with you this afternoon, this passage is something that I've really been wrestling with lately. It disturbs me. It sometimes even interrupts my sleep at night, "Lord, have I completely surrendered to you lately? I know I fall short of this so often and for that I ask for your forgiveness. May my life be a constant worship service to you. I completely surrender."

While you and I constantly worship and continually surrender ourselves, the truth is a lot of us aren't surrendering/worshipping the right thing/the right person. So I ask you, when was the last time you allowed worthy worship to disrupt your life? When was the last time you allowed it to disrupt your checkbook? The way you treated people? Your schedule in order to spend more time with God?

Likewise, Paul reminds the early believers, "I appeal to you therefore, brothers and sisters, by the mercies of God, to present your bodies as a living sacrifice, holy and acceptable to God, which is your spiritual worship" (Romans 12:1).

Worthy worship is constant and knows no determined destination. Worthy worship is a way of life, but secondly, worthy worship is Christ-centered. Jesus continues to talk with the woman at the well in verse 22. He says, "You worship what you do not know; we worship what we know, for salvation is from the Jews."

In this part of his conversation, Jesus makes a reference to himself. He calls the Samaritan out on not really knowing what she worships, but that worthwhile worship is directed to the one who paves the way for salvation. It's to be Christ-centered. It "comes through the Jews" was another way of saying that Jesus was Jewish and He alone is the way to a relationship with God.

Again, the Samaritan's heart of worship had been there, but it was directed towards the wrong object, the wrong recipient; therefore, it was lost.

A couple weeks ago my landlord called me up and complained that her company had not been receiving our monthly rent check. Of course, this was news to me and caught me by surprise because there was no doubt in my mind that the bills were being paid. After all, the fault is never on my end! I made a few phone calls and checked back in my records and sure enough the check had been sent in. We couldn't figure out why they hadn't been receiving our money, but then it dawned on me to verify the address I had been sending it to (that's important!). Sure enough, the address was off by one letter.

All along I had made the effort, but that effort had been directed toward the wrong place. As a result, it had been lost, and in essence it was meaningless. That was the case for the Samaritans. Their worship was meaningless and lost, but I believe it's also the case for us today. We may go through the motions of worship, but the heart is empty. We can even worship good, "godly things" such as preaching, ministry, theology, and seminary education, but if it's not all for the glory of Christ, we will fail and our efforts will remain meaningless. God wants nothing to do with that. I like how Louis Giglio put it. He said, "Guard your worship and evaluate all potential takers!"[2]

I like that because our worship is for Christ alone. One of the five basic beliefs of the Reformation was *Solo Christo*, which means, "in Christ alone." It was the reformers' prayer that the church would be restored to the worship of "Christ alone." And that's as applicable today as ever. When it comes to a relationship with a boyfriend or girlfriend...*Solo Christo!* When a professor challenges the authenticity of scripture...*Solo Christo!* When we're presented with a decision between popularity and truth...*Solo Christo!* When it comes to our preaching of the Word week in and week out...*Solo Christo!* Again, when was the last time you allowed worship to disrupt your life?

In verse 23 of our text, Jesus says, "But the hour is coming, and is now here, when the true worshipers will worship the Father in spirit and truth, for the Father seeks such as these to worship him" (John 4:23).

Catch what he says again, "true worshipers will worship the Father in spirit and truth." You ask, well who or what are "true worshipers"? They are those who realize that Jesus is the truth and the one and the only way to God the Father. But true worshipers who worship "in spirit and truth" completely surrender their heart, mind, and soul to the one and only true God.

Lastly, we see that worthy worship is a continuous decision to surrender. God isn't interested in the half-hearted, somewhat-

---

[2]Louis Giglio. *Don't Waste Your Worship: Wired for a Life of Worship: Part 3*. August 7, 2007. http://blog.worship.com/worship/louie_giglio_wired_for_worship_series.

committed Christians. In fact, He wants nothing to do with that person. Rather, He is seeking true worshipers who will continually decide to surrender themselves before his throne.

You see, the first time the word "worship" is ever used in scripture is found in Genesis 22 when Abraham is asked by God to sacrifice Isaac upon the alter. In verse five, Abraham says to one of his servants, "Stay here with the donkey; the boy and I will go over there; we will worship, and then we will come back to you" (Genesis 22:5).

It's consistent throughout the Bible. The true definition of worthy worship looks like complete surrender. Because we know what Abraham was asked by God to do. He was asked to sacrifice his only son and surrender his own desires to the throne of God. That day, Abraham offered God worthy worship. And completely surrendering doesn't cost one thing; the price is everything. The disturbing truth is that worthy worship disrupts every bit of who we are, but only if we let it. That's the challenge for us today. When was the last time you allowed worthy worship to disrupt your life?

You know, I've been married for almost two years now. God has blessed me with an intelligent, beautiful wife that leaves me wondering to this day, "I sure hope she doesn't wake up one day realizing she could have done so much better!" But ever since June 27, 2008, my life has been completely changed and disrupted. Marriage has been somewhat of a struggle because of the constant and strenuous decision I must make as a person to surrender my desires, my needs, and my agenda to God.

I know that as a follower of Christ the world can offer so many more enticing and seemingly worthwhile distractions. So sometimes I need to stop for a moment, drop what I'm doing, look at my wife, and verbally tell her how worth the fight she is to me. Maybe we need to verbally affirm our allegiance to the one worthy of true worship. As much as I love my wife, how much more significant it is it to surrender to Jesus Christ who paid our eternal debt upon the offensive cross?

I think the Psalmist writes out our invitation perfectly today by proclaiming, "O come, let us worship and bow down, let us kneel before the Lord, our Maker! For he is our God, and we are the people of his pasture, and the sheep of his hand. O that today you would listen to his voice!" (Psalm 95:6-7).

26

"MINISTRY IS IN THE STUFF"
Mark 8:27-38

Brandon Grady

I don't quite get it! Why is ministry so confusing? The wonderfully interesting, yet unarguably regular scenes seem to roll by month after month, and I say that only having been a pastor for just over a year. Worship is facilitated, spurring people to freshly sense God in courageously intense ways, hopefully leaving a lasting impression. Church business, for better or worse, is transacted by committees who invest, to differing degrees, their measure of knowledge and ideas to stimulate the church's growth, while at the same time maintaining its practically essential operations. Some individuals weekly prioritize Christian Education through intentional study in Sunday school or Vacation Bible School, as well as gaining other learning via guest speakers or other biblical and intellectual resources. Continually and without forgiveness, the stages of ministry evolve in people's personal and collective lives too. They might include enduring unspeakable hardship, realizing great joy, searching for identity, acutely being aware of the need for something more, being ready to give up, being terminally ill, being hopeful for the future, being content where one is now and wistfully longing for the past. Stuff! So much Stuff!

Okay, maybe I understand why ministry is so complicated. It's largely because we're all human beings created by God, some of whom have professed a faith in Jesus Christ, yet all of us at a different place in our faith journey. And that conundrum, to me, is not wrong, but rather exciting! Truth be told, if we were all in the same place there wouldn't be any room for sincere discussion, passionate debate and avid opinion. But wait, I forgot the most important entity. There wouldn't be room for Jesus if we individually knew it all, and collectively, we were crammed into a narrow tunnel of thought. We just need to make sure Jesus is leading our lives, regardless of their current timbre. As ministers we must deal with all our stuff and try to be with everybody else in their stuff. What an uncomfortably intimate dichotomy we face.

Obviously, ministry comes with a cost. In Mark 8, Jesus reminds us who he is so we know who's in charge. He then relieves his readers of any doubt about who he is by illustrating to the disciples, especially to Peter, his assertive power. Next, he gives a charge to the disciples and the rest of the crowd to follow him. And finally, he encourages, yet admonishes his audience to not be afraid of serving him at all costs. So for us as ministers, I see four keys to living this account according to Mark, and thereby living in the stuff of the harmonious mystery of ministry. I've tried to make this easy for us friends. Easy, because it's important. All these words you'll notice end with the "ation" suffix. It is a miracle I can even tell you that, because I can't spell! Anyhow, the keys are *preparation*, *affirmation*, *dedication* and *participation*.

Let us start with *preparation*. To undertake any task, we must have an idea of where we want to go. Jesus couldn't have preached half of what he did to the disciples, or anyone else, had he not established who he was and made darn sure they realized the immense greatness with which they were dealing. Preparation is the foundational crux, yet often forgotten thirsting root for any ministry. It involves carefully intentioned organization and planning. It declares consideration for others to make an idea or program happen, as well as expresses encouragement for attending those events. Preparation allows us to thoroughly enjoy the fruit of our labor. You might especially be aware of its necessity when you are planning a trip. Honestly, it's probably not going to be as effective if you just go. Now we're not talking about a simple jaunt over to the supermarket, but a long vacation or business trip. Chances are, unless you're really adventurous, you're going to take steps to develop some kind of basic framework. Well, ministry works the same way. A framework with God as its outline is inordinately essential to bask in ministry's rich awesomeness.

Something else to consider, preparation involves sound communication. We must rely on the network around us to foster a sense of togetherness and not try to do it all by ourselves. Jesus has called us, even if we make mistakes, to pick ourselves up and keep trying. I encourage all of us to think about always properly preparing ourselves for the stuff in ministry. Here's the reality…if we don't, we cannot be surprised or disappointed when more people are not coming to our churches or that ideas glimmer and die. An idea is only a stone unless it's joined with other stones to form a solid foundation.

The second key to live in the stuff of ministry is *affirmation.* Consider our scripture again. Jesus couldn't possibly have won over the hearts of his disciples, nor the rest of the crowd in Philippi, nor any of his hearers ever in history for that matter had he not affirmed at least a portion of who they were, and sincerely encouraged their future living by speaking so succinctly and firmly. Now certainly he wasn't all that affirming of Peter by calling him Satan. But even that was a gesture of calming assertiveness to wedge awareness in the disciple's minds about how most people were actually going to treat him. And when Peter tries to refute Jesus' wisdom, it's no wonder why he's a little ticked off. It's almost as if Jesus is saying to Peter, "Brother; don't try to sugar coat the reality of this whole situation to make everybody feel better!"

Friends, affirmation simply cannot be halfway. It doesn't have to be warmly soft. It can be vehemently paying someone a compliment, or supporting an impassioned plea either by yourself or someone else, as Jesus was doing here. Affirmation is better to be overdone, rather than to not be mentioned at all because it's assumed. What happens if we don't feel affirmed? It's pretty simple. Ministry, even with the best laid plans, will not take flight without some affirmative energy to get it off the ground and keep it sailing along. Also, genuine affirmation cannot be replaced by anything else. Expressions such as thanks, good try or it all came together, just don't cut it! You still haven't actually affirmed a person's effort, as well intentioned as those thoughts might have been. That is why many times, I may over affirm my own congregation. Not because I am trying to butter them up, (I realize, just like any other family of faith, we have our challenges), but because Jesus does not call me as a pastor to emotionally hit people over the head every week. We should all adopt appropriately timed affirmation friends as supportive pillars of the church for one another, and for people we come in contact with when we get the chance. Jesus couldn't possibly have walked with his disciples in their stuff, without affirming their current place, and encouraging them to follow and suffer along with him if necessary. For ministers of the gospel, suffering in certain stuff can reveal surprising faith. All people are the church! We are merely its shepherds. We need to join the disciples in looking to Christ's light to guide us together.

The third key for living in ministry's stuff is *dedication.* So now the framework has been laid, and we have positive direction and are going to move forward. But none of it can happen without true dedication. Hence, I point us to Jesus' insistence that the disciples willingly take up their cross and risk a life of following in divine obedience. Dedication involves awareness of a ministry, keeping up to date with its current goings on, and making sure to be a living sacrifice when necessary. Friends, we cannot have an idea then not agree to dedicate ourselves to making it happen. Admittedly, dedication can be time consuming. It can involve large expenditures of energy, emotion and attention. Dedication, to a certain extent, should exhaust us, but at the same time invigorate us! It also absolutely inspires others to pitch in and work hard, similar to the qualities of a sports team. In a special feature on the DVD of the movie, *The Natural*, baseball legend Cal Ripken Jr. talks about his view of success. Even though he is one of the greatest individual players in baseball history, what mattered most to him was succeeding as a team. In the interview he says, "I'd much rather be referred to, not as an individually great player or someone who tore up the record books, but someone who came to the ballpark and said, 'Okay, I'm here, I want to play, what can I do to help us win today.'" Any Baltimore Oriole who saw Cal throwing himself on the ground to stop a ball, putting in extra effort with other guys to help them improve, and speaking at certain engagements to inspire confidence in yearning souls to try a little harder benefited from being around his example day in and day out. Ripken's dedication is well documented because he played 2632 consecutive games, becoming baseball's well known "Iron Man." His dedication rippled through his clubhouse and on the field. He embodied the principle that when one guy sacrifices for the team, pretty soon, everybody does. That's what the church should be about. Living in the stuff of ministry means seeing when there's a need and asking how we can work as a team to help out. Let us dedicate ourselves to people in our ministries friends, and even the strongly annoying and the apparently fruitless stuff can, in the end, taste delicious!

The final key is *participation*. Now this key seems the most obvious, and yet, it is the one often conveniently discarded. Bottom line, a church's ministry will not flourish if there is nobody participating! And that is our job as persons called out by God. That is, to communicate to others participation's sincere importance. Notice, I didn't emphasize the church as a business, but a ministry. Ministry without participation becomes downright discouraging. Many churches are struggling with declining membership, and I will not deny our efforts should be channeled to effectively reach out to bring more people in. However, we need also to encourage the congregants we do have to participate in the nurturing faith of the nourishing spirit-filled community in order to fully realize profound edification in our ministry. Now does that mean everyone will participate in every church program? No! But perhaps we can think of small steps, just as Jesus did, to invite, not turn away people from the transforming church. Our task is to model Christ's example so people will not be ashamed but be proud of sharing agape love with everyone. The level of our participation needs to be measured by our authenticity, not our busyness! To live in the stuff of ministry, we must name areas in which we really can grow, not dwell on ones that will set us up to fail. Remember, Jesus warns the crowd not to invest in anything that obtains them personal gain, but prospers them in a spirit-led divine will. So please prayerfully consider how you can help your ministry take that next step by participating healthily in its stuff together with Jesus in a way you might not have before.

I'd like to conclude with a story depicting an interaction between a first grade teacher and one of her male students on the first day of school. Accustomed to going home at noon in kindergarten, the boy was getting his things ready to leave for home when he was actually supposed to be heading to lunch with the rest of the class. The teacher asked him what he was doing. "I'm going home," he replied. The teacher tried to explain that now that he was in the first grade, he would have a longer school day. "You'll go eat lunch now," she said, "and then you'll come back to the room and do some more work before you go home." Well, the boy looked up at her in disbelief, hoping she was kidding. Convinced of her seriousness, he then put his hands on his hips and demanded, "Who on earth signed me up for this program?"

Brothers and sisters, as ministers and Christians, I'm sure we all want to ask that question many times when we enter new ventures, establish firm principles, and examine fresh perspectives. There is no doubt ministry can be a scary proposition. Yet, divine blessing can nourish our doubt and our souls can be filled! Therefore, let us take up our cross and follow Jesus fearlessly just as the disciples did in Mark's gospel. Let us support one another in fortified determination and live in the stuff of ministry through preparation, affirmation, dedication and participation. Let us walk with Jesus, being led by the Holy Spirit, and being supported by God, as we truly enjoy the vast mystery, as well as the beautiful tapestry ministry really can be! Come. Don't be afraid. Jesus is waiting. Are you ready?

27

"YOU ARE THE LIGHT"

Matthew 16:25-26

Alyssa Haller

First, let me say what a blessing it is to be here today with all of you in this beautiful sanctuary. It is truly an honor to be here at the Festival of Young Preachers, and I'd like to thank the people who put this event together and for inviting me to be a part of it. I also have to thank those people from my home church who came to see me today. I am truly blessed to have your support.

It is every person's desire to live a successful life and leave his or her own individual legacy. Every person strives to leave the world a better place after their time on earth has ended. But a worthwhile life is defined in so many ways. Some would say success is having a bestseller book written about your life after you have passed. Others may claim that a mark of success is having millions of people know your name all over the world. Or maybe the mark of a truly worthwhile life is having time itself measured by the year of your death. Well, when it comes to meaningful lives, I know of only one that has accomplished all three of these feats and countless others–Jesus Christ.

The story of Jesus' life, contained in the Bible, has sold more copies than even the *Harry Potter* series, and rightfully so considering it is the most beautiful story ever told. In his short life, spanning just over three decades, Jesus became the greatest teacher the world has ever seen. He gained many followers and from his birth has showered the world with an abundance of miracles. The life of Jesus Christ continues to impact the world each and every day thousands of years after his death. His life remains the most cherished life in all of history, the one example of a perfect being. Christians all over the world study Jesus' actions and strive to live in his ways.

The fact remains that Jesus was perfect, so striving to live like him is a daunting task. In his perfect lifetime, Jesus was able to completely resist the temptations of Satan and live a life without sin. When tempted after forty days of fasting, Jesus refuses to give in to Satan's demands. Even at his weakest, Christ refuses to create food for himself or test God in any way. Instead, Jesus sends Satan away and claims that only God is worthy of worship and service. For us, however, striving to live in the sinless ways of Christ requires constant confession. Every week, every day, and every hour we must ask God to forgive our constant sinning. Then and only then can we take complete comfort in the fact that God has already forgiven us. Through the life and death of Jesus Christ, God has rectified the sinful nature of humans. We have been saved.

Trying to be perfect will wear you down quickly and completely, and it will often leave you in worse shape than when you began. Instead of aiming for perfection, we should turn to the word of God to find out what the Lord requires of us. We can take comfort in Micah 6:8 which says, "He has told you, O mortal, what is good; and what does the LORD require of you but to do justice, and to love kindness, and to walk humbly with your God?" Read in those terms, when we listen to what God wants us to do, the all-consuming task of living a Christian life becomes less impossible. As long as we dedicate our lives to mercy and justice and listen to God's will along the way, maybe striving to live like Jesus isn't so hard.

I'm sure at some point of your spiritual journey you have stood in awe of the miracles Jesus performed throughout his lifetime. From turning water into wine to feeding 5,000 people with one child's lunch, Jesus Christ caused miraculous events to unfold everywhere he went. So how can those of us here today and Christians all over the world striving to live like Christ recreate his deeds? Jesus is known as a miraculous healer. Many of his miracles instantly rid victims of paralysis, leprosy, and other plagues. Therefore, in order to live like Jesus, we should heal. I'm not saying that every time you meet a blind man you should offer to smear mud on his eyes. No, instead we should focus our efforts on the spiritual healing of the people around us. We should recognize when a friend needs help, realize when there is a plague upon their heart, and we should heal as Jesus healed.

One of the best ways to heal does not require us to tell a crippled man to walk. In fact, one of the best ways to heal is to just listen, and to tell those in suffering that you understand their pain. More importantly, tell those in suffering that Jesus feels their pain, that he desires to take it upon himself and lift their burden so that they may be healed. A friend that loses a loved one, a good person that makes poor decisions, and any person that strays from the path of righteousness will require spiritual healing. This is when as servants, messengers, and disciples of Christ, we should heal in his name.

In addition to healing, we should live our lives in service to others. In Mark 10:43-44, Jesus tells us in his own words how to live righteously. He says, "Whoever wishes to become great among you must be your servant, and whoever wishes to be first among you must be slave to all. For the Son of Man came not to be served but to serve, and to give his life a ransom for many." Jesus came to serve others. Christ came to serve all people in God's name, eventually giving his life for the salvation of sinners. For that reason, to truly live like Jesus we must give of ourselves to others. When we use all of our talents and abilities for the benefit of others, we just might find that striving to live like Jesus does not require miracles but results in them.

In using our talents and abilities, we must be like Jesus as he walked on water. We must have faith. Faith that all our endeavors in the name of Jesus Christ will be blessed by God and succeed as miracles here on earth. We must strive to have faith like Christ as we set about serving others. Often it is hardest to have faith in Christ when we lose faith in ourselves and our ability to do work in his name.

On one of my annual mission trips to the Appalachian Mountains, I did construction work on a small laundry room. The Appalachian Service Project staff showed my crew the work site and anticipated that the project would take no more three days. Our task was to replace the floor in the laundry room which was ready to collapse under the weight of the washer and dryer. We were there to make the area safe for the family, especially the children living in the home. As my crew began working to lift out the old floor we discovered that the many layers of flooring (held together by everything from screws to masking tape) and the very cramped work space created hidden challenges. It was hard for the crew to work in the small room all at once, and soon some of youth began to feel useless waiting for their turn to work. Attitudes worsened, and due to the unforeseen difficulties and our own inexperience, we fell further and further behind on our deadline to get the job done.

One afternoon my crew was about to make major strides in our work by putting in the first layer of the new floor. However, when we loaded the new flooring into the house, we discovered that the measurements were about an inch off and the entire floorboard would have to be redone. The new floor was the last sign of hope for my work crew. We had based the rest of our plans for the week on the new floor being installed that evening, and when we encountered another road block my entire crew was crushed. That afternoon no one spoke on the drive back to our mission center. We played no music; we told none of our usual jokes. All in all, we had lost our last ounce of faith. Throughout the evening the other members of my work crew and I complained to our friends about our hardships. We focused on ourselves and our weaknesses rather than how we could channel our abilities to accomplish something for the family in need.

The next morning on the drive to our work site, we wondered who we were serving and how we were attempting to go about our service. We realized in unison that we had forgotten our purpose in Appalachia. We had not traveled so far and worked so hard to satisfy ourselves. Our goal that week was to live like Christ and ultimately serve others. When we realigned our focus and began to serve faithfully, we were able to accomplish a week's amount of work in two days time. I truly believe that a miracle took place that week. It was a miracle in the shape of a laundry room built in faithful service to others by a minister, an oral hygienist, and five teenagers with no construction experience. Perhaps studying the miracles Jesus performed and turning that knowledge into action in our lives doesn't require miracles on our part. Maybe for us it is as simple as having enough faith to humbly follow the Lord's will and striving live like Christ.

"For those who want to save their life will lose it, and those who lose their life for my sake will find it" (Matthew 16:25). Beginning a life as a follower of Jesus Christ always requires a recognition that you are called. You are called to sacrifice your sinful ways. You are called to heal the sick, and you are called to work in faith. You are called to live your life for him, and lastly, you are called to tell others the story of Christ. Christ is using you each and every day in your actions and in your words to lead others to the light of salvation. In studying the son of God and proclaiming the good news of his life and death, you become a teacher, a healer, and a miracle worker. Matthew 5:16 says, "Let your light shine before others, so that they may see your good works and give glory to your Father in heaven. I urge all of you to leave here today with renewed faith in yourselves and an unfailing faith in Jesus Christ because "You are the light of the world!"

28

"HIGHLY UNLIKELY"
John 4:5-24

Kara Hildebrandt

An odd, an unusual, an unlikely sequence of events. A highly unlikely situation is where we find Jesus and a Samaritan woman. An unlikely story to have relevance in the 21st century. We have different cultural norms, have different struggles, have a different concept of the world from the 1st century. An unlikely story of any relevance to us yet we must examine its intricacies and complexities with respect to what it means to worship God.

Why is the story highly unlikely? In reading through the gospels we are acquainted with Jesus speaking with people who are the oppressed, who are in need, who are the outcasts, who are the enemies of society. These are the stories we are used to reading, hearing, knowing. Yet from the very beginning this story is different. This story grabs a reader's attention. Jesus walks to the city of Sychar in Samaria...an unlikely place to find a Jew. Jews were not commonly seen in Samaria because they were considered a disgusting people. A worthless people. Yet the Jews were not the only ones filled with hatred. It was not just Jew against Samaritan. It was also Samaritan against Jew. They did not want to see a Jew in their vicinity. The relationship between the two was so hostile and hate filled that the closest modern day example is the animosity between the Jews and Hamas.[1] They would rather see each other lying in the street dead. The relationship is defined by hatred, pain, loathing. That is the relationship between Jews and Samaritans. For Jesus to walk into Samaria is unthinkable but he does not stop there. He sits down near Jacob's well at noon. An unlikely place, an unlikely time...sitting, watching, waiting, asking for water.

When an unlikely person a women comes to draw water from the well. And it is here that Jesus asks for the basic necessity of life...

[1]Amy Jill-Levine, *The Misunderstood Jew* (New York: HarperCollins, 2006), 149.

water... The Samaritan woman turns to him and states the obvious. "How is it that you, a Jew, ask a drink of me, a woman of Samaria?" (John 4:9). A modern day rendition of this question would better be suited to "Are you serious? Do you honestly think that I am going to give you a drink? Have you completely lost it in thinking that you would want me near you? You hate me...I hate you...We don't speak to each other. We have not, do not, and will not give each other what we need. At this abrupt statement, Jesus confidently answers back, "If you knew the gift of God, and who it is that is saying to you, 'Give me a drink', you would have asked him, and he would have given you living water" (John 4:10). Jesus is asking the woman to look beyond his Jewishness, to look beyond the hatred, to look beyond the ideologies, to look beyond the cultural norms. Jesus is offering a completely different understanding of how to see each other, of how to understand God, of how to understand neighbor. However, the Samaritan woman cannot fathom what he is saying, so she responds skeptically...as we all would. She wants to know how, where such a living water, where such a society, where such a people could exist. If today we said that a member of the Taliban would give a U.S. citizen water we would laugh, we would say impossible. We would say what a dream. If we said that Hamas and the Jews were joining together in peace, we would say it was only a fantasy.

The Samaritan woman looks at Jesus and says, who do you think you are? Do you think there is something different about you, that you could bring together two groups who hate one another. And why do you... a Jew want anything to do with a Samaritan and why would I want to have anything to do with you? Jesus responds again with a statement of life, not judgment, not I am better because of culture, but instead "those who drink of the water that I will give them will never be thirsty. The water that I will give will become in them a spring of water gushing up to eternal life" (John 4:14). In this moment Jesus shows an unlikely love of reconciliation, a love for the other, a love that quenches the hatred, a never ending love that satisfies need. And the Samaritan...She begins to think maybe this is something I want yet she is still unsure because of a foundational problem. She says, "Sir, I see that you are a prophet. Our ancestors worshiped on this mountain, but you say that the place where people must worship is in Jerusalem" (John 4:19-20).

Jesus response to her is an unlikely one, and at first glance it seems he is holding the Jews above the Samaritans or even speaking directly about himself when he says "You worship what you do not know; we worship what we know, for salvation is from the Jews" (John 4:22). To a Samaritan these would be fighting words, these are the words of hate, these are the words a Samaritan would expect from a Jew, these are the words that do not build a relationship but instead eliminate the prospect of loving one another as God loves. Yet when we closely examine the text further, Jesus is offering a new way, a different way of understanding worship, of understanding God. Jesus offers an unlikely alternative. When he says "But the hour is coming, and is now here, when the true worshipers will worship the Father in spirit and truth, for the Father seeks such as these to worship him. God is spirit, and those who worship him must worship in spirit and truth" (John 4:23-24). Jesus is saying worship is no longer about the right place, the right action, about being divisive, but worship is to be about glorifying God.

Worship is about a diverse people coming together, a people who have different ideas, are different culturally, have different beliefs, are different in understanding what it means to worship God because it is first and foremost about glorifying God, about loving neighbor, acknowledging that God is with us in a multitude of ways, and even though we are different God's spirit is with us and somewhere in what we say and what we do there are pieces of God's truth.

God's truth is somewhere in our worship. Jesus speaks to the fundamental task of loving neighbor, showing compassion, giving water to our enemies, but he goes further in delving further into what we hold sacred, what defines us. He directly challenges our understanding of worship. Jesus is not content with just loving our enemies or quenching our hate. We are not to just show respect and love our enemies in public. We are not to just give them water, show compassion when they are hurting, stop by the side of the road and help, but we are to do something even more unlikely. Jesus is calling us to the most unlikely of actions. Jesus is calling us to have respect for our enemies, those we dislike and those we disagree with in how they worship.

The 21st century church is not far removed from the Jewish and Samaritan animosity. In fact, we may understand it just as well as the Samaritan woman. We enjoy claiming we are a part of the one universal holy catholic church and that we worship God yet we allow our differences to breed disrespect, polarize our ideologies, and disregard how each other worship. We use language of us versus them, we begin to convince ourselves that we have the right way to worship, we worship correctly, we know what God wants, we are the ones who truly worship God. Others must be mistaken; we refuse to participate in each other's worship because we can't agree with how we pray, if the songs are right, we can't agree with who is leading, and if the sacraments are taken correctly. We allow our diversity to destroy our relationships. It is in this place that we hear the words of Jesus calling us to an unlikely place, a new place of understanding worshipping.

We are called to the unlikely place of respecting, of participating in each other's worship, learning from our differences, allowing ourselves to be challenged by the things that make us uncomfortable, that we don't understand. We are called to be a people united in our diversity, called to challenge each other, called to love one another, called to build each other up in the ways we worship because worship is not about us, how it makes us feel, about what we are comfortable with, worship is about God and what God does.

Howard Marshall, a New Testament scholar at the University of Aberdeen, says that worship is about looking beyond the human actions and remembering that "From the beginning it is God who takes the initiative in the creation of the world and the people in it, in providential care of them and in communicating with them in various ways. The Bible is the story of what God does and how people respond to him, both positively and negatively."[2] Worship is about God and not about us, which is what Jesus is stating in his unlikely words to the Samaritan women, "But the hour is coming, and is now here, when the true worshipers will worship" (John 4:23). We are the unlikely ones who are called by God to worship God in our diversity.

Thanks be to God. Amen.

---

[2]Marshall, I. Howard, *The Westminster Theological Wordbook of the Bible* (Louisville: Westminster John Knox, 2003), 543

29

"SILENCE THE FLUTES"

Mark 5: 21-43

Joshua Johannes

As a young pastor who really loves the church and the Christian faith in all its many forms, it seems as if there are a few things that always come up in conversation. Chief among these things is the future of the church. Last year, before Easter, *Newsweek* featured an article called, "The Decline and Fall of Christian America." The article, written by John Meacham, was surprisingly cordial, but a few things really stuck out. He noted that the percentage of self-identified Christians has fallen 10 percentage points since 1990, from 86 to 76 percent. The percentage of people who say they are unaffiliated with any particular faith has doubled in recent years, to 16 percent; meanwhile, the number of people willing to describe themselves as atheist or agnostic has increased about fourfold from 1990 to 2009, from 1 million to about 3.6 million.[1]

As a young pastor, these facts, statements, and statistics have at best been challenging to me. At worst, however, these statements have been extremely discouraging to me. It was during a night of discouragement and distress that this particular text came alive for me. In it I have found the hope of Christ for our present situation.

Our story begins as Jesus Christ is stepping out of his boat onto the Galilean coast. As he steps, I am sure that in the distance he can see the crowds coming toward him. I know nowadays there is nothing better for a preacher than a crowd, but here in Mark the crowds are left in mystery as to whether they are a good thing or a bad thing. So I imagine they can hear the footsteps approaching them. I picture it almost like a swarm of locusts consuming a plentiful crop. This crowd advancing on him is full of quite desperate men and woman. They are the mentally and physically ill, they are demon possessed, and they are hungry for what they can get from Jesus.

---

[1]Jon Meacham, "The End of Christian America," *Newsweek*, 04 April 2009.

But amid this crowd, it seems one person is able to stand out. Whether he is out in the lead or has the loudest voice or a way of getting attention, a man named Jairus is heard above the others. Jairus is like no other in this crowd. Jairus was a ruler of the synagogue, one of the most prestigious and powerful positions in this Jewish Galilean society. He is not mentally or physically ill. He is not demonic; however, I am sure at face value his desperation makes him look very much like those around him. And as he comes up to Christ here, he comes crying out, "My little daughter lies at the point of death. Come and lay your hands on her, that she may be healed, and she will live." Much to Jairus' pleasure, Christ agrees to come with him, but now they must work their way through this massive crowd in order to arrive back at Jairus' home.

I imagine Jairus was so panicked pushing his way through the crowd. I imagine he was sweating and panting and pleading. I imagine every moment of working through this mob drained Jairus of everything he had. So I can imagine Jairus' reaction when he turns around to see that Jesus is no longer following him but has stopped. Amid this overpowering crowd, Jesus has ceased walking and now the disciples are perplexed as they pass through a collage of arms and legs and faces. They have to check their steps to make sure that they do not crush anyone. Then the text says that Jesus stopped and asked, "Who touched my clothes?" It's funny the texts says the disciples responded by saying, "You see this multitude thronging you and you ask who touched you?" Essentially the disciples are saying, "What do mean? I touched you, he touched you. Everybody in the crowd touched you!" But as they look about it becomes apparent that something different has taken place. They can see a woman trembling on the ground in fear. The text tells us that this woman has had a flow of blood. This flow of blood is a common experience for women, but what is uncommon is that this woman's flow has continued longer than it should. Twelve years longer than it should. Leviticus tells us that such women are unclean. Not only are they unclean, but everything they touch and are touched by becomes unclean. The only decision for a community to make is to separate itself from this person. They do this often by making the unclean remain outside and away from the people. They can't be around their families. They can't go into synagogue. They truly can't do anything. For all intents and purposes, this woman is dead. She has spent the last twelve years of her life personally, socially, and spiritually dead. She has spent the past years walking about daily experiencing death.

This woman has good reason to shake in fear. She has reached out and touched someone. You see, by reaching out and touching this man, she can potentially make him unclean. Her touch will force him to have to go ritually purify himself and be unclean until evening. However, she believes that if she can just touch the edge of Jesus' garment, she can be made well. And as her filthy, unclean, defiling fingers touch Jesus, corrupt Jesus, something else happens. This woman who had the power to bring uncleanness upon Jesus has been made clean by this touch. It's as if this woman's uncleanness, her ability to defile has been overpowered by Jesus power to cleanse. So now this woman stands here fearing and trembling, knowing that she has broken the rules. She fears what this man will do to her. But Jesus doesn't bring her words of condemnation. Rather, he says, "Your faith has made you well."

We have to realize that as this is going on, there is still another story taking place. We have Jairus standing toward the front of the crowd. I'm sure that at least five percent of Jairus is overjoyed for this woman right now, but the other ninety-five percent is thinking we have got to go. The text tells us that while Jesus is still speaking, while he is still saying to woman "Daughter, your faith has made you well. Go in peace, and be healed of your affliction," another crowd shows up. This crowd comes from Jairus' home. They come to tell Jairus that his daughter is dead. They have come interrupting Jesus message of life with a message of death. They are not bad people either. They are not pessimistic, negative, or mistaken. They are just honest. They come with the truth; the truth is that there is a dead girl who needs to be honored with mourning and a funeral.

This crowd comes to inform Jairus of the unfortunate news of death. They are too late. There is no point in bothering this "teacher" anymore. The girl is dead. Jairus has to be torn. If they hadn't have been thronged by this crowd and stopped by this unclean woman, maybe then they could have made it. But Jesus looks over at Jairus and says, "Don't be afraid, just believe." And quite possibly the most amazing part of this story is that Jairus believes. Think about it. No matter how sick a person is, we rush them to the hospital. But we don't often take dead bodies into the emergency room. Adding to that, in this culture and time you did not keep a dead body with you for days. No, a dead body is buried as soon as possible. Jairu's actions need to turn from outreach to mourning.

Instead, he follows Jesus back to his home. There, the funeral service has already begun. There are mourners wailing outside to display the sorrow of this situation. They exchange their mourning for momentary laughter when Jesus suggests the little girl is just sleeping. Jesus ignores them and brings Jairus, his wife, and some disciples into the room with the child. He then looks at the cold body of a twelve-year-old girl and says to her, *Talitha cumi,* "Little daughter, arise." She has been saved. Jairus' plea has been answered, and Jesus tells them to feed the child and our healing stories come to an end.

Recently, my soul has been very distressed. It's been distressed because of a message I have heard from good people. It is distressed because I have heard from people within and people without the church that church is dead. That religion is dead. That it is time to put the church to rest. Rip our clothes, shave our heads and bury these old buildings. My distress this morning is fleeing because I have learned that we should always show caution in declaring something dead when Jesus is just around the corner.

I have heard that there are no new people in the church; there are new people at the lake and at the bar, but not at the church. As I hear these facts about the direction of our world and the forecast of our church, I hear it like the sound of funeral flutes in my ear–flutes that play so loud and so powerful that they drown out our worship services. But despite the power of the flute, I hear something else also. I hear a gentle voice in my ear saying to me, *Talitha cumi,* "Little daughter, arise."

Today, let's not let the funeral outside convince us there is no life in the house. Do not let that flute cause you to miss out on the life inside. As I think about Jairus and his family, I know there came a point that Jairus finally had to go and open the door of his home. And I imagine that after he opened the door, he had to shout out into the crowd, "Silence the flute! End the funeral! Here she comes!"

As young people of the Christian faith, let's not let the funeral outside convince us there isn't life on the inside. Don't let the sound of flutes drown out the voice that is calling out to us, *Talitha cumi,* "Little daughter, arise." But let's walk out as the little girl did–shocking those who have declared us dead. Let us silence the flutes with our life, with our love, and with our salvation. Amen.

30

"HOW WE ARE TO LIVE"
1 Corinthians 13

Katie Lynde

Good morning everyone! Today's scripture reading comes from the book of 1 Corinthians. This is a pretty common scripture that many people know by heart. Presently, I am in the process of memorizing this text since it will be a part of my wedding this October. These verses of love provide instructions on how to live life in relationship to those around us. It addresses those we love such as family and friends, brothers and sisters in Christ, and married couples.

Instead of telling you a lovely tale of a couple of their wedding day expressing their love to their church, family, and friends, I instead want to tell you a story about my aunt who was recently in a car accident. My Aunt Kathy is a strong woman. She has worked her way up the ladder and broken through the glass ceiling in her career. She is a successful college dean, has a great marriage, and is a wonderful mother to my cousin. My aunt is also very fit at the young age of 54, running 5-10 miles per day. And as if running wasn't enough, she also goes to the gym to work out most nights after dinner.

On the evening of December 29, 2009, my aunt was walking to the gym when she was hit by a car as she started to cross the road at the crosswalk. Had she not stepped back a few inches before being hit, she would have died on impact. Instead, because of these few inches, both her legs were broken and she was rushed to the hospital for emergency surgery to put rods in her legs.

When I received the phone call telling me what happened, my whole world stopped. I had spent the day picking out bridesmaid dresses with my sisters and girlfriend. I was having a great time in my own little world when BAM, just like that my world was turned upside down. I was crying, and I was angry at this man who hit my aunt. Because he was in such a hurry to make the traffic light, he broke both my aunt's legs, taking away her ability to run, walk, and stand. Even though I was happy my aunt was alive, I let anger overtake me and I wanted justice.

So how does this tie into 1 Corinthians? Well, in this story about my aunt, I was not demonstrating the love that is explained to us in this text. I love my aunt, but could not love the man who injured her. It wasn't until a few days later I learned more about how the man reacted after hitting my aunt with his car. I learned how sorry this man had been as he held her alongside the road, calling 911 and my uncle. He kept apologizing and had the guts to still call for help and call my uncle to tell him that he had just hit his wife and she needed immediate emergency care. When I hear this, I think, WOW! How hard that must have been for this man to do all that he did. In all that happened, this man demonstrated love to my aunt even after he accidently messed up.

1 Corinthians tells us that, "Love is patient," and for all I know patience is what this man needed to learn by not being in such a hurry when driving. Love is patient with us as we make mistakes and wrong turns. True love stands by us and doesn't abandon us or leave us stranded when we mess up. It patiently waits for us to pick up the pieces and continue on. As 1 Corinthians 13:2-3 says, "If I have prophetic powers, and understand all mysteries and all knowledge, and if I have all faith, so as to remove mountains, but do not have love, I am nothing. If I give away all my possessions, and if I hand over my body so that I may boast, but do not have love, I gain nothing."

This can also tie in with Jesus' beatitudes in the Gospel of Matthew. To have and demonstrate the qualities of the beatitudes is great, but if you don't practice them with love, then it means nothing. Everyone has heard of people trying to "buy" the love of someone, often times a parent trying to buy the love of a child when all the child really wants is love. Material stuff is great to an extent, but when you are in a near death accident you want more than just your sweet sports car, your designer clothes, your big house, and your vacation home. You want your family, your loved ones to be there by your side.

When I think of family and how my parents taught me to treat my family, this verse pretty much sums it up, "It bears all things, believes all things, hopes all things, endures all things. Love never ends" (1 Corinthians 13:7). Families stick up for each other. They trust each other. They always hope for the best. Let's face it, it is tough work to be in a family, but it is also way worth it to know that you have the constant love of your parents, siblings, aunts, uncles, and grandparents. This love is demonstrated to us by our parents and families, but comes from God and his love for us. God is just like that parent or sibling who is always there for you no matter what, always in your corner cheering you on.

This love is also expressed through our church families. When I began my freshman year of college, I came home for fall break with a lot of questions and concerns for my minister Liz. I talked to her about changing my major to religious studies and pursuing the ministry. She greeted me with open arms, and my congregation supported me in becoming licensed within my denomination. All my church family took an interest. They wanted to hear what was going on, what I was thinking, and they wanted to hear me preach.

Through the support, love, and guidance of my church family, I preached my first sermon in December 2008. It took a lot of hard work and planning, but in the end I delivered a short, successful sermon. And even though we got out of church early because the service ended up being so short, everyone in my congregation was happy with what I said and happy to see me in the pulpit. My congregation demonstrated the love of 1 Corinthians 13 to me. They were patient and kind, and they had my back. They were there to support and love me no matter how bad the sermon went.

One of my favorite singers is Jana Standfield. Her songs are encouraging and challenging. One her songs, "Love Only Knows," describes the power of God's love shown to us through Jesus:

> Love knows no color.
> Love knows no race.
> Love knows no country.
> Love knows no faith.
> Love plays no favorites.
> Love doesn't care who or what or why or where.
> Love knows no titles.
> Love knows no names.
> Love knows no history, no pride or shame.
> Love keeps no secrets.

Love builds no walls.
And I believe there's love in us all.[1]

These are powerful lyrics. This song makes love that much bigger, not by telling us all that love is, but rather what love isn't. And I believe this is true of God and our relationship with him through Jesus Christ. Are these not the good qualities we like to attribute to God? Do we not want God's love to be as this song describes? Love knows no color, race, country, or faith. Love doesn't play favorites or care about what titles we hold, what our names are. Love builds no walls. Most importantly, love is in us all! Everyone has the spark, the love of God inside them waiting to illuminate their entire being. Love is patient enough to wait for us. Just as a parent waits for his or her child to come home...love remains.

It is through Jesus' teachings in Matthew 5:1-12 and 1 Corinthians 13 that we as Christians can grow in our faith and relationship with God. And it is with these words that I conclude: "Now faith, hope, and love abide, these three; and the greatest of these is love" (1 Corinthians 13:13).

---

[1]Jana Standfield, "Love Only Knows," from the album *Brave Faith,* Relatively Famous Records, 1998.

31

"THE COST OF DISCIPLESHIP"
Mark 8:27-38

Michael Oellig

Before I get started, I would like to thank the Academy of Preachers for hosting and providing this opportunity for individuals like myself to explore the ministry of preaching. Secondly, I would like to thank my spiritual mentors, in particular Brother Brandon Grady. Lastly and most importantly, I would like to thank Jesus Christ for coming into this world to show us by example.

....

Today, the media coerces us into what we should do or believe. They want us to buy every new gadget, read *Cosmo*, *Living* or *"O"* magazines which tell us how to live our lives or what side of any particular story we should believe. While I do not believe the media is inherently bad, certainly *"O"* magazine might have a good article on how to do something romantic for your spouse. Obviously, God did not send Christ here to give us romance tips. I think, however, that there is a more important point. I believe we must be able to differentiate between how they want us to believe or live and how the Bible tells us to believe or live. You see, the media has filled us with ideas of what the American dream is. We must now live in a large house, have two cars per driver in each household, and have 2.5 children. Haven't we lost what the original American dream was all about?

Many early Europeans came here due to religious conflict. It was the dream of the Pilgrims, Puritans, Anabaptists, and others to make a better life here where they could worship freely and do the work of the Lord as they saw fit. What if we had the same feeling of religious freedom as we worship or do the work today? Today many churches have become a media outlet; they create, produce, market, and sell church as a product to individuals. Many churches want us to believe that our Christian walk is an individual decision, and we walk in and out of church as if we are going to a movie theater without ever knowing our neighbor. Discipleship starts in strong Christian community and is rarely cultivated by individuals in isolation. How is it that we can restore the true American dream of vigor for discipleship in our communities?

In Mark 8:31, we find Christ talking about his purpose on earth. He says he must suffer, be rejected by the religious authorities, and be killed, and be raised from the dead after three days. Peter, one of Christ's disciples, rebukes him for what he is saying. Peter doesn't like the thought of suffering and death. Christ responds to Peter, "Get behind me, Satan! For you are setting your mind not on divine things but on human things" (Mark 8:33*b*). You see, Christ wants us to know that following him requires sacrifice and commitment.

All too often our secular lives are clouded by the media. The media likes to report bad news because bad news sells. Unfortunately, too many of us do not want to hear news of good deeds, "true" Christian acts of love, or peacemaking initiatives. We are so confused; we no longer live lives like Christ, but rather, use the Bible to justify our actions or the actions of others. The Bible has been used to justify slavery, war, and polygamy. Oftentimes, we hear someone say they have been blessed by God. We later find out they own a new Mercedes Benz. As consumers, when we buy something, do we ask how we will use that object for Christ's ministry? If we can't give an honest answer, then we probably don't need it. If we were to purchase a larger house with extra room, do we purchase it for more comfort or do we purchase it to help someone in need who may need a place to stay? We must reject Satan's motives in our lives and start accepting the motives of Christ. We must learn how to reject excess in our culture and accept the way of the Lord. Our hearts are not to be partially devoted to Christ, but rather, wholly devoted to Christ.

Jesus continues his teaching in Mark 8:34-35 by saying, "If any want to become my followers, let them deny themselves and take up their cross and follow me. For those who want to save their life will lose it, and those who lose their life for my sake, and for the sake of the gospel, will save it." It is a call to reject our personal ambitions and follow Christ. We are to take up our cross and follow him. We are to sacrifice our lives in his name. We will have no eternal gain by profiting from the world, but we will gain eternal life by following in the ways of Christ.

I believe that Christ illustrates what it means to really follow him in Luke 18:22. In this parable, a rich young ruler asks Christ what it takes to enter into the kingdom of God. Christ instructs him to sell all that he owns and give it to the poor. To the ruler, selling everything he owned was the ultimate sacrifice. As the wealthiest nation in the history of the world, what are we willing to sell in order to enter the kingdom of heaven? Some may charge me with heresy for saying that we do great things as a nation, but I ask you, do you donate your money after all your bills are paid or before they are paid? To those of you who give before the bills are paid, how much time have you given directly to the Lord in service? The point is we will not be able to keep all the commandments, and more than likely, we will not live a life of poverty so that we may help others. The choice to follow the Lord must be an intellectual decision, and perhaps discipleship is not for everyone. While recruiting followers, Jesus calls Simon and Andrew in the first chapter of Mark. Christ calls the brothers out of the fishing business, and they left everything and followed him. Can we say this is true about our lives as we follow Christ? Are we ready to sacrifice our careers, ambitions or lives for a career in discipleship? These brothers had no fear; they wanted to follow Christ.

The cost of discipleship may be beyond our comfort level. We may not want to accept a more fundamentalist view of Christ's life. Some may say, "Christ suffered for us, so we don't have to suffer any more." We must accept that Christ's disciples lived simple lives and sacrificed a great deal of their personal ambitions to follow him. The Christian walk is not an easy walk. It is not a path for everyone. The requirements are great for those who wish to live a Christ-centered life. We must be ready to donate our time. Time can be spent in prayer, meditation, self-examination, or Bible study. Time also needs to be spent ministering to the poor, the blind, and the sick. We need to be humble servants of the community. Our time is equal to money. While financial giving is important, American churches have allowed financial giving to replace living by Christ's example. We can't buy our way to heaven. We must take up our cross and follow him.

In a nation filled with an erroneous view of the Christian life, we must learn how to differentiate between what is pious in God's plan and the myths created by the media. We must take up our cross and follow Christ, even in the times of great suffering. If we cannot wholeheartedly surrender our hearts, minds, and souls to Christ, we will never be able to follow him. We must be able to reject the luxuries and excesses of life. We must be prepared to die defending our actions in the name of our Lord and Savior Jesus Christ. We must give up our time, money, and resources to better humanity. I challenge all of us to thoroughly examine ourselves and decide if we are going to take up our cross and follow Christ. Amen.

32

"LETTING JESUS DRIVE"

Mark 8:27-38

T. J. Pancake

Three years ago, my sister left home to go to Nashville, Tennessee to attend college. There she developed a strange affinity for country music. I'm not really sure how that happened; however, now Carrie Underwood has ended up on my iPod. In one of her most famous songs, she sings: "Jesus take the wheel…take it from my hands. Because I can't do this on my own. I'm letting go."

I don't know about you, but I hate asking for and receiving help. You can just ask my mom. She will say, "Hey, you want help writing your paper?" I reply, "No mom, I got it." "You want help applying for that scholarship?" "No mom, I got it." I love being the sole decider of my own fate, like the idea of having all the glory and all the blame. But here's the problem: God can't be sitting on the throne of my heart if I am. I can't serve both myself and the true Lord. Anybody else ever had that problem?

God says in Exodus 20:5, "For I, the Lord your God am a jealous God." In this verse, God is bold and unwavering in his declaration of intent for the lordship of our souls, which is difficult for some of us to deal with. And so the Lord Jesus gives us a road map for becoming submissive disciples at the end of Mark 8. Mark splits the passage up into three main sections, the first being verses 27 to 30:

"Jesus went out with His disciples to the villages of Caesarea Phillipi. And on the road He asked His disciples, 'Who do people say that I am?' They answered him, 'John the Baptist; others, Elijah; still others, one of the prophets.' 'But you,' He asked them again, 'Who do you say that I am?' Peter answered Him, 'You are the Messiah!' And he strictly charged them to tell no one about Him."

Jesus sets up the situation in divine order, beginning with the foundation of allowing him to lead. The first step towards truly following anyone or anything of substance is to understand and respect that person. Who in here hated calculus class in high school?

Well, then pray for me because I have another semester. My teacher is notorious for being incredibly boring, but she knows a ton about calculus. But if instead, I had a very interesting calculus teacher who actually knew nothing about calculus, I would be very entertained every day during 6th period, yet at the end of the year, my report card would display a big fat F. The interesting calculus teacher may be really cool, but he's not powerful, whereas Jesus wasn't exactly the most popular guy in Jerusalem, but he was definitely the most powerful. And we want to follow him because he is powerful, not because he's cool. Blindly jumping on the Jesus bandwagon is not only unwise, but Jesus himself abhors it. He says in Revelation, "Because you are lukewarm, and neither cold nor hot, I am about to spit you out of my mouth" (Revelation 3:16).

So Jesus expects us to know who we are following and be in a relationship with him. It's interesting that those who saw him from afar misunderstood him, yet those closest to him, who communed with him day in and day out, they were the ones who understood his majesty. If we only know of God, but we don't truly know God, we may mistake his character. I know that many of you are preachers, or preachers to be, and I'm sure you're thinking, "T. J., I'm a preacher; it's my job to know Christ." But I encourage not to tune me out just yet. God is more than multi-faceted. God is infinitely faceted. To fully comprehend a being which created each and every one of us, and knows the number of hairs on our heads is impossible. If you think you know everything about God, read the last couple chapters of Job. He makes it very clear that he is beyond our understanding. So I pray that we would all delve deeper into God's mysterious being when we write our sermons, and that we would not just look for applications in the text, but look for God in the text. That way, we can have a deeper and stronger root in God. Warren Wiersbe says of the onlookers in the passage, "Instead of diligently seeking for the truth, the people listened to popular opinion and followed it, just as many people do today. They had opinions instead of convictions, and this is what led them astray."[1]

What Wiersbe says here really resonates with me. I want to be a man of convictions, not opinions. Convictions move mountains… opinions move lips. Convictions are unshakable…opinions quake

---

[1]Warren Wiersbe, "An Exposition of the New Testament," in Bible Exposition Commentary (Wheaton, IL: Victor Books, 1989).

in their boots. Being convicted is different than having opinions. So let's jump back into the text, verses 31 to 33: "Then he began to teach them that the Son of Man must undergo great suffering, and be rejected by the elders, the chief priests, and the scribes, and be killed, and after three days rise again. He said all this quite openly. And Peter took him aside and began to rebuke him. But turning and looking at his disciples, he rebuked Peter and said, "Get behind me, Satan! For you are setting your mind not on divine things but on human things" (Mark 8:31-33).

Isn't this the same guy who just a few verses earlier, in a moment of divine inspiration, called Jesus the Christ? But here Jesus is illustrating through Peter how easily we forget God's will and focus on ourselves.

In middle school, every year I attended a retreat called "Believe." I absolutely loved it. It changed my life in sixth grade, and then it changed my life in seventh grade, and in eighth grade, it changed my life again! But as I think back, it really hadn't changed my life in sixth grade, or else my life wouldn't have needed to be changed over and over again. I suffered, and sometimes still suffer, from what is commonly known as the mountaintop syndrome. This is a deadly problem for Christians in comfortable America, and it refers to when you go to a retreat, festival, or camping trip, and you truly experience God and his wonders and live on this incredible mountaintop with God's presence for as long as your there. Then you get back and you see your friends at school, or your coworkers at the office, and then you fall right back into your comfortable, normal life in the real world.

The Israelites wrote the book on the mountaintop syndrome. Immediately, after following a pillar of fire and crossing a parted Red Sea, Moses went up on the mountain to be with God, and the Israelites decided that they wanted to worship a golden calf! Moses found them, he broke the tablets inscribed with the Ten Commandments, and then God punished them. Just as a side note, I find it ironic that the Israelites break the first commandment and Moses breaks all ten! The Old Testament is littered with stories of the straying children of God, constantly having to be reined in.

In Mark, Jesus shows us how he feels about this shifting of our spiritual eyes back on to ourselves. His rebuke of Peter is so serious that he calls him Satan. This is Peter! The Rock! That's Jesus' main dude, and he just called him Satan? Peter let his own selfish wants rapidly creep in and poison his thinking instead of focusing on God and his will. Jesus says, "You are not setting your mind on the things of God, but the things of man." Aren't you glad that never happens to us? But the truth is, it does. We don't reach out because it's uncomfortable, or we let our relationships become too important, or we focus more on our performance than God's message.

In the final portion of this passage, Jesus specifies more tangible ways to follow him:

"He called the crowd with his disciples, and said to them, 'If any want to become my followers, let them deny themselves and take up their cross and follow me. For those who want to save their life will lose it, and those who lose their life for my sake, and for the sake of the gospel, will save it. For what will it profit them to gain the whole world and forfeit their life? Indeed, what can they give in return for their life? Those who are ashamed of me and of my words in this adulterous and sinful generation, of them the Son of Man will also be ashamed when he comes in the glory of his Father with the holy angels.' And he said to them, 'Truly I tell you, there are some standing here who will not taste death until they see that the kingdom of God has come with power.'"

In the sixth century B.C.E., there was a wrestler by the name of Milo of Kroton. Milo was an Olympic champion, and his fame spread far and wide, but it's how he got there that people remember. When he was younger, his father gave him a calf, and each day Milo would take his calf and lift it and carry it in to show his father. As the calf grew, so did Milo's muscles, but each day he continued to carry his calf to show his father. Eventually, the calf became full grown, and Milo of Kroton was carrying around a bull.

Every day Jesus asks you to pick something up. It's not a calf; it's a cross. Jesus is telling us that we must bear suffering to follow him. When we allow ourselves to suffer for Christ's sake, we show Jesus that it is His will we are following. We must deny ourselves and our comforts daily that we may strengthen our spiritual muscles and become heavenly champions.

The next point Jesus makes can sometimes be confusing. Whoever would save his life will lose it, but whoever loses his life will save it. In his book *Drops like Stars*, Rob Bell talks about what he calls the art of possession. He uses the example of his guitar saying, "I play a little, and I can make a fair bit of noise. But my friend Joey? He comes over and starts playing my guitar and evokes sounds out of it I simply cannot. There is a difference between ownership and possession. I own the guitar, but Joey possesses it in ways I can't."[2] There is a difference between ownership and possession. He goes on to talk about Paul who claimed that he had nothing and yet possessed everything. We can own the whole world and possess none of it, and we can try to be the owners of our own lives only to learn we possess none of it. In following the true Lord, we may own nothing, we may be made fun of, we may lose the life that makes us comfortable, yet we will posses everything.

Jesus ends the passage in 9:1 by giving those listening hope to see the kingdom of glory. And see it they do. Immediately after this passage plays out, Peter, James and John accompany him to the mountaintop where they witness the transfiguration of Christ. God always gives us hope. We endure suffering and hardship when we deny ourselves to follow our Rabbi, but through perseverance the glory of God will shine upon us. In 1 Peter, he talks about suffering leading to glory nine times in a five chapter book. He obviously thought it was an important point to get across. The suffering comes first. We sacrifice our lives for our Lord, and he will bless us.

As I was writing this sermon, I titled it "Letting Jesus Drive." In the *Message* translation of this passage Jesus says, "Anyone who wants to come with me has to let me lead. You're not in the driver's seat; I am."[3] Does everyone have their car keys with them? If you have them, take them out. If not, just imagine that you have them.

Let us pray: *Father, I pray that you would allow us to let you take the lead in our lives. We're not in the driver's seat; you are. Amen.*

---

[2]Rob Bell, *Drops Like Stars* (Grand Rapids: Zondervan, 2009), 94.

[3]Eugene Peterson, *The Message* (Colorado Springs, Alive Communications, 2005).

33

"RECOVERING THE ART OF CHRISTIAN DISCIPLESHIP"

Mark 8:27-28

Brandon Perkins

On February 29, 1948, Romanian born Pastor Richard Wurmbrand was arrested by Communist police for his unwavering devotion and commitment to God. While thousands of his fellow clerics sought safety and security by renouncing their faith in God, Wurmbrand willingly endured the suffering of one who stood for Christ. His numerous books tell of how over the next fourteen years he willingly endured unspeakable tortures and unbelievable pain for his faith. Yet in all that he suffered, he never allowed his faith to waiver, but used what he had been through to strengthen and propel his ministry forward.[1]

However, as I survey the current portrait of 21st Century Christianity, I cannot help but notice that the type of faith embodied by Wurmbrand and others seems to be ancient history. A strange shift has occurred in our churches today. The Church that had for centuries given its life for the Gospel now appears to have shied away from messages of sacrifice and suffering in favor of messages of safety and prosperity. Yet while the church remains comfortable in our grand houses of worship, Christ and the world are waiting for the Church to be the Church. There are lives to be saved, souls to be changed, families to be restored, persons to feed, diseases to cure, children to teach, and yet we sit.

Over the past two days, the next generation of great preachers from across this country have filled the halls of this hallowed ground and have proclaimed the Word of God. We have heard messages proclaimed telling the marvelous stories from the life of Christ. Our joy has been renewed, our hope restored, and our faith enriched. However, after we leave this place, and return to our colleges,

[1]Richard Wurmbrand, *Tortured for Christ* (Bartlesville, OK: Living Sacrifice Book Co., 1998), 20-34.

seminaries, and pulpits, will our lives really have been changed because of our being here this weekend? Will we leave here better equipped to serve our master, or will we have simply wasted our time, energy, and resources? Will we preach the Word in season and out of season, or will we shy away from the Gospel message? Will we be prepared to serve our fellow man, or will we be focused on our own agendas? It is here this morning that Mark invites you and me to leave the life of fellowship behind us and embrace the call to discipleship.

The Gospel of Mark carefully crafts and details the life of Jesus not from the picture of a king like Matthew, not from the personality of the Son of Man like Luke, and not from the persona of the God-man like John. Mark's pages are peppered and punctuated with Christ as the servant of humanity. Mark's theology is clear, for he writes in his Gospel in chapter 10, verse 45, "For the Son of Man came not to be served but to serve, and to give his life a ransom for many." Therefore, if we are to possess a ministry that is to meet the needs of all humanity, then Christ tells us that our focus cannot be predicated on self-fulfillment or personal satisfaction, but that it must be rooted and grounded in service. That's why the hymn writer Raymond Rasberry penned these famous lines, "You may seek earthly power and fame, the world might be impressed by your great name, soon the glories of this life will all be past, but only what you do for Christ will last."[2] Therefore, it is here in Mark's eighth chapter that we find the portrait of how one is to walk in this walk of Christian Discipleship.

Our text this morning unfolds as our Lord and Savior Jesus Christ is in the little mentioned territory of Caesarea Philippi. As the Bible records, this region is only mentioned twice in the New Testament; however, it is here that one of the most important dialogues in the New Testament takes place. Christ asks his disciples in Mark 8:27, "Who do people say that I am?" And it was his disciple Peter who answered, "You are the Messiah."

This brings me to my first point this morning. The world that we live in is riddled and perplexed with confusion. Every time we turn our heads, there seems to be another would be savior on the scene. Men and women are placing their hopes in people like Barack

[2]Raymond Rasberry, "Only What You Do for Christ Will Last," 28 Dec. 2009, http://www.lyricday.com.

Obama or their educations or their jobs. And it leaves preachers to ask themselves, "What can I say? What can I say when I try to proclaim God's Word, but men say who is this God you serve? What can I say when I preach the divine message of Christ and the world degrades him to a mere man? What I can say when I try and live out the words of this holy book, but the world tells me that this Word has no power?"

My brothers and my sisters, I am persuaded, convinced, and convicted this morning that despite the unpopularity of our message, this generation of preachers must proclaim like Paul when he says, "At the name of Jesus every knee should bow, and that every tongue should confess that Jesus Christ is Lord" (Philippians 2:10-11).

Secondly, our text is tailored to teach us that if we profess that Jesus Christ is the Savior and Lord of our life and that our life's desire is to serve him, there are three things that Christ calls us to do on this Christian journey.

The first thing Christ calls us to do is learn the discipline of self-denial.

Christ says in the text, "If any want to become my followers, let them deny themselves." What Christ is saying here is that on this Christian journey it is not enough just to say you are a disciple of Christ, for the true make and model of a Christian disciple is characterized by humility.

There is a danger when a man or woman of God cannot walk in humility. This Gospel that we preach is not about us. However, it is very easy and tempting to let man, titles, and ego fill our heads with the notion that we preach this glorious Gospel by some power and authority of our own. The preacher must never be found guilty of praising and finding glory in himself, but instead should declare like Paul, "If I proclaim the gospel, this gives me no ground for boasting, for an obligation is laid on me, and woe to me if I do not proclaim the gospel!" (1 Corinthians 9:16). Furthermore, in times when we are tempted to follow our own plans, our life's declaration should be like that of Christ when he uttered these words in the Garden of Gethsemane, "Not my will but yours be done" (Luke 22:42).

Christ then says, "Take up your cross and follow me." Since the formulation of Judeo-Christianity, the Church and its members have endured persecution. It was the second century church father Tertullian who said, "The blood of the martyrs is the seed of the church."[3] But if Tertullian is correct, then why is it that the message of unconditional sacrifice is no longer preached? Most of Christianity has all but lost the ideals and faith that compelled persons such as Peter the Apostle, William Tyndale, and Dietrich Bonheoffer to give their very lives for this Gospel. Yet in this passage, Christ tells us that we must take up our crosses. Furthermore, it states the words "their cross" to imply that every believer–no matter what age, shape, or color–has a sacrifice to make for this Gospel. I cannot bear your cross and you cannot bear my cross, but we must all bear our crosses, for Thomas Shepherd pens these famous lines,

> "Must Jesus bear the cross alone,
> and all the world go free?
> No, there's a cross for everyone,
> and there's a cross for me."
> The consecrated cross I'll bear
> till death shall set me free;
> and then go home my crown to wear,
> for there's a crown for me."[4]

So Lord, if my cross gets me mocked and ridiculed, I'll bear it. Lord, if my cross causes my family and friends to leave, I'll bear it. If my cross causes me to lose all material wealth, I'll bear it. If my cross causes me to lose my very life, I'll bear it because no cross equals no crown.

Once a believer has resolved and purposed in his heart to live a life of self-denial and has further resolved to live a life of unconditional sacrifice, the last thing Christ calls us to do is live a life of wholehearted service. Christ closes his statement by uttering these two words, "Follow me."

We see that Christ does not say follow me first, but last. This implies that although many want to follow Christ on this Christian journey, many will never be able to because they have not conformed to the image of a follower of Christ. Many are far too concerned with their own agendas, plans, and proposals. This morning Christ says that if you truly want to be my disciple, your life's testimony must be like that of Isaiah. When God needed someone to go and do his will, I heard Isaiah say, "Here am I; send me."

---

[3]DC Talk, *Jesus Freaks DC Talk and The Voice of the Martyrs: Stories of Those Who Stood for Jesus, the Ultimate Jesus Freaks* (New York: Bethany House, 1999), 22.

[4]Thomas Shepherd, "Must Jesus Bear the Cross Alone? 28 Dec. 2009, www.library.timelesstruths.org.

My brothers and my sisters, if we are to leave Louisville better than when we arrived, our lives must be spent following Jesus.

I hear Christ saying…

Follow me when you're alone with no support like Abraham.
Follow me when all you have are dreams like Joseph.
Follow me when you're second guessed like David.
Follow me when you're persecuted like Daniel.
Follow me when you've messed up like Jonah.
Follow me when you're stoned like Stephen.
Follow me when you're exiled like John.
Follow me when you're crucified like Peter.
Follow me when you're beheaded like Paul.

I hear Christ saying …

Follow me as I cure AIDS in Africa.
Follow me as I feed the hungry in Asia.
Follow me as I eradicate poverty in South America.
Follow me as I bring peace to Iraq.
Follow me as I teach the masses around the world.

I hear Christ saying…

Follow me as I save sinners.
Follow me as I restore those who were hurt by the Church.
Follow me as I renew the faith of doubters.
Follow me as I reignite the joy of the depressed.
Follow me as I encourage the persecuted.
I hear Christ saying…

Follow me until you reach that city that sits on twelve foundations, with three gates in the East, three gates in the West, three gates in the North, and three gates in the South. And when we get to that city, I want to hear him say, "Well done good and faithful servant, thou hast been faithful over a few things, I will make thee ruler over many things" (Matthew 25:21).

That's why today I can sing and make this declaration: I have decided to follow Jesus. I have decided to follow Jesus. I have decided to follow Jesus. No turning back. No turning back. Amen.

34

"JESUS' CALL TO DISCIPLESHIP"
Mark 8:27-38

Krista Phillips

It was just over three weeks ago that we stood on the threshold of Christmas morning, a time when we were constantly being reminded that Christ was made incarnate, our Savior was born of flesh and became like us. This passage from Mark is a good dove-tail to the Christmas story, a reminder to us of the reason behind the birth of our Lord and Savior. The passage I just read is the first time in the Gospel of Mark Jesus predicts his rejection, suffering, death, and resurrection, and he uses this prediction to teach a lesson about the necessary actions one must take in order to be a disciple.

After Jesus' prediction, we see Peter being Peter, and too often act just like him. We have read the story. We know what Jesus went through on our behalf, yet we tend to only talk about Jesus being a precious gift that gives us eternal life rather than talking about the cross and the suffering and the death.

So why does Peter rebuke Jesus? Peter does not want the Jesus who is to suffer, to be rejected, to die. Peter's idea of the anointed one is a lot like ours in that Jesus is full of glory and renown, not pain and suffering. We claim to follow Christ, but we only pray when the going gets tough and we need help. We are so quick to share the beauty and the good times but not so quick to forget about the hard times. This is why Jesus turns back to Peter and says, "Get behind me Satan, for you are setting your mind not on divine things but on human things" (Mark 8:33). How guilty we are especially during and around Christmas to have our minds set on human things and not divine things. Our minds are on the gifts, the shopping, the money, the friends, and our families coming and going, and every once in a while during the Christmas season we are reminded of Christ. That reminder leaves, and our focus returns to the human things. During Christmas we are often guilty of having our image of the Messiah as nothing more than that precious gift, the child in the manger, and the miracle of the virgin birth.

Jesus rebukes Peter because Peter understood the truth that he was the Messiah, the anointed one. He is one who is set above all things, and Peter refused to believe Jesus had to suffer and die. Peter did not want to believe that the suffering was coming, but Jesus wanted to let him know that it was real and that it wasn't going to be easy for them.

Our minds cannot continually be set on the idyllic picture of Christmas. The reality is Christ was born to face tough times; Christ came to be rejected by the elders, the chief priests, the scribes, and to suffer on the cross and die. Thankfully, we are reminded that the story did not end there. Christ overcame the rejection and suffering by conquering death and rising from the grave on the third day. This is a hard truth to swallow at times because it means acknowledging that we choose to follow a Savior who served us all the way to his death. It means we are faced with daily questions about how and why we live our lives the way we do and how we can truly believe what the Bible has to say.

In order for us to be a follower of Christ, one of his disciples, Jesus tells us to do three things: to deny ourselves, take up our cross, and follow him (Mark 8:34). These three commands are radical and tough. They mean that day in and day out, in everything we do, we are to remember the one who came to us and died for us. It means getting dirty in the efforts to change the world around us and dusting oneself off again and again. Following Christ means that when the going gets tough, the tough show God's love.

The first requirement Jesus requires of his followers is to deny yourself. This means to take an honest look at yourself through the eyes of Christ. As today's disciples, we must realize the things of this world that continually hinder us from growing closer to God and walking in Christ's footsteps. To deny ourselves means to give up the worldly ideas that Jesus accused Peter of having. We must deny the ideas we have about what makes us happy, successful, and intelligent, and we must turn and look to see what Christ had to say about such things. To deny ourselves means to deny the world. It means that we acknowledge that following Christ means we have been set apart; therefore, we must set standards for ourselves that are above the declining standards of the world. Denying oneself means making a choice to turn away from your selfish ways and to be more concerned with those around you than you are with making a gain for yourself. Denying oneself for Christ is the first step towards discipleship and understanding what it is to be set apart.

The second step Jesus calls us to do is to take up our cross. One of the most beautiful things about our Savior is the fact that we are not told to straighten out our lives before we receive anything. Jesus calls us just as we are. He does not call us to simply pick up our cross; the scripture says to "take up" our cross. When I hear the words "take up," I think about digging up a bush or tree, cutting the roots out from something and physically digging it up and changing where it is. The difference between picking something up to move it and taking it up is an effort to change where it is rooted and how it will grow along the way. If we pick up our crosses, our burdens, our trials and carry them with us, they are never gone. Consequently, we will never open ourselves up to the power of the Holy Spirit to change and use those crosses in our lives. If we "take up" our crosses, we are digging up all the attachments we have with them, and we are making a conscious effort to refuse being rooted in whatever is holding us back from growing closer to God and walking in a way that is Christ-like and set apart from the world.

Jesus does not only call us as we are, Jesus called the twelve disciples to come as they were: Peter and Andrew from their boats to drop their nets, James and John to leave their father's boat, Philip and Nathaniel to get up and come in faith believing that Christ is the Son of God. The disciples were all called in the midst of their lives to stop what they were doing, take up their crosses, to come as they were, and to follow him. They chose to take up their crosses instead of being rooted in their own ways of life. They chose to learn the ways of Christ along the way. We too are called from the troubles of this life to take up our crosses and come as we are to follow Christ. As disciples we make a choice each day to learn something new about this Christ-like way of living and then we choose to put it into practice.

If we were to simply pick up our cross and continue to focus on our problems instead of pressing on through the hard times, our commitment to being a true disciple would be nowhere near what Christ intended for it to be. Taking up our cross means that we acknowledge the rejection and suffering of Christ and realize that because of our commitment to be disciples grounded in the truth and love of Christ we too will face rejection and suffering at times on our journey of life. As theologian Dietrich Bonhoeffer talks about in his book, The Cost of Discipleship: grace is not cheap; it is costly. He writes, "Cheap grace is grace without discipleship, without the cross, without Jesus Christ: living and incarnate."[1] Today this is living a worldly life, sinning because we can, and sinning because everyone tells us God is going to forgive us anyway. The grace of Christ on the cross is not cheap by any means. It cost Jesus his life.

The last thing Jesus tells us to do is to follow him. The text says "If any want to become my followers, let them deny themselves and take up their cross and follow me" (Mark 8:34). Jesus' disciples did just that; they followed him. The disciples followed Jesus into storms. They followed him as he performed miracles, and as he showed mercy and grace to those he encountered. They followed him as he would preach and teach anyone who would listen. They followed him from land to sea, from town to town, from house to house, from the peak of his ministry to the cross, and then from the cross to the tomb where they found it empty. Following Jesus is more than just retelling the stories of his life and ministry. Following Jesus means going where the Spirit leads in today's time and being able to share stories of how we followed Christ into a vocation, into a relationship, into an organization, or into an event. And then we must be willing to share with others how our journey with Christ has transformed our lives.

Following Christ also means that since we choose to deny ourselves and take up our cross, our lives reflect the life of Christ. Following Christ means imitating Christ, teaching and preaching the Word, feeding the hungry, clothing the naked, giving to the needy, and loving those who feel unloved. Following Christ means that we walk the walk, which is his walk. It is not a once in a lifetime choice, it is a daily necessity, especially in the world in which we live. It is so easy to get caught up in the ways of the world and forget about being set apart, to forget about the God we serve, to forget that we are called to be different and to bear the light.

So why make the decision to follow Christ? It is what Christ calls us to do. It is not just how we think or what we say, it is in everything that we do. It is God's way of having a voice and action in this "sinful generation." It is hope for the generations that are to follow us, and it is a common ground which we share with people all across the world. As Christians we always talk about being Christ-

---

[1]Dietrich Bonhoeffer, *The Cost of Discipleship* (New York: Macmillan, 1966), 45-46.

like, being set apart, and yet according to most public opinion polls, 75% of Americans claim to be Christian. Do we act like a nation that is predominately a Christian nation? Do we love our neighbors as ourselves? Do we treat our bodies as if they are temples of the living God? Do our actions reflect those of Christ? If we claim to be Christians, Jesus says we have to act like it. We have to deny the world, take up our cross, and follow him. Jesus does not give us a choice between the three, it is an all-or-nothing deal. If you want to be a follower of Jesus you have to do these things.

Jesus follows these three instructions to the disciples with two questions: "For what will it profit them to gain the whole world and forfeit their life? Indeed what can they give in return for their life?" (Mark 8:36-37).

There is a story of a pastor who met a couple that had just moved into his community and were looking for a church home. "Tell us about your church," they said. "We might be interested." Of course, what they meant by that was: tell us about your programs, your activities, your facilities–what do you have to offer us, in other words? How does your church compare with the others we've visited? The pastor smiled and said, "Oh, you'll love our church. If you come to our church, we'll kill you."

Well, that wasn't exactly what the couple was expecting to hear. At first, they were stunned and speechless. Finally, the woman chuckled politely and said, "I assume you're kidding." The pastor said, "Not at all." Then he went on to explain that to follow Jesus Christ is not to add another line to your résumé, but to give up self-interest in pursuit of Christ's kingdom on earth. He said the church is not a shopping mall where you pick up the things you need, but a mission outpost from which you go out in service to Christ and his kingdom.

To be a disciple of Christ, we lose ourselves; we lose the world around us and gain something greater. We gain a relationship stronger than any other, one with our Creator, one with the precious child that came to live among the lowest of the low, in order to change lives. The call to be a disciple of Christ is a radical call. It is radical for us because it was radical for Christ. As disciples we follow a savior who was willing to risk everything, including his life, so that we may have eternal life. We give ourselves to the service of Christ, forfeiting our lives as the world knows them, and gaining a life that is the only true life.

Christian discipleship is a long, tough road. It is a road we are all called to follow, yet as we see in the world around us, those willing to lead others down that road are far and few between. Therefore, we need to be willing to take up our cross and follow Christ as we are, boldly and radically. We need to become a generation ready to preach and walk Christ's message of discipleship because we care about the world we live in, the generations of Christians that are rising behind us, living with us, and those who have gone before us.

In this passage from Mark, Jesus teaches us what it means to be a disciple of Christ. Now the choice is ours. In this New Year, may we show the world around us what it means to be a disciple of Christ, loved by God the Father, in fellowship with the Holy Spirit, and in the grace and mercy of our Lord and Savior Jesus Christ. Amen.

35

"THE LORD'S PRAYER"
Luke 11:1-13

Anne Marie Roderick

When I was eighteen years old, I graduated from high school and moved to New Orleans. I lived there for almost eight months, working on post-Katrina relief efforts. I came to New Orleans a person of very little faith. I had been raised going to church with my family, but since my early teens I hadn't really believed in God, or that the Bible was holy, or that religion was anything more than a human-made invention to explain why things are the way they are. It was more than a year after Katrina and the streets were still filled with damaged, deserted homes; former residents of New Orleans were scattered all over the country trying to get home to rebuild their lives with little or no money to do so. I was confused, angry even, that people could have faith in a God who would allow so much destruction, so much tragedy.

Just two months before I left New Orleans, I became good friends with a young man that I had been working with. Joshua was the son of two Baptist preachers; he was firm in his identity as a Christian, and it came up in our conversations a lot. He was never too earnest or overzealous, but we would have long conversations about faith. I would ask Joshua all kinds of questions–are the stories in the bible supposed to be real, why does God allow so much suffering, if God created the world, then who created God–the basic questions people ask when they don't understand faith. And although I wish I could say that my intentions were sincere, I think a big part of me hoped that Joshua would get tripped up on one of my questions and would have to admit, that contrary to what he had believed his whole life, there actually was no God. But Joshua didn't relent; his answers were moving and deeply honest. Sometimes he admitted that he didn't know the answers to my questions, nor did he have any way of proving to me that his answers were right; but he could feel them in his heart and that was all he needed. As I continued to talk with Joshua, I began to reflect on these questions in my own heart. This was a turning point in my faith journey, when I finally began to feel God moving in my life.

One day, I came to Joshua and asked him a question, as I had many other times. At this point, he knew that my attitude, my intention in asking the question, had changed. He knew that I was sincerely struggling to find answers that I could hold on to. After I asked my question, Joshua turned to me and said, "I don't know. Why don't you ask God?" "What do you mean?" I said. Was there some direct line to God that I didn't know about? "Why don't you pray about it?" Joshua responded.

I went back to my room that night with a resolution to pray. I knelt down by the side of my bed as I had seen children do on TV and as I had vague memories of doing when I was a child. I clasped my hands together near my heart, bowed my head, and said, "O God–." Nothing else came out. I tried again, "O God–." And still nothing. For the last several weeks my mind had been racing with thoughts and questions, but now that I finally felt like I believed in God, I didn't have anything to say. There was so much to ask, so much to catch up on, but I was speechless. I thought I might give up and try again another night. After all, who was I to think that it would be easy to get in touch with God after so many years of not returning God's phone calls? But then, out of the depths of my mind, arose the Lord's Prayer. Before I even knew it, I was reciting the prayer, out loud. And that was it. I prayed the Lord's Prayer, the only piece of scripture I knew by heart, and I went to sleep. And the next night, I found the words to pray my own prayer.

When I received the list of scripture passages that we could preach on for this Festival, the Lord's Prayer stood out. I hold onto this prayer as the first prayer I ever truly prayed, as the first conversation I ever had with God. Yet there's still so much about it I haven't explored. When I told my friends at school that I was coming to this Festival and that I had chosen to preach on the Lord's Prayer, they were less than enthusiastic. "Everyone knows the Lord's Prayer," they said. "Don't you want to preach about something people don't know so well?" "How can you preach a prayer? Isn't the whole point of the Lord's Prayer that you pray it?" Although they didn't say it outright, I suspect that buried in their comments was another concern: Who are you to think that you can offer something new and meaningful about one of the most widely used pieces of Christian scripture? Although I understood and agreed with my friends' concerns, both the spoken and unspoken ones, I still felt pulled toward this topic. Preparing to preach is the best way I have found to let the spirit guide me in understanding the scriptures. The Lord's Prayer is familiar, maybe even over familiar to some of us, but it is not always explored deeply. This is the problem with memorization–we can know something without really knowing it at all. Even in New Orleans the prayer just came out of me. Why did that happen? What does the Lord's Prayer really mean?

Maybe the Lord's Prayer offers us more than something we can just recite. Perhaps we recite the Lord's Prayer when we have nothing else to pray; when our hearts are too heavy, too scared, too shy, or even too full. When I was in New Orleans, I prayed this prayer because I didn't know how to pray. As carriers of the Gospel, we can take these words that have been given to us and use them when we don't have words of our own.

Last year, I attended an interfaith conference in Chicago. There were twenty young people from around the country who had gathered together to share stories about their faith traditions. Throughout the conference each faith group had a chance to worship on its own, so on Sunday morning I got together with the rest of the Christians. There were only twenty people at the conference, and only four of us were Christians, so it was a small worship group. We were from a variety of denominations, and from very different kinds of churches. We didn't know how to worship in a way that would make everyone feel comfortable. Soon somebody suggested that we read scripture and offered a passage. We all read along and then each of us shared a reflection on the passage. It was okay, but it didn't really feel like worship. Even though we were reading scripture together, it didn't feel like we were having a collective experience of God. Finally, somebody suggested that we repeat the Lord's Prayer. Surely all of us knew it, and we all felt comfortable reciting it despite denominational differences. We closed our bibles, looked around at one another and recited the prayer. Our voices came together as one voice. For the thirty seconds that it took us to recite the prayer, we felt connected to one another in Christ; we felt unified. Our denominational differences didn't matter; the size of our group didn't matter. We had spoken a prayer together with a common love for God in our hearts.

The Lord's Prayer is universal; it offers us a way to commune with another, to worship with one another, to find fellowship when we don't know how to do it on our own. Maybe memorization isn't that bad after all; it offers us something to tap into when we're alone and we don't have words to pray, and when we're with others who don't pray as we do. These are the gifts of reciting the Lord's Prayer.

But now there is something else about the Lord's Prayer that keeps nagging at me. Almost all Christians know and recite the prayer, but are we even sure that that's what Jesus meant for us to do with it? In the Gospel of Matthew, Matthew quotes Jesus as saying, "When you pray, pray like this," not, "When you pray, pray these exact words." In Luke's version, Jesus says, "When you pray, say…" and then he says the Lord's Prayer, but are we supposed to believe that Jesus meant for us to pray the exact same prayer every time we pray? Jesus only offers the Lord's Prayer after his disciples ask him to teach them to pray. So maybe the prayer is more of a lesson, an instruction, a guide, or an invitation to come closer to God by deepening our own prayer lives. Perhaps this is our model for prayer.

"Our Father who art in heaven, hallowed be thy name." Here, Jesus shows us how to address God as holy. "Thy Kingdom come, thy will be done on earth as it is in heaven." We acknowledge the imminence and power of God. "Give us this day our daily bread." Jesus encourages us to ask God for what we need to be sustained, for our share in the world. "Forgive us our trespasses as we forgive those who trespass against us." Jesus teaches us to ask for forgiveness and to reflect on whether or not we have forgiven those who hurt us. "Lead us not into temptation, but deliver us from evil." Jesus instructs us to ask for God's help in keeping us safe from that which is unknown to us. And finally, he shows us again how to name the vastness of God's presence in the last line.

While the Lord's Prayer is complete and can certainly be prayed as is, we can also accept the prayer as an instruction. Jesus is guiding us to create our own complete prayers. Each time we pray, we can consider the questions that Jesus poses in the Lord's Prayer:

- How would you name God's holiness?
- How would you describe the imminence and power of God?
- What is your daily bread?
- What forgiveness do you seek?
- Have you forgiven everyone who has hurt you?

- And finally, how would you ask for God's help in protection from that which you do not know?

These are big questions. They can't all be addressed in one prayer, but they are questions that will enrich our prayer lives if we think about them, because they are questions that Jesus raises as he teaches us to pray.

So the Lord's Prayer offers us more than a prayer, it offers us a whole way of praying.

I would like to invite all of us to try experiencing the Lord's Prayer together. We are a group of denominationally diverse people; we may be at different places in our prayer lives; but we all have the Lord's Prayer. Jesus gives us this prayer so that we can pray when we don't have the words to do so on our own, so that we can pray with others we might not normally pray with, and so that we can learn to pray as fully as Jesus wants us to. Let us repeat this prayer now as if we are hearing it for the first time; using whatever version you know best. And I invite you to take it with you after we leave and to use the many gifts this prayer offers us. Please bow your heads with me. Let us pray…

Our Father, who art in Heaven
Hallowed be thy Name
Thy kingdom come
Thy will be done, on earth as it is in heaven
Give us this day our daily bread
And forgive us our trespasses, as we forgive those that trespass against us
And lead us not into temptation
But deliver us from evil
For thine is the kingdom, and the power, and the glory, forever and ever. Amen.

36

"CARRYING THE CROSS"
Mark 8:27-38

Daniel Rudy

As a young child growing up, my father told me many things. One of the things he told me most frequently was, "Dan, stop assuming things." Now, when I had grown into a young adult, Dad also reflected that one of the easiest ways to get me to do anything generally was to tell me not to do it. It is with this in mind that I start my sermon with an assumption. It would seem pretty safe to assume that most of the people in this room have at one time confessed that Jesus is their Savior and have committed to live their lives under his Lordship. I should think that this is a fairly safe assumption to make at an event for young Christian preachers and their mentors. As people who are gathered together to learn how to communicate the gospel both to those who have never heard and those who know it best, it would seem pretty self-evident that we ourselves would have heard the gospel and acted on its life-giving message.

This action may have come at different times for each of us. Some of us may point to a dramatic conversion experience that followed a revival service. Others may have been brought up in the church and came to know Christ through the services of the church or through confirmation or baptism. Still others may have experienced a gradual growth in Christ Jesus without being able to point to a dramatic turning point in their journeys. Growing up in a tradition that baptizes adults, one of the greatest turning points for me was when I decided to commit my life to Christ and entered the transforming waters of baptism at the mature age of eleven. Looking back twelve years later, I can safely and honestly say that I had absolutely no idea exactly what I was getting myself into that day that I promised to follow Jesus despite the excellent work of my pastor in preparing me for that.

Sisters and Brothers, knowing what I know of my own story, I wonder if Peter and the other eleven disciples had any real idea what they were getting themselves into when they left their fish nets, tax booths, and old lives behind to follow Jesus. I suspect that they thought that it might be glamorous to follow this great teacher around the country healing and driving out demons. After all, whatever following Jesus was about it would sure be better than the drudgery of fish nets. Things certainly seemed to be going well for the motley crew that followed Jesus at the beginning of the journey.

What may have seemed like an easy road for the disciples took a turn on the road to Caesarea Philippi. As they were walking down the road with Jesus, he asked them, "Who do people say that I am?" I imagine that this question produced some head scratching. "He is just now getting around to asking who the people think he is? We've travelled all over this country. Well, that's a dumb question. He is a great teacher, a healer." The disciples give some reasonably safe answers about who others say Jesus is, but Jesus responds with another question, "Who do you say that I am?" This is a question that Jesus asks not just to those twelve disciples who walked with him down the road that day, but to you and me and to every person who may claim him throughout the ages. It was not good enough for the disciples to know who others say Jesus is, just as it is not good enough for us to know who our pastors, professors and spiritual teachers say Jesus is. Who do I say that Jesus is? How do I understand his life and ministry, his death and resurrection, his presence through the Holy Spirit, and his coming again in glory? How does that understanding impact my life as a believer?

After Jesus asks this question, Peter blurts out to Jesus, "You are the Messiah." And with Peter's confession, the world that the disciples knew shifted. When Peter says that Jesus is the Christ, I thing that Jesus decides the disciples are ready for some of the hard teachings that he has for them. "The Son of Man must undergo great suffering, and be rejected by the elders…and be killed, and after three days rise again," he said. Jesus, the Messiah and the Lord, will suffer and die at the hands of mere sinful mortals. I think we ought to stop and think about that. It is somewhat easy for us to come to grips with because we know the end of the story. We have read about Jesus' passion and death. But those twelve on the road that day had no clue what was coming for them. They expected an easy walk to glory. And if Jesus suffering and dying was not shocking enough for these disciples, he offers them the same cup that he will drink from. "If any want to be my followers, let them deny themselves and take up their cross and follow me. For those who want to save their life will lose it and those who lose their life for my sake and the sake of the gospel will save it."

Sisters and brothers, here is the crux of the matter. Everyone who calls himself or herself a Christian has at some time accepted Jesus Christ as Savior and Lord. How many of us sincerely thought that a literal cross might await us at the end of the road? Did we think that the road ahead would lead to our suffering and maybe even our literal death? I do not ask these questions in an effort to frighten you. I too did not really understand these things on that day when I promised to follow Jesus and descended into the waters of baptism. I too would rather have an easy life on earth followed by eternal reward in heaven. I must admit that there are times that I look at those around me and lust after worldly things. I like to be dressed in the latest fashions. I like to have my fill to eat and then some despite what you see at the pot luck line. I like being a part of the group. But Christ calls me to follow him, not to be like everyone else.

Mennonite scholar John Howard Yoder defines the cross as the price that we pay for our non-conformity to the world. The Apostle Paul said that we are not to be conformed to the world, but transformed by the renewing of our minds. I have to wonder, if it is easy for me to follow Christ, and I do not stand out from my neighbor in any practical way, am I really following Jesus? If my moral judgments are the same as those who have never heard the name of Jesus Christ, am I really being transformed by the Holy Spirit? Sisters and Brothers, if our faith does not lead us to stand out from those who do not know Jesus then our faith is lacking.

In Matthew's gospel, Jesus said that not everyone who says to me, "Lord, Lord" will enter into the kingdom, but only those who do the will of the Father. We should not expect an easy path in this Christian walk that will lead to social respectability and riches on this earth. Christ calls us out of the world and into the reign of God, and if following him down the path of non-conformity does not lead us into any uncomfortable situations, than I have to ask whether we have been transformed at all.

I will leave you with one final story. As I said earlier, I committed my life to Christ when I was eleven years old. I did not understand what it really meant to pick up my cross until I was nineteen and served on a two week delegation with Christian Peacemaker Teams in the West Bank. For those of you who do not know, Christian Peacemaker Teams is an organization that engages in active nonresistance and documentation of human rights abuses in international conflict zones. I journeyed to the West Bank because I felt called to participate in the reign of God breaking into the world in our time. I felt called to witness to the transforming love of Jesus Christ in a place that is so known for its oppression and its militarism.

One day while I was in the West Bank observing a protest by Palestinian villagers in a rural shepherding village, the Israeli Army came into town and detained many of the men in that village. An Israeli Captain, whom we had interacted with the day before, said to the CPTers that we would have to leave within five minutes or be arrested. Now, me being the southern boy baseball player that I was at the time decided we were not going to leave in five minutes. So, if I am going to get arrested, then I am at least going to get my money's worth. So I looked the Captain right in the eyes and said, "Fine sir, I'll talk to you in five minutes." Well, fifteen minutes later, we were still standing there and as some others arrived to observe the action, we went up into the hills to decide what we were going to do. We could call all of the media outlets that we worked with and go back down into the village and get arrested in a blaze of glory, or would could play it by ear and do our best to stay out of jail. As our group decided how to respond to the threat of imprisonment, the words of the third verse of the hymn "I Have Decided to Follow Jesus" popped into my head. Humming the words, "The world behind me, the cross before me, no turning back, no turning back," I said to my fellow CPTers, "I am up for whatever you are."

God gave me the courage to face the cross of non-conformity. Not everyone's cross will be the same as mine. Indeed, God will likely have other crosses for me to bear as I go forward in faith following Christ Jesus. But my prayer for all of us this day is that as the church of Jesus Christ when we are called to pick up our crosses and follow Jesus that God will give us the courage and the strength to follow Christ on the road to Golgotha, onto the cross and into the resurrection. Let it be so. Amen.

37

"THE GREATEST OF THESE"
1 Corinthians 13

Christian Smith

When I think about this passage of scripture, I think about my own childhood. After all, I was a child up until a few months ago (legally speaking)! I think about all I've been through, all I've experienced, and all I will yet go through.

When you look up the definition of "child," it is defined as a person between birth and full growth: a son or daughter, a baby or infant. These are all considered children, yet we are considered children of God.

As children, we want to be loved. We want to be nurtured by our families. We want to be loved by God. We want to be cared for and protected. But I'm here to tell you, God loves us! God loves us in a mighty way!

Some people show their love by giving gifts. Some people show it by simply saying, "I love you." Some people show it be attending different events, showing support, and demonstrating concern. Some people show love by just giving you a hug. But God showed the ultimate sacrifice of love when he sent his son to die on the cross so that we don't have to carry the burden of sin.

In verse 11, the text says that when we become adults we should put away childish things. What are childish things? Well, childish things are anything that is not of Christ. Anything that is hindering you from having a personal relationship with God is a childish thing. Whether it is gossip, backbiting, or talking about people in a way that isn't Christian, all of us need to put away some of these childish things.

Childish things are spiritual as well as physical. This is why we are all "children" of God. Not one of us is perfect in the eyes of God; therefore, by definition, we are not full grown. By definition, we are "children." We all need guidance, protection, and love. And who better to show that love than your parents.

When Jesus was born, the angel came to Joseph and said, "You will be an earthly father which means you will guide, protect, and love this child." Even though he wasn't the one to make Jesus, he was his father just as all of us are fathers or mothers or brothers or sisters to someone in this world. Whether it is by birth or by the blood of Jesus, we call each other brothers and sisters in Christ.

When I look at this scripture, it says the greatest thing is charity. What is charity? It's a gift given with no intention of getting anything in return. Charity is what you give someone when you don't expect anything back. Charity is love. When you mom says she love you, she doesn't expect you to clean your room, even though she may want you to. By saying she loves you, she means she loves you with an abiding love, an unrelenting love. Love is something no one can take, and you can't give your love to someone else. You can't give the love that my father has for me to anyone else in this room. It belongs to me. God's love belongs to you. He protects you. He gives you guidance. This (holding up the Bible) is his book of guidance. He didn't just write it because he was bored one day. This book is for guidance and correction. Personally, I don't like correction. But that's what this book is for. It is for discipline. It is for teaching us what we do wrong and how. It helps us to learn from our mistakes. If God didn't want us to learn, why did he give us this book?

In school they say you can do this, but if you do it, this will happen. The Bible says if you are saved, you will go to heaven. It's called evidence/consequence. The evidence of your actions is that you've done wrong. The consequence is that you'll be disciplined. The evidence that God loves us is that he sent his son. The consequence is that his son had to die on the cross. Some people ask, "What is the evidence of this preaching event?" The evidence is that we have 92 young preachers here to preach the Word of God. We have people here to support us. We have mentors here to introduce us and encourage us. The consequence is that someone will come closer to knowing Jesus as their Savior. Someone will deepen their relationship with God. Someone will realize what God has called them to do.

A lot of people say that youth don't do anything.My experience is that youth don't do anything because they are not given an opportunity. Youth don't do anything because they feel like they don't have enough support from their family and friends. But you have to realize that God loves us still. He loves us even when we don't do what we're supposed to do. He loves us even when we turn against him. He loves us.

You see this stole I'm wearing. It's very colorful. But I also have a different stole that I brought with me today. This is something I received at the General Assembly of the Christian Church (Disciples of Christ). This stole has hands on it. Some people ask me what the hands mean. They mean different things. This side means all the things we have done. Each color represents a different sin we've committed. If we were judged by the sins we committed, none of us would be going to heaven. I know I wouldn't. Luckily, there's another side. There's a side in which there may be different shades of green, but it's all green. This shows what God looks at when he sees us. God sees every sin the same. He sees lying, stealing, and killing the same way. It doesn't matter. And if God were to judge us personally, we would all be in trouble. But God looks at us as a people, as a community he created to praise and worships him.

If God loves us this much, why can't we show how much we love God?

I was recently talking with some people about how we praise God. Some people praise God in the darkest days. They want to life up the name of Jesus and pray and ask God to help them. Some people only praise God when God is blessing them. But I'm here to tell you that we should bless God all the time. We should praise God when we have that extra $20 in our pocket. We should praise God when we get that new house or that new car or that new suit. But we should also praise God when things are going wrong. We should praise him when our school work isn't going as well as we think it should. We should praise God when we're just not feeling well. We should praise God no matter what is going on.

38

"CONVERSING WITH CHRIST"

John 4:1-42

Kevin Stamps

In recent years my family has grown. My marriage and subsequent fatherhood has added several members to our family, and my brother's marriage and subsequent fatherhood has done the same. Spaces that used to be ideal for family gatherings are now being abandoned in favor of larger venues. Furniture is being shifted, chairs and tables added, and superfluous objects are being removed in order to make room.

This truth became all too evident this past Christmas. We went back to the house that used to be my great-grandmother's before she passed. Her son, my great uncle, now lives there. This was the first time we'd had Christmas there in years. We quickly discovered that a space that used to be perfect for our family is now entirely too small. As we gathered in the small kitchen in order to eat, we quickly realized there wasn't enough seating. We did the proverbial "kid's table" thing and set up a card table with folding chairs. I thought this would solve the problem as my children and my younger sister would be relegated to that position while we "adults" sat at the big table. But I was wrong. I ended up relegated to that table along with my wife and children. A grown man, college graduate, minister in the Methodist church, and here I was sitting at the "kid's table." I tried to make the best of the situation by joking about it, but I soon was able to understand why kids hate sitting at the small table: you aren't part of the action.

You want seconds? Better ask the adults to pass some to you from the big table. Want a refill on your tea? Plead with the adults to pause their riveting conversation long enough to indulge your needs. You aren't really part of the action when you're at the small table, and the worse is that you aren't part of the conversation. It's a terrible feeling to know that your thoughts and your input aren't needed. I may be over exaggerating slightly to prove a point, but it honestly feels like your presence isn't necessary. I think we can assume the woman in this passage felt very similar.

A woman in ancient Palestine who's been married five times, a Samaritan, and obviously disliked because she is drawing water alone in midday instead of the cool of the morning, was never part of the conversation. This woman, sort of like me at Christmas this year, often found herself relegated to the "other" table, the "other" position, and the "other" social order. This was a woman with few rights and privileges and for a male Jew to be speaking to her was unbelievable. For the first time in this woman's adult life, she's part of the conversation. Our understanding of this woman's social class is confirmed when the disciples return and marveled that he was talking to her. The disciples wonder why Jesus is giving her the time of day, and I bet the woman wondered the same thing. In fact, she asks, "How is that you, a Jew, ask for a drink from me, a woman of Samaria?" (John 4:9).

The woman is asking, "Why do you care about my existence?" It's nice to be included in the conversation. Jesus invites this woman in to speak and to learn and he teaches her that not only will he give her water that will be a perpetual spring, but that the very man she has encountered is the Messiah incarnate. How does one respond to this paradigm shift? How does one go from being a second class citizen to being in a conversation with the Messiah?

I'm reminded of Charlie Bucket from *Willy Wonka and the Chocolate Factory*. Poor Charlie wanted a golden ticket so he could enter the Wonka factory and take a tour. We observe as Charlie agonizingly watches the news as the first, second, third, fourth and fifth golden tickets are found, all by undeserving brats! Poor Charlie has nothing to hope for. Like the woman in our passage, he is poor and lower class, a mere speck on the face of the earth with no real significance. However, if you're a fan of the movie you know what happens! One of the young people had cheated and had their ticket revoked. Walking down the road, Charlie finds a piece of currency lying in a storm drain and he uses it to buy one last Wonka Bar; then his entire world is changed. Like this Samaritan woman, he will never be the same. Charlie finds the golden ticket and runs to tell his family of his good fortune. The Samaritan woman finds the Messiah and runs to tell her town of her good fortune. In both instances, the only proper response to such good news was to become a herald of good news for others.

Christ invites all people of all nations into the conversation. The categories and labels the world has placed upon your life are of no relevance to the cosmic conversation that Jesus invites us to participate in. When we begin to dialogue with Jesus, we quickly realize that the trivial conversations we have everyday are of no eternal value. Dinner plans, appointments, bills, cleaning, and even harmless banter are all understood to be rubbish in light of conversing with Christ. Christ is talking about the human condition: pain, love, sex, suffering, death, and the real fabric of life. It is in the midst of this conversation with Christ that we realize somewhere along the way we've stopped talking about what matters and have focused on superfluous and meaningless subjects.

Jesus invites us to join a conversation that has weight and sustenance. When was the last time you confessed your sins to another Christian? When was the last time you dealt with residual grief in your life or addressed the guilt that plagues you daily from some situation in your past? What is the status of your relationship with God? These are the topics that come up when we converse with the One who makes all things come to the light. Jesus doesn't introduce himself or even ask the lady concerning about her identity. He goes straight into the weighty subject of her multiple marriages and subsequent divorces. No one ever said the conversation would be a comfortable affair!

The woman at the well makes the same mistake we do in our churches. She asks about the "how" of religion instead of the "who" of our faith. She asks Jesus about where the proper place to worship is, on the mountain or in Jerusalem? In nearly 2,000 years nothing has changed. Our Western mode of thinking is pragmatic and calculates the quickest and most efficient way to do anything, including worship. Contemporary music vs. hymns, robes and clerical vestments vs. casual, gothic cathedrals vs. modern spaces, all of these issues seem to dominate the Christian dialogue and yet Jesus says, "It doesn't matter."

The hour is coming, promises Jesus, when mountains, temples, rituals and clerical regalia won't matter because we will be worshipping in spirit and truth. God is looking for worshippers like this. I am led to believe that if God desired for us to worship in exactly one manner, in exactly one vein of theological tradition, then he would've laid out such desires in the scriptures. But all Christ tells us is that a day is coming when we will all worship in spirit and truth. At the time of Jesus' earthly ministry, the general consensus was that the prophetic voice had ended; it had been so long since they heard the voice of a prophet. Good news was scarce. The Spirit was commonly associated with prophecy, so for Jesus to say that true worship is done in spirit and truth, he is offering this woman a very hopeful glimpse of the future of worship as well as the present reality of having the Christ stand before her.

True worship must not focus on rituals and dead traditions but on offering a voice of hope in an otherwise hopeless world. You have been married five times and the man you are with is not your husband, and yet I'm still willing to offer you a perpetual spring of living water so that you will never be thirsty. Of course, Jesus isn't talking about physical thirst. He's speaking of the thirst of the human heart. Jesus says that he offers a remedy, a thirst-quenching antidote to the human condition, and we can find it when we worship in spirit and truth and converse with Christ. Amen.

39

"A SPIRITUAL RELIGION"

Micah 6:6-8

Brooks Talbott

The scene is a courtroom. God has put Israel on trial. And to prove his case, God calls in the witnesses. He asks the mountains to be witnesses against his people. Mountains never change. They remain constant for thousands of years, but God's people do not.

God cannot count on them anymore. Even though the people had promised to be faithful and true, even though they had pledged God their love, they turned their backs on him. Tears begin to stream down God's cheeks as he says, "O my people, what have I done to you? In what have I wearied you? Answer me!" (Micah 6:3). The people can say nothing. The Israelites are embarrassed. They realize they stand without excuse. God certainly had done nothing to hurt them. On the contrary, he had always blessed them and helped them even though they didn't deserve it. The people feel ashamed. They realize their need to get back into a proper relationship with God, so they ask, "With what shall I come before the LORD, and bow myself before God on high? Shall I come before him with burnt offerings... with calves a year old...with thousands of rams...ten thousands of rivers of oil...my firstborn?" (Micah 6:6-7).

God says, "I have told you, O mortal, what is good; and what does the LORD require of you but to do justice, and to love kindness, and to walk humbly with your God" (Micah 6:8). These words are some of the most important in the Bible. In fact, they are so important that they are etched in the main reading room in the Library of Congress in Washington, D.C.

As future leaders in the church, I believe this passage is one that we must have etched in our memories. It's a passage that will stay with us through the best of times and the worst of times. And if we're really going to be leaders in the church, then we need to take the last verse of this passage and boil down our lives to these three actions: do justice, love kindness, and walk humbly.

Today I want to speak to each of the future leaders in this room, and I want to give us a taste of what it means to be a Christ-like leader by looking at Christ's example as indicated in Micah 6:6-8. Now I know there's a lot of people here listening who are very smart and could probably be world class communicators. But neither of these things matter if you do not appreciate the Word we have been called to teach. We can have all the intangibles, all the tricks, the best teeth and hair and be able to speak eloquently, but at the end of the day, if it is not the Word of truth that comes out of our mouths, then we are worthless.

Adolf Hitler was a great communicator, yet his message was terrible. Is it your ability to communicate well? No, though it helps. If the source of your message is not a deep humility in the face of God's grace, then it doesn't matter. Take a look at what Jesus says to the Pharisees who communicated well but had the wrong message. In Matthew 23:23, Jesus speaks to the Pharisees using some very strong words. He says, "Woe to you, scribes and Pharisees, hypocrites! For you tithe mint, dill, and cumin, and have neglected the weightier matters of the law: justice and mercy and faith. It is these you ought to have practiced without neglecting others."

The Pharisees had a practice where during times of fasting they would wipe dirt on their faces and exaggerate their features as a way of showing the people how holy they were. They would lead the people into thinking there was only one way to be holy: to live by the letter of the law and make sure everyone knows it. So these men who were supposed to be guiding the people to God were actually guiding the focus of the people to themselves and not to God! In the next verse, Jesus even calls them "blind guides" (Matthew 23:24).

Sadly, we have plenty of blind guides in the church today. Some time ago I turned on the news to find some members of the Westboro Baptist Church picketing a soldier's funeral. They were spewing all kinds of hate, yet they proclaim Jesus Christ as the head of their church. I also read an article on the "health and wealth" gospel where thousands come and give their money to ministers hoping that God will bless them and heal them.

You see, these people do not walk humbly. They do not live mercifully. They do not live justly. Can you be humble, have mercy, and live justly without having a personal relationship with Jesus Christ? No. And if we aren't careful in our leadership, it can be easy to slip right into the opposite actions God describes as good for us. What are the opposites of those he mentioned?

The opposite of humility is arrogance. In church leadership, arrogance can make us believe we know all about God and we are closer to him than anyone else. I have seen this happen first hand. If you have gone to Bible college, you have been this person at some point.

When we look at justice, we find that the opposite is corruption. When corruption begins to sneak into a church leader, their motive for working for the kingdom of God changes. Church leadership can become such a position of power we begin to confuse God's agenda for our own. This can literally tear a church apart. The glory of the church shouldn't be focused on one individual. It should be focused entirely on God.

The opposite of mercy is abuse. Sadly, this is the most difficult for me. We see in the news about children who are hurt by a pastor in the church. Or we see articles about a pastor who has stolen from the church. A pastor who has no honesty and integrity is a "blind guide." As the leader of a church, it is your duty to put on Christ and deal with these issues accordingly. I think it's easy to forget that we are messengers of Christ, and we need to show Christ's love to everyone.

The truth is we are all guilty of being a "blind guide" from time to time. We all fail Christ. We all fail his church. We all fall short of what God expects of us in Micah 6:8!

Yet, God knows this, and he will offer us a second chance. Will you live the kind of life that is worth Jesus hanging on the cross to die for? And honestly, if you don't want to do that, then you shouldn't be in ministry. God's people deserves better than that. God deserves better than that.

In Psalm 51, we get the idea that the only thing which matters to God now is coming to him humbly, mercifully, and justly with the right heart. He no longer takes delight in sacrifices, or burnt offerings. And although it is true that, as teachers of the Word we have a higher responsibility, sometimes it's easy to get the wrong impression of what God expects out of leaders in the church. Unfortunately, many leaders in the church feel they have to do everything right or God will punish them. But Christians are in a covenantal relationship with God in which the law has been placed within our hearts! Obedience for Christians is to the indwelling Holy Spirit, not to the letter of the law. His grace is sufficient for us.

Sometimes we think that leadership is about completing a checklist, but ministry is so much more than that. It is about an appropriate understanding and appreciation for who God is. It is a continued remembrance that the good news you get to share with the world was bought at a very steep price.

When Jesus was in the Garden of Gethsemane on the night of his betrayal, he looked up at God and asked God for another way. And though we don't get God's answer in the text, we know it was, "No." Jesus' answer was, "Your will be done." Let us never forget as leaders how our sins were paid for at a high price. In the great sweep of history, humility, mercy and justice were demonstrated most clearly when Jesus hung on the cross. He could have called legions of angels, but he didn't. The creator of the universe hung on a cross, and he challenges us today to live as he did.

My challenge to you as leaders is this: live a life that's worthy of the cross. Live one that says "my freedom was bought at a price, and I can do nothing else but live humbly, pursue justice, and treat others with mercy." God has already done it, and we have the amazing opportunity to join in his good work.

The day Jesus was resurrected the disciples could finally see him for who he was. They finally understand what he'd been telling them all along. "Lord, what should we do now?" Jesus looked and them and at us and says, "Love mercy, walk humbly, and act justly."

40

"THE BEST SPOILED ENDING EVER"
John 2:12-22

Alex Williams

When I was younger and much more immature, I liked to provoke my friends. Whenever one of my friends would ask a group of us if we had seen a particular movie, I would jump in and say "Yeah! It was awesome until so-and-so died at the end!" Of course, chances were I had not actually seen the movie and that whoever I said died probably didn't. I used to do things like that to get a reaction. No one likes a spoiled ending. Well, excuse me for reverting back to my "immature ways," but I hope to do a bit of spoiling this morning.

The story I like best in the Gospel of John comes in the 2nd chapter. Do you remember the story of Jesus running amok in the temple? I love that story! Can you fathom what it must have been like to be a bystander at the temple when Jesus entered and was appalled at what he saw? People were selling cattle and sheep and doves. They were profiting from a sacred religious festival! Thousands of people came from out of town. Because many of them would travel long distances, they would not bring their own animals to sacrifice. Those who did bring their own had to have the religious leaders inspect them to make sure there were no imperfections. As a way to raise money for temple upkeep, the religious leaders would discriminate and tell them their animals were not worthy to be sacrificed. This would force a lot of people to buy animals on the premises.

Imagine going to church and seeing someone selling lottery tickets. "Get your 'scratch and win' tickets right here! Pay $2 for a chance to win $10,000! God wants you to give as much as you can! Pay 2, win 10! Give it to God!" Yeah, I can see why Jesus was irate. More than that, I can picture him wide-eyed, his blood boiling with righteous anger, and the veins in his chiseled neck bulging as if the pressure from his rage would make them pop!

I've never been a fan of comic books, and I know very little about any of them. But when it comes to the Incredible Hulk, what

I do know is that you didn't want to make him mad. I think the same could be said about Jesus. I would not want to be a money changer in the temple, of all places, when Jesus arrived. Jesus began flipping tables and scattering money. He brandished a whip he made from rope and chased the merchants and money changers from the temple. He yelled at them, "Get these out of here! How dare you turn my Father's house into a market!"

John doesn't say what the disciples were doing as Jesus cleared the temple. Did any of them join in the ruckus and flip tables? Were they admonishing the money changers too? Each time I envision this scene, the disciples play the same role. They stand there, mouths hanging wide open, shocked that their Master is cracking a whip, tossing money around, throwing tables, and chasing people. As his disciples took all this in they remembered what was written in Psalm 69: "For the zeal of your house consumes me."

Do you feel that way about church? Do you have an eagerness, a fervor, a passion for church? There are definitely days when I don't feel mentally prepared to come and stand before God and worship him in a communal setting. There are days when I am preoccupied by things to do around the house, things going on at work, and things going on within the family. All of that can be a distraction for me at church. When I am able to focus my whole being on God, when I can give him everything on those Sunday mornings...what an experience! I don't ever want to leave church!

Pay close attention to John 2:18, where it talks of the Jews demanding a sign of Jesus' authority. These Jews were the religious leaders and most likely included the temple police, scribes and Pharisees. Jesus' outburst more than upset them. They approached him and demanded to know where he got his authority to act and try to destroy their profitable business. They wanted proof; otherwise, I imagine they were going to run him out of town.

You see, that's the problem with being one of the religious leaders. They were blind. They didn't know who they were dealing with. All they wanted was physical proof of who Jesus was and why he acted the way he did. They wanted a sign. Do you know what their sign was? First of all, Jesus gave them two. Those leaders were well educated about the scriptures. They not only knew them but were able to use them to their advantage. But in this instance, they completely missed the fulfillment of one of God's prophecies. Malachi 3:1-3 says that the Lord whom the people seek will suddenly come to his temple and will purify the Levites.

In Numbers and Deuteronomy, God sets apart the tribe of Levi from the other 11 tribes giving them the distinction that only Levites were allowed to be priests. In his prophecy, God is saying that Jesus will come to cleanse the temple of sin and corruption and to rebuke the religious elite, including the Levite priests. This is precisely what happened. That was their first sign.

Since they missed that one, Jesus offered another one. He responded with a *mashal*, a veiled saying that is often in the form of a riddle. These sayings were things the religious people should have been accustomed to hearing...Jesus said, "Destroy this temple, and I will raise it again in three days!" This wasn't just some little shanty we're talking about. This is a big stone building with a stone courtyard. Furthermore, we're not talking about Extreme Makeover: Temple Edition coming in and building it up in three days. We're talking about one man. The scoffs and laughter Jesus must have endured. Everyone knew it had taken 46 years to build the temple, which, by the way, still wasn't finished. They knew there was no way it could be rebuilt in three days. But Jesus wasn't telling them to literally destroy the temple, even though that is how they understood it.

Jesus' *mashal* contained several words that had a two-fold interpretation. The Greek word for "destroy" that Jesus used is applicable to the tearing down of a building or the destruction of the human body. Also, the Greek word for "temple" refers either to the sacred shrine, which included the outer courts, or the physical frame of a man viewed as the dwelling place of the Spirit. The Greek translation of "raise it" implied reconstructing a building or the resuscitation of an individual.

I haven't been to a movie theater in at least two years. I think the last movie I saw in a theater was "Bee Movie," but I could be wrong. It was a cute little movie, and what made it halfway decent was that I didn't know much about the storyline. No one at work talked about it. All my co-workers were either into the overly dramatic chick-flicks or the rock 'em, sock 'em, thriller, shoot 'em up movies. In other words, "Bee Movie" was too tame for them. I didn't have to worry about anyone ruining the story, or more importantly, the ending.

Friends, we now come to verse 22 – the spoiler. The Gospel of John has 21 chapters. We're only in chapter two, and we have the spoiler for the entire Gospel. Verse 22 says, "After he was raised from the dead, his disciples remembered that he had said this."

Jesus' disciples had an epiphany. It all finally clicked for them. They remembered Jesus promising those religious leaders in the temple that he would raise the temple in three days, only now they understood he had been referring to himself! Those religious leaders wanted proof of Jesus' authority. Jesus met their demand with the warning that by destroying him he would rise from the dead three days later. That would be their proof.

I hate a spoiled ending as much as the next person, but I am so relieved to be able to read the Gospel of John and find out so early on that the good guys win! Do you know what that means for us? It means that when we put our faith and trust in Christ to be our Savior, our Lord and Master, we will be included as one of the good guys. We will be on his winning team!

For those of us who are believers in Christ, God has taken off our blinders. He has graciously allowed us to see that Jesus is the Son of God, who was sent here to die for us. John 2:22 makes it known in this story that Jesus will die. But then it says that Jesus will rise from the grave. Did you get that? I'm not suggesting that you don't need to read the rest of John's gospel, but this is the most important part of the story. Jesus was crucified. Jesus rose from the dead. He did exactly what God said would happen.

Sin is very problematic for God. It's against his nature and he doesn't tolerate it. Jesus hated how the religious leaders had desecrated the temple and turned it into a marketplace. A violation of God's dwelling called for extreme measures. Oftentimes, people picture God as this gentle, meek God that is warm and cuddly, like a lamb, and that he loves us and only wants good things for us. This is true to a point; however, in this passage Jesus displayed the side of God that can be overlooked. He exhibited the awesome power of God.

Sometimes people need a little smack on the hand to get them to stop misbehaving. Other times it takes a swift kick in the behind to get their attention. God chose to play the part of the lion. He chose to display signs of his power and greatness. And like fools, with their hearts hardened from their sin, the Pharisees, priests and others at the temple missed those signs. But be reassured for there is a God who says, "I am the same yesterday, today and forever." There is a God that spoke to ancient people using signs and wonders. That same God still uses signs to speak to us. We have the ability to see those signs. Have you noticed them? Or like the religious leaders of the temple, have you been caught up in the busyness of life and missed some of the most amazing things God has done for you?

God loves you, and God most certainly wants to bless you beyond comprehension. But all too often we miss those blessings. We miss those creative signs God gives us. God deserves more than our attention. He deserves more than our love and admiration. He deserves everything we could possibly give and then some.

In John's account of Jesus, long before Jesus was crucified, John spoiled the story for us. John slipped it in, like a whisper, about how Christ died and then was raised to life. This was God's greatest sign of all time. He sent his only Son to purify us from our sins by offering himself as the ultimate atoning sacrifice.

Learn from the mistakes of the religious leaders Jesus confronted. They missed the signs because their focus was on material things. They were more concerned about their social status and how they were able to appear as religious and be part of society's upper crust instead of being true servants and available to do God's purposes. That is a big reason why they were confronted by an angry Jesus.

We shouldn't make God discipline us. He doesn't like it, but he will lovingly do it for our own good. Sometimes we may get our hands smacked; other times we may need that kick in the rear. However, one thing holds true. We are to trust in the Lord with all our heart and not trust in our own understanding. In everything you do and everywhere you go, acknowledge God. He will make your path straight. If we acknowledge him, God has spoiled the ending for us too.

41

"THE LEFT BEHIND SERIES"
John 4:1-42

Lonnie Winston

Many times in our lives we have left behind something of great use or value to us. On many occasions, we have left behind all sorts of things for known and unknown reasons. The phrase "left behind" simply means to depart or not take along. Who in attendance at this Festival today left behind a few things in order to get here? Obviously, you and I brought everything we deemed necessary to make it through this conference, but what is important to us for survival is not always important to Jesus. Therefore, many times in our lives, he will say to us, "Leave it behind."

As Jesus' humanity takes hold on his body from his journey through Samaria, he finds a seat on Jacob's well. As Jesus sat weary, thirsty, and needing a drink, a Samaritan woman arrives while Jesus is at the well with her water pot to draw water. As Jesus begins his Salvation 101 Class, the woman seems interested and puzzled at the same time. As he continues to speak, the more interested she becomes, but she can't understand why this is happening. First, during this time, Jews and Samaritans didn't associated. Second, men never approached women. Finally, no one would have been at the well during this time. The tradition indicates that women would come early in the morning and late in the evening so they would be comfortable drawing water. But this Samaritan woman came during the hottest time of the day. It would have been hot, muggy, and uncomfortable.

Many times in our lives we live in ways that aren't pleasing to God. As a result, it makes us feel uncomfortable. This woman's discomfort enabled her to understand, to think outside the box and tear down social and cultural barriers. Basically, Jesus was telling her the only way she could understand was to, "Leave it behind!" Many of us are dealing with issues we must leave behind so that God can use us entirely.

You may say, "Well, God is using me now!" But what if you just left behind the mess that is weighing you down? As the woman leaves behind her sexual indiscretions, Jesus reveals himself to her as being the living water. Once Jesus does this, she leaves in excitement and joy, even leaving behind her water pot. But she now doesn't have to worry about physical water because she has encountered a spiritual spring that flows forever.

Many of us are just like this woman. We believe we need material things to make it, but all we need is spiritual things to survive. As the woman arrived on the scene, she had her water pot ready to use; however, when she experienced Jesus, she left it behind unused. Jesus is looking for us to leave behind those things that burden us so we can leave with joy and excitement and declare the good news of Jesus Christ. My brothers and sisters, this is what the Samaritan woman did after encountering Jesus.

Isn't it good to know that Jesus will fix it after while! When Jesus fixes it, he will put a clap in your hands, a spring in your step, and praise in your mouth. If you don't believe me, look at the Samaritan woman. She said, "Come see a man who told me everything I have ever done" (John 4:29). I don't know about you, but I want to see this man!

As I say good afternoon, I'm reminded of another woman named Helen Keller. She came into the world born physically blind and deaf. She was very defiant, mean, and hateful growing up. She was also very demanding and got what she wanted from her family no matter how she acted. Her family responded to her disability as a charity case instead of disciplining her and teaching her how to behave. As she started school, she met her match as her teacher Ann Sullivan came to her house and began to work with her. It took some time, but Ann Sullivan got Helen to leave behind her defiant moods, childish behavior, and poor attitude. As a result, Ann helped Helen learn sign language, and she went on to become the first deaf and blind person to earn a Bachelor of Arts degree.

Once Helen Keller left behind her issues and her past, she was able to be used by God. Helen and Ann's friendship continued to grow, and Helen developed a loving and caring relationship with Ann Sullivan. One day after Ann had a breakthrough with Helen, she asked Ann, "What is God's name?" When Ann spelled God into Helen's hand, the young girl smiled and her fingers spelled a reply. Helen said she always knew God was there, and now she knew his name! I have to smile thinking of Helen and her knowledge about God. Helen came into this world blind and death, but she left behind her issues and could eventually see and hear a wonderful Savior.

Perhaps there is someone here today who just can't figure it out. There are times I like to be all by myself and just tell Jesus all about it. And when I come out of whatever it is, I have a personal relationship with him and a testimony to share. As we see in the text, this is how some of the men responded. They couldn't understand the woman's testimony, so they got Jesus to stay a little while longer. As a result, many came to believe.

My dear friends, no matter how you do it, just come to Jesus. He came that you and I might live and live abundantly. It's because he lives that we can face tomorrow. It's because he lives that all fear is gone. It's because he loves me so much he sent his only Son that I might have eternal life. They hung him high, they stretched him wide, he hung his head, and then he died. But that's not how the story ends. In three days he rose again. Now that's love!

Passion & Death

42

"EVERY WITNESS NEEDS A GOSPEL"
John 19:31-37

Zachary Bailes

The sun was high in the sky. Forty years ago the parking lot would have been filled, but today there were only a few cars in the lot. I perspired through my shirt. People snapped pictures of the infamous building we were visiting. I felt lost. I felt pain. I felt sadness. A wreath hung from the balcony, looming over us as though there was a mysterious energy pulsating. As I wandered through the Lorraine Motel I eventually came upon a spot where I overlooked the balcony. In that spot I stood near the place where Dr. Martin Luther King, Jr. breathed his last. In that place, a pool of blood and a clenched cigarette were all that remained. In that remnant, hope and hate met.

Rev. Samuel "Billy" Kyles reflected upon that day saying, "And they said, 'We will shoot this dreamer and see what happens to his dream.' That's where the witness comes in. The witness will tell all who will listen, 'Yes, you can kill the dreamer, but no, you absolutely cannot kill the dream.' And so that witness has taken me through all of this for the last forty years. I know that's what I'm supposed to do, and that's what I do."[1]

Every witness needs a gospel.

When Martin Luther King, Jr. breathed his last, his dream did not die with him. It is true, we have not arrived at the fullest realization of his dream, but we catch glimpses and the dream is still alive. For Kyles and others it is not the dream itself that energized the movement. It is the witness not of a death, but of a life.

I can tell you neither the weather nor how many donkeys were around the day our rogue witness watched Jesus die. Jesus had been convicted and was sentenced to death. It was a disgraceful death. He, the sarcastically named "King of the Jews," suffered an abysmal death. Yet, I can't tell you who our witness was. Who was he? Or,

[1]Rev. Samuel "Billy" Kyles, interviewed on the Tavis Smiley Show, 1 April 2008. Available from www.pbs.org/tavissmiley/archive/200804/2008041_kyles.html.

who was she? We don't know what this witness said, but it may have sounded something like: "And they said, 'We will crucify this dreamer and see what happens to his dream.'"

When Jesus breathed his last, his dream did not die with him. It is true, we have not arrived at the fullest realization of his dream, but we catch glimpses and the dream is still alive. For our witness and others, it is not the dream itself that energized a movement. It is the witness not of a death, but of a life.

Every witness needs a gospel.

There was no Twitter at Golgotha, updating the Roman Empire on who had been killed. There were no written documents detailing who had been killed. The Gospel writer needed someone to corroborate the story told, he needed a witness. That witness spoke the truth–Jesus died.

Every witness needs a gospel. When I say gospel I'm not speaking of Matthew, Mark, Luke, or John's writings. I'm not speaking about good news. I'm talking about something of prime importance. You're only a witness when you have special information. You have seen something that others have not. Perhaps this witness didn't see only Jesus' death. But, the witness saw the life of Jesus. Perhaps the witness didn't only proclaim how Jesus died, but how Jesus lived.

What do you see? What of utmost importance do you see in the world? Because throughout history I see that God is deeply connected to this world, the world we often times condemn. I see that God's love knows no color, no creed, no boundary. Need examples? Jesus was born to a young woman who faced societal judgment. Martin Luther King, Jr. was born into the Jim Crow South. In Jericho there lived a prostitute named Rahab who assisted Israelite spies. Priscilla was a tentmaker who became a teacher of the early Christian faith. If you need more examples, we'll chat later.

The gospel we know doesn't call us to a crucifixion on the cross or on a balcony. The cross we carry isn't up to a hill called Golgotha, the "Place of the Skull" where with a name like that you can't expect anything good. We are called to a gospel that is always and at once tied up in our lives. The gospel is not a book. It is not words on a page that describe the gospel we witness. What we witness are lives lived as we teeter between belief and unbelief.

Every witness needs a gospel.

As I stood in the Lorraine Motel, I wondered how I could be a witness. As I listen to the story of Christ's death, I wonder how

I can be a witness. After all, to call yourself a witness is to see the events firsthand. I didn't see the crucifixion of Christ. I saw neither Mary weep nor soldiers take the hyssop and offer the wine. How can you be a witness?

As a gospel witness our responsibility is to see the world. To see opportunities to love. To give hope to the hopeless. To love the unloved and foster faith for the disillusioned. Our witness begins here. Proclaiming the word through the movement of our hands and our desire. The witness we hear about in the gospel tells that Jesus did die. That Jesus did not hide for three days in a tomb. But that Jesus suffered, died and was buried. That the good news of resurrection is alive and possible. As radical as the resurrection was, so too is the proclamation of such radical ideas as hope, peace, and love.

When we make ourselves a witness we proclaim that the gospel of resurrection is just around the corner. When we see a broken body, there is hope for healing. When we see the blood of injustice, we will apply the gauze of God's golden guarantee: righteousness and justice.

How often do righteousness and justice seem so far away? How discouraged do we become? I offer no remedy for discouragement. I offer no solution. Discouragement happens. Weariness happens. The fact is I could explain how to overcome discouragement, but it won't make you feel any better. We find comfort in the arms of community. While we are called to hear stories, we must also be willing to tell our own story. We cannot carry our burdens alone. Discouragement is a season we all pass through.

This ebb and flow between storyteller and witness is always at work. We need those willing to stand up and tell a story of hope, struggle, oppression, or redemption. We as people all across the globe and in this room need to hear stories. Story after story we might soon find out that we aren't so different. We all struggle. We all share joy, fear, and triumph. For it is the witness of Christ's death where soldiers, Mary, Peter, and a rogue witness are brought together.

If the twenty-first century is to be any less deadly than the twentieth, witnesses must stand up and speak out. Senses of justice must become more acute. An appreciation for the fragility of life must become deeper. We must become, as a global community, more caring and compassionate. This will not happen without witnesses.

The hope of our gospel, our important news, will take us to unknown places. For some it has taken them to the ends of the earth, others to edge of their hearts. For Rev. Samuel "Billy" Kyles, who was present when Martin Luther King, Jr. died, it meant putting one foot in front of the other. For Fannie Lou Hamer it meant forming the National Women's Political Caucus in 1971 and speaking for inclusion of racial issues in the feminist movement.

Proclaiming the dream will not be proclaimed by words alone. Our powerful propositions will be the movement of our feet. We will shape our world with dream-inspired hands. We will, with our souls, go to the world with a message of love and redemption. For our greatest witness is not that we are timid, but that in darkness, in the middle of chaos, when there is no hope, we hear each other. We hear and we act. We do not wait because we know that the story is no longer a tale but a call for action.

Who will tell your story? Whose story are you proclaiming?

As we proclaim we must realize that this has not always been a fair game. Even as the witness tells of Jesus' death, the Roman Empire looms over the early Christian world. But we don't even need to look to the Bible for those stories that have been overlooked. We don't need to look past yesterday to hear stories to which a deaf ear has been turned.

To proclaim we must listen. It can be hard to hear the stories of those who suffer. Many suffer from an ailment called shame. Their burden is one that they did not choose. Their burden is one placed upon them by those who could not listen, even to themselves. But you have heard a story of a man that hung on a cross. He was born to a young woman, unmarried parents, and challenged the status quo. Shame was the game for those around him.

Yet for our obscure, no-name, out of the blue, run of the mill, Jack or Jill of all trades, quickly-fading, never digressing witness, that gospel was love! A new way of relating had come. No longer did we have to control through shame, but we could liberate through love.

The image of the wreath hanging from the balcony remains fresh in my mind, but the Lorraine Motel cannot contain all that is a dream. Neither can a cross on a hill. For the dream is within me and within you. Yes, you can crucify the dreamer, but you cannot crucify the dream. Amen.

43

"MIDNIGHT IN THE GARDEN OF GOOD AND EVIL"
Mark 14:32-42

J. C. Campbell

"But the raven, sitting lonely on the placid bust, spoke only,
That one word, as if his soul in that one word he did outpour.
Nothing further then he uttered–not a feather then he
fluttered–
Till I scarcely more than muttered 'Other friends have flown
before–
On the morrow he will leave me, as my hopes have flown
before.'
Then the bird said, 'Nevermore.'"[1]

Deep in the Garden of Gethsemane, past the sweet perfumes of freshly pressed oils, radiant greenery, tranquil olive trees, and furrows of ancient foliage, lives darkness, despair, and anguish. In the midst of the illustrious scenery of Gethsemane we find weakness, brokenness, and loneliness. It is the beginning of the end. The ultimate act of selflessness, obedience, and love begins here in this very dark garden. Here at this place that represents all things naturally pleasant and all things spiritually corrupt, Jesus reveals his ultimate humanity and supreme glory. Most scholars, preachers, and Christians alike would argue that the cross is the climatic unveiling of the glory and obedience of Jesus Christ. It has been said that not until the cross did Jesus reveal himself as man willing to suffer and God willing to save. However, if we bend back the branches of those old olive trees, and we tiptoe lightly so as not to disturb the sleeping disciples, we find the true Jesus revealed.

Jesus Christ, since his emersion in the waters of the River Jordan, was thrust into the service of God. In this service, we find the raw,

[1]Edgar Allan Poe, *Complete Tales and Poems of Edgar Allan Poe* (New York: Vintage Books, 1975), 943.

unadulterated truth of suffering, temptation, and evil. According to the Gospel of Mark, "And the Spirit immediately drove him out into the wilderness. He was in the wilderness forty days, tempted by Satan ..." (Mark 1:12-13*a*). Immediately after God's divine recognition of Jesus, he is thrown to the Lion of all lions to be tested and tempted. Needless to say, he proved himself worthy, able to say to Satan, "Nevermore."

In the continuous growth of Christ's ministry, he is constantly tried and tempted by the Pharisees and Sadducees, who mock him and plot against him without compassion or mercy. They criticize him for sitting with the tax collectors and sinners. In Mark 3, the Pharisees and Herodians hatch a vile, wicked plan to murder Jesus. Furthermore, the religious leaders accuse him of being demonic. The list goes on and on. Their ultimate goal is to stump Jesus in a war of words, ritualistic pomp and circumstance, and ultimately give themselves and the public a reason to kill him.

In our service, we will be tested by some vicious people. We will be questioned and analyzed every second of our lives. There are people who plot and plan and watch your every move just to see when you will fall, and when that time comes, baby, they want to be the first ones to have their foot on your chest. They will scratch, claw, and dig for any dirt they can find, and they will break the law and their backs to persecute you. It is a shame, but people like this–back stabbers that smile in your face and all the time want to take your place–will always hate and they will always exist.

It is a rough road ahead for our Savior. Many traps have been set, but not executed. Many plans plotted, but not initiated. Unfortunately, it is only a matter of time. Is it not enough to say that he was tempted by Satan himself in the wilderness, tested by the hardened hearts of the religious society? But what seems to bother Jesus the most, to test him, to wear on his patience, is the ignorance of the twelve disciples. In Mark 4, Jesus calms the winds and the waves and says to the disciples, "Why are you afraid? Have you still no faith?" (Mark 4:40) The disciples later reply, "Who then is this, that even the wind and the sea obey him!" (Mark 4:41*b*). When Jesus entrusted the disciples with the knowledge of God, they still didn't understand. They preferred to argue and bicker about who would be the greatest and who would sit to the right and left of Jesus. Through their ignorance, unfaithfulness, and weakness, they tested Jesus.

Sometimes it is hard to believe that those who claim to be our friends and stick by us are the very ones that test us. It is a shame that our confidants and good buddies are wishy-washy and sometimey. It is painful to realize that when we need someone to lean on, when we need a shoulder to cry on, when we need to vent, our friends are nowhere to be found. The disciples did this very thing. They experienced life with a man that they hardly ever knew.

These factors in Christ's ministry lead him to the ground of the garden. Gethsemane symbolizes the realization that Satan not only has tempted him in person but continues to tempt through the evil plots of the Pharisees, the double-mindedness of his disciples, and the consciousness that this suffering would be one of loneliness. Jesus could not trust the hypocrisy of the Pharisees to comfort him. He could no longer lean on the words of his disciples who could not clearly identify him or his power. They could not follow simple instructions. In Mark 13, Jesus repeatedly commands and warns his disciples to watch and be alert. Again, in the garden he commands them to sit and pray. He confesses to them his supreme sorrow and pain, "I am deeply grieved, even to death; remain here, and keep awake" (Mark 14:34). They completely ignore this confession and allow the flesh to win.

What Jesus does next is profound. He goes behind the berry bushes, drops to his knees and prays for mercy from Golgotha, "Abba, Father, for you all things are possible; remove this cup from me; yet, not what I want, but what you want" (Mark 14:36). He pleads with God to take away this cup of pain, humiliation, suffering, and loneliness. But, in a glimpse of hope for humanity and the brazen boldness and authority of Jesus Christ, he declares that God's will shall be done. He returns to find his disciples sleeping. He chastises them and declares, "Could you not keep awake one hour? Keep awake and pray that you may not come into the time of trial; the spirit is indeed willing, but the flesh is weak" (Mark 14:37*b*-38). Here Jesus gives them advice he just followed himself and tries to stress the importance of prayer and obedience. Yet, they fail him again. Through all Peter's talk of loyalty, Judas' back-handed betrayal, and the weak eyelids of the disciples, Jesus is convinced that only his faith and obedience will see him through.

In a bold move that would rival Butch Cassidy and the Sundance Kid, Jesus confronts his destiny. He boldly, through obedience and of prayer, accepts the way that John the Baptist prepared for him. Jesus is now the voice crying out in the garden, making his path straight to Calvary. He is without friends, without family, and without God. But he fought on and did not wave or bend. Aren't you glad to know that although we can be double-minded and conflicted, Christ always remains faithful? Why? Wouldn't any human being break under the pressure of being lonely, misunderstood, demonically sought after, talked about, lied to, abused, and misused? Wouldn't any human being just give up! The answer is YES! But Jesus is not just any human. He went through the trials saying, "NEVERMORE." He suffered on Calvary saying, "NEVERMORE." He was humiliated and accepted evil saying, "NEVERMORE." He died a sinner's wretched death, our foul, disgusting death declaring, "NEVERMORE." But early Sunday morning, he rose with all power and authority in his hands declaring, "NEVERMORE."

In Genesis, we see the desolation of paradise. Adam and Eve sin by eating the fruit with the knowledge of good and evil and are cast out of the Garden of Eden. It is so profound that Jesus must accept the knowledge of good and evil in his prayer and meditation and consciousness of suffering in the Garden of Gethsemane. Jesus is purifying paradise. He is being obedient as the second Adam and leaving the garden not by punishment but with power.

Today we must understand, like Jesus, that without test there is no testimony. Without pain there is no power. Without struggle there is no strength. Without sacrifice there is no paradise. Without calamity there is no celebration. You say, "How do you know this is possible?" I tell you that Christ made it possible. He is the perfect example for us right now. We can defeat persecution, we can reject temptation, and we can command Satan to flee. We can stand on the promise of God and boldly declare, "NEVERMORE!"

44

"THE GARDEN SECRET"

Mark 14:32-42

Chris Dodson

"It was the sweetest, most mysterious looking place any one could imagine."[1] Or so Mary thinks when she first enters into the "secret garden" in Frances Burnett's novel. As Mary wanders along the path of grief, she encounters a world both beautiful and strange. As she gazes at flower beds, unsure if their contents are dead or alive, she stumbles upon a world both familiar and disconcerting. There is something about it that is both ideal and out of place.

As we view Jesus, wandering the paths of a very different garden, these same senses of comfort and discomfort stir within our souls. As we read Mark's account of this story, this unsettling feeling only seems to grow. Jesus, overwhelmed with sorrow, collapses to the ground. He prays desperately for another way to be found because he knows God can do it. His grief is great enough that he feels he could die then and there, far short of any cross. In fact, Mark's account is too disturbing for the other gospel writers. In Luke, there is no room for a Jesus who collapses to his face overwhelmed with sorrow and grief. In Matthew, Jesus does not appeal to God's full ability to find a different way. In John, Jesus doesn't pray that the cup of suffering will pass at all, but his request is turned into a rhetorical question emphatically answered in the negative! Should it pass? No, never! But before we flee to the comforting images of a divine being gracefully accepting human punishment, let us try to hear the very human voice of Mark. Perhaps, we will hear a word of comfort even in a most uncomfortable story.

This is the most human portrait of Jesus depicted in the four gospels. In John, Jesus weeps beside the tomb of Lazarus, but there is something about Mark's account of Gethsemane that makes Jesus so entirely relatable, in ways the lofty language and ideas of John's

---

[1]Frances H. Burnett, *The Secret Garden* (St. Petersburg, FL: Worthington Press, 1991), 78.

gospel cannot. Jesus knows what is coming. He has predicted it for quite some time. And as he enters into the garden of Gethsemane, Jesus leaves the majority of his disciples behind, presumably to keep watch for trouble. However, the hour is late, and they will spend these last moments of Jesus' earthly life not alert to their Lord nor the wicked workings of men, but asleep.

Jesus takes Peter, James, and John with him, but they will fall away as well. He can hardly go any further. Finally, he collapses. He falls prostrate, exhausted and overcome. He does not lift his head to pray, but with his face crushing the grass he cries out to God. God, it would seem, is the only one Jesus has left. His friends have nothing to say, and God has nothing to say.

Haven't we all been there? We cry out to God in grief and fear, in apprehension and ambiguity, and our friends and loved ones have nothing to say. Even God seems to be as silent as they are. And we cry out, "God, give me wisdom! God, give me strength! God give me something because I'm drowning here!" And not even a cricket dares disrupt the silence of the response. And we feel utterly alone.

This is the portrait of Jesus in this text. He is alone and afraid. He could boldly predict suffering when it was a distance away, but it is entirely different when the moment is upon him. Now the way seems more treacherous, but he will stand. He will go to the disciples. Jesus will tell them to rise because the time has come for him to accomplish the will of God. Whereas the spirit was willing and the body was weak before, the body has been brought into alignment and things will progress as planned.

At last we arrive at the secret locked away within this garden. Despite your trials, your sufferings, your discomforts with your lot in life, take heart. If you will kneel for a moment beside an overcome Messiah, take heart. For as you kneel beside him, you will see that he suffered too. If you kneel beside Jesus in the Garden, you will see the violence of his suffering. And if you lift your eyes for a moment, you will see that same Jesus overcoming the world. If his suffering indicated not the end of the world but its renewal, how can we view ours any differently? So take heart.

Ludwig von Beethoven was born in 1770. His father was a drunk and a fanatic, but he overcame this to become a great musician and innovative composer. In 1802, Beethoven's life seemed to be going so well until something unexpected happened. He began to lose his hearing. He was devastated and depressed, but he overcame. In 1823,

Beethoven completed his Ninth Symphony. The final movement of this symphony is accompanied by a chorus singing in German, "Be embraced, you millions! This kiss for the whole world! Brothers, beyond the star-canopy must a loving Father dwell."[2] The lyrics became known as "Ode to Joy." Beethoven had a rough beginning, a disappointing middle, but a rousing finale. My friends, sorrow and heartache can be overcome.

I still wonder where God is in all this mess. Mark tells us that on the cross Jesus cried out, "My God, My God, why have you forsaken me?" But it seems as if God withdrew from the narrative well before then. Where was God when Jesus was on the cross? Where was God when Jesus was spat upon and whipped? Where was God when Jesus was falsely accused? Where was God in Gethsemane when a very human Jesus weeps and begs? I wonder if God isn't exactly where he should be: kneeling beside Christ.

We know there are many catastrophes which God does not prevent. But as my fellow Truett student, Kendall Renfro, reminded us in one of our chapel services, "There is no tragedy which God does not mourn." So I wonder if maybe the tears of this human Jesus are also the tears of God mourning what is to come. And I wonder if in the midst of our own anguish God is kneeling beside us as well. Perhaps moments of divine silence can be filled with pastoral presence if we stop demanding prophetic protest. There is a time for presence and protest, but if we let God impart what he desires, we will be blessed. Christ somehow received the strength to stand and go forth, and he called his disciples to do the same. It was the silent comfort of the divine which enabled Christ and which will enable you.

So we who are disciples, let us rise, let us go. The hour has come. In a few hours we will depart this place to return to the trials and tribulations of life. For some, it may be the rigors of schoolwork. For others, it may be the frantic pace of the work place or something entirely more severe. But no matter the trials you return to, kneel first beside Christ. Kneel first in the comforting presence of God, and take heart. He has overcome the world. Thanks be to God.

---

[2]Ludwig Beethoven, "Ode to Joy" as found in the Fourth Movement of his *Ninth Symphony*, 1823.

45

"THEY CALLED IT A WASTE"
Matthew 26:6-13

Thomas Gricoski

They called it a waste. The disciples looked at this act and called it a waste. This was a simple act of generosity and hospitality that you would afford to any guest at your table, anointing his or her head with some oil. They called it waste because it was too much. A single drop would have sufficed because this oil was so precious. But she wasted it, all of it, in one moment, giving it all away, without holding anything back. The disciples are smart; they have spent time with Jesus; they heard him preach the Sermon on the Mount. "Blessed are the poor..." (Matthew 5:3). They remember the rich young man who came to him on his knees and said, "Teacher, what good deed must I do to have eternal life?" (Matthew 19:16). "Sell your possessions, and give the money to the poor" (Matthew 19:21). They saw him walk away sad because he had many possessions. Perhaps Matthew himself, the tax collector, remembered how Jesus came to him and called him. Matthew, in his heart, may have looked at this woman and said, "What a waste. She wasted her chance at eternal life by not selling this oil to give to the poor. A single drop would have done." They called it a waste.

We too might look at our lives and find something we would call a waste. In coming to this Festival, every single young preacher has taken a risk. Every single one of us has come with our hope poured out into a jar that we are ready to pour out onto the world. We know that the world, and even those in the church, might call it a waste. Jesus' controversial phrase in verse 11, "you always have the poor with you, but you will not always have me," has been abused from both sides. Jesus' words have been used in defense of having great works of art and beauty, great technology, at the expense of charity. It has been used on the other side when people say, we don't need any of that; all we need is to give everything we have to the poor. We hear these criticisms and we doubt ourselves. We look at the years of dedication that we pour into this preaching craft. We amass our debts. We amass our doubts. Is it worth it?

I remember a friend of mine from high school who had his first preaching experience in our senior year. Now he is a preaching pastor. His family wanted him to be a doctor, but he wanted to be a preacher. The difference of opinions gave him doubts. When he came up to the podium in front of the thousand people who had gathered for the worship service, he shuffled his notes, tripped over his words, stumbled, mumbled, and fumbled his message at times. When he came down, I'm sure he had more doubts than ever. Is it worth it?

Jesus looks at this act and calls it good. Jesus looks at the woman with the oil, and he calls this good. Perhaps the woman thought she was only going to perform a simple act of hospitality, to anoint the guest with oil to soothe his head from the heat. When she approaches him, however, something inside of her wells up, and one drop will not do. The whole of it is necessary. Mark records that she broke the vial so that all of it had to be used right there at once. She came in love to give herself to the Lord. Perhaps she did not know it, but she was doing something grander even than that.

There are three types of people in the Hebrew Scriptures who are anointed with such a precious ointment. The priests are anointed because they make an atoning sacrifice for the forgiveness of sins, and so they are consecrated to the Lord's service. The prophets are anointed with oil so they may preach the word of hope, repentance and consolation to God's people, to bring them back to a right relationship with God. The king of Israel is anointed because he is called to love the people, to serve the people, to feed the people, and to defend the people.

Jesus gives another interpretation to this act. "She has done it to prepare me for burial." Prophet, priest, king? Yes, but the kind of king who dies; the suffering servant king. Jesus looked at this woman and her deed, and perhaps Jesus saw himself. Jesus had been going about the countryside for a year or more. To every single person who came up to him and asked, Jesus doled out a drop of his love for their healing, for their reconciliation, for their life. Everyone who asks receives. But when he came to Jerusalem he saw that something more had to be done. His whole span of ministry will be concentrated into a single, grand moment of pouring out. Jesus will pour out his life on the cross; Jesus pours out his blood, when only one drop would suffice. All of it, given in an instant, to make such a beautiful deed. Jesus calls this good.

Jesus looks at what he has called us to do, and he calls it more than good. He calls it worship. We have come here as young preachers to pour out our lives for God's people. That is what we do. I believe that, indeed, God is pouring us out. God pours us out for the life of the world. He has collected us from the ends of the earth, and he has purified and refined us, and he has made us precious in his sight. He has made us beautiful, so that he can pour us out for the life of the world which he loves. So that even in the life of the stumbling and bumbling young preacher, who might at first hold himself or herself back, out of fear or doubt ("Maybe I should have studied plumbing or pharmacy or something useful!"), he want to pour us out.

There comes a moment in a young preacher's life when he or she must say, "A drop will not suffice; God's people deserve it all." God's Word comes gushing out in ways that we do not expect, in ways that a parent could not have dreamt, in ways that only God has known. God works through these beautiful deeds to anoint his Christ in the world. Christ, messiah, means "the anointed one." The world and those who have known Christ, but have perhaps forgotten him, often see Jesus as only a man and wonder if he ever even existed. When the woman poured the oil on Jesus' head, he became in the eyes of all in the room, the anointed one, the Christ.

When preachers stand up to open their mouths to pour forth the Word of God on the world, Jesus becomes the Christ in the hearts and minds of all who hear this word with faith. All of the good works of charity, social justice, and building up the Kingdom of God… all of it comes through love. How can we love unless we are inspired? How can we be inspired unless we hear? How can we hear unless someone preaches? These beautiful acts of preaching inspire more beautiful acts of love, until the whole world is transformed into the Kingdom of God. Jesus calls this good. Jesus calls this worship.

From the beginning of time, God has been pouring himself out. God poured out his Word in the beginning and made the heavens and the earth. God poured out his breath and gave life to Adam and Eve. God poured out his promise and made Abraham and the chosen people.

God poured out his glory and became one like us in the incarnation. Jesus poured out his life in ministry, and he raised the dead and healed the sick. Jesus poured out his life in one grand gesture on the cross and forgave our sins. God poured out immortality on our mortal flesh to raise Christ from the dead. God poured out his Spirit on the Church to make many people into one. God pours out his Spirit on preachers, teachers, ministers, mothers, fathers, brothers, sisters, sons, daughters, and all God's people, to make this world his Kingdom.

Some call it a waste. God calls it good.

46

"THE FINISHED WORK"
John 19:28-30

David Malcolm McGruder

It is an interesting reality that many of the greatest works of history's most noble and honorable men are works that were left unfinished. Works that, either due to death, illness or other circumstances, were left undone. They were full of resplendent promise and august potential, yet rendered partial, fractional and incomplete.

The great theologian, St. Thomas Aquinas, cited a spiritual experience in worship as the source that lead to the abandonment of his greatest work–*Summa Theologica* –in 1273. *The Mysterious Stranger* was a promising text that took the late Mark Twain 20 years to write three versions of and yet he finished none of them. Martin Luther King, Jr.'s Poor People's Campaign, which aimed at eradicating economic injustice in this country, was cut down in its infancy with Dr. King's assassination in 1968. There is even speculation among many scholars and academicians that the gospel of Mark is incomplete.

We could go on to investigate the French novelist Honoré de Balzac's *La Comedie Humaine, Plato's Critias,* Leonardo da Vinci's "The Last Supper," Johann Sebastian Bach's "The Art of Fugue," Franz Schubert's "Symphony No. 8 in B Minor," Mozart's "Requiem," Hemingway's *Garden of Eden,* Nietzsche's *The Will to Power* among others, and there we would discover great works begun by great men, works that have stood the test of time and the fickle nature of human interest, works that even in their partial and fractional state-have revolutionized the modern world, and yet they are not finished works.

From the nineteenth chapter of John's gospel, there vociferates a glorious affirmation: the greatest work in all of human history, the work of salvation wrought on the cross of Calvary through Jesus Christ, was a finished work! It was a mighty work, a grueling task, a challenging work, but thanks be to God, it was a finished work!

I raise the question then today: Because history has certainly been kind to the aforementioned men, what would history record of our Christ had he come down through 42 generations, been born of a virgin, increased in wisdom, stature and favor with God and man, walked the face of the Earth for 33 years, and yet never finished his work? What would the landscape of religious history look like if Jesus, Immanuel, Mary's baby, had come and worked many miracles, opened blinded eyes, unstopped deaf ears, gave the paralytic their ability to walk, healed leprosy, raised the dead and this had been the totality of his mission and ministry. How well would we speak of Christ had he made the decision not to drink of the bitter cup and the work go unfinished? Would he really be worthy of worship if on the night that he was betrayed Jesus had broken bread but never his body, or if he blessed the wine but never shed his blood? Would our gathering here be in vain if Jesus had been marched from judgment hall to judgment hall, ordered to be put to death by Pontius Pilate, led to Golgotha's hill with an old rugged cross on his back and a crown of thorns on his head, and there, under the weight of sin and the agony of crucifixion, he decided to abandon the redemption project on Calvary? What would we say of Jesus had he started but never finished?

John 19:30, though it presents us with a terrible scene, bares good news. It gives us reason to rejoice and be exceedingly glad, for the redemptive work of Calvary, the salvation of all mankind, the crux of our faith, that work, was a finished work. What we see there is what the Greek philosopher Aristotle would have called a "TELOS"[1] or an end. We see there the working out of a purpose started long ago in the heart of God. Before the worlds were ever framed by the word of God, before the concept of purpose was conceived in the minds of men, the purpose of Christ was already accomplished–a lamb slain from the foundation of the world. It was a finished work! But what constitutes its completion? What characterizes its finality? What determines that the work is done?

First, the work would not have been complete if Christ had not died in our place. Gustaf Aulen calls this reality of the vicarious nature of Christ's death, "the most evident and most inscrutable of all spiritual realities."[2] It was the fulfillment of scripture, the redemption

---

[1] *Telos* (from the Greek τέλος for "end", "purpose", or "goal") is an end or purpose, in a fairly constrained sense used by philosophers such as Aristotle.

[2] Gustav Aulen, *The Faith of the Christian Church* (Eugene, OR: Wipf & Stock Publishers, 2002), 208.

of man from his own sin through someone and something that did not belong to him: something higher than man, something greater than man that was given because God loved man.

The finished work was vicarious in nature. The sins of humanity placed Jesus there. The transgressions and iniquities of all humankind – past, present and future – forced him there upon that cross. Our rebellion against God, our lack of moral astuteness and ethical uprightness, our degenerate nature, man's inhumanity to man, our sin put him there! But he finished the work!

He bore our burden for our sake. He became sin for our salvation. He died in our stead, bled on our behalf, hung in our place. Isaiah says it most profoundly: "he was wounded for our transgressions, he was bruised for our iniquities: the chastisement of our peace was upon him; and by his stripes we [as a human family] were healed" (Isaiah 53:5). Thank God he finished the work!

Second, not only was the finished work of Christ vicarious in nature, but the work could not be complete unless it was voluntary in nature. Sin put him there, but it would require love to keep him there. Our attention is arrested by verse 30 where the author declares, "He gave up the ghost." The breath of life was not snatched from him. There was no mortal blow, no fatal stroke. He simply laid down his life and finished the work!

The voluntary nature of the finished work at Calvary reveals the beauty of Christ's divinity, for even in death he was God over death. Even at the point of destruction, he was still God enough to Make 'Ol death behave. No one and nothing could take his life from him: no pain, no agony, no centurion, no suffocation from crucifixion. He laid down his life. He gave himself to reconcile the world to himself. He finished the work!

He chose to go, to give his life, to become the propitiation of our sins. He didn't have to do it. He could have come down. At the point of decision, he could've made another choice, but he decided to save others because he would not save himself. He finished the work!

Finally, the completion of the work of the cross hinged upon its victory. Reinhold Niebuhr postulates that, "the good news of the gospel is that God takes the sinfulness of man into himself, and overcomes in His own heart what cannot be overcome in human life."[3] He was victorious, able to accomplish what even the strongest

---

[3]Reinhold Niebuhr, *The Nature and Destiny of Man* (New York: Scribner, 1943), 153.

and greatest of men could not. Without the shedding of blood there could be no remission of sin, but what type of blood was strong enough to redeem of all of mankind? The blood of sheep and goats couldn't do it. Turtle doves couldn't do it. Certainly human power could not accomplish and achieve redemption on its own. It took something greater. It took something more. It took Jesus. And there at the cross he finished the work!

As aforementioned, the word for end in the Greek is the word *telos*. It is the word used by the philosophers of the Aristotelian tradition, crucial to the works of Kant and Hegel. In and of itself, the word *telos* connotes a sufficient end, but it is not the word employed by Christ. Christ uses the phrase *tetelestai* ... It is finished. In the Greek that phrase does not simply suggest completion, but it implies a perpetual perfection. For Christ it was not enough for the work of salvation to be sufficient, but the work had to be completely completed, forever finished, eternally accomplished. It had to be perfectly done. Seeing that all was accomplished, he finished the work!

It is finished. It will forever be finished. Nothing else can be done to complete the work. Nothing else can be done to un-do the work. It is finished. His grace stooped low and his mercy bowed down to help us. It is finished! Captivity was lead captive; the myth of Satan's power was outlasted. Evil was overthrown. The gates of hell can no longer prevail. The grave was stripped of its victory, death no longer has a sting. It is finished! Sins were forgiven, the debt was paid, the account was settled, our souls were pardoned, and we were set free. It is finished!

47

"ALABASTER BOX"

Matthew 26:6-13

Kimberley Proctor

If you have ever heard the song "Alabaster Box" by CeCe Winans, you will remember that she painted a pretty vivid and realistic picture of this particular story. The song tells the story of a woman who walks into a room full of people and everybody stops what they are doing. They don't do this because of anything spectacular about her, but they are in shock and begin to whisper things about her because they don't consider her good enough to be in the presence of Jesus Christ. Some commentaries suggest that this woman was Mary, the sister of Martha and Lazarus. When you read another version of this story in Luke 7:38-47, you find that this woman is described as a woman of the city, or in other words, a lady of the night, a streetwalker, a prostitute, a sinner. So it is assumed that this woman is Mary Magdalene. But as she enters this room to make her way to Jesus, the disciples look down on her and consider her not good enough. But this woman did not come to Jesus in the same way that other people came to Him. She did not come to ask for anything–not healing, forgiveness, salvation, nothing. She did not come to *get* anything from him, but came to *give* everything to him–her praise, worship, and adoration.

Mary brought with her a bottle made of alabaster, which was a gemstone used to make bottles that would hold costly perfumes and ointments. The unique thing about an alabaster jar is that when a potter molded and shaped the bottle, the only way to get the perfume back out was to break the bottle.[1] And after breaking it, she poured the contents over Jesus and anointed him. The people immediately ridiculed her for breaking the jar and "wasting" the perfume because they considered her to be foolish for not selling the perfume and giving the money away to help the poor. But Jesus came to her defense, proclaiming that her deed was honorable and her legacy would be profound.

[1]http://thealabasterbox.wordpress.com/2007/11/27/the-alabaster-jar/#more-26.

Mary had to press through some obstacles, but she was determined to give her best. She did not simply pour out this perfume or give a portion, but because it had to be broken, she gave all of it. Can you imagine how the fragrance filled the room? If there was anyone who had not noticed her when she walked in, the smell of the perfume as it consumed the room surely would have grabbed the attention of every person. Throughout the Old Testament, you will find it mentioned how burnt offerings and sacrifices released a sweet fragrance that would please the Lord, and the New Testament says that fragrance is released from those who love and serve the Lord.

She filled the room with extravagant love (Mark 14:3), kind of like when you walk into a room, the Light of Christ in you should fill the room like a sweet fragrance. People can't help but notice you. Yet they criticized her and felt that she wasted what she had. I can remember when I first told my family I was going into full-time ministry. My brother said I wasted time and money getting a college degree. He insisted that I was throwing all that hard work away for some pipe dream or something that wasn't needed and wouldn't bring money. He has since changed his opinion of my ministry and is now one of my greatest supporters. But at the time, I was determined not to allow disapprovals or lack of support hinder me from doing what I believed in my heart was my destiny.

There will always be someone who will mock and ridicule you for serving God. People will not understand why you are doing what you are doing – why you would rather go into the ministry instead of finding some lavish, better paying job. There will be people who will not share in your excitement or share your vision because they do not understand exactly what God has placed in you to do. But do not allow those things to become stumbling blocks for you.

I've learned that it can be difficult to put into words what you know and believe in your heart, so you must come to a point where you stop trying to explain things just so it can make sense to other people. What God has for you is for you only. There is no need for a full, drawn out map with explanations of your ministry. You have to be like this woman, who ignored the comments, the stares, the ridicule, and disapproval of the people in her path in order to get to Jesus and pour out everything she had before the Lord.

Mary's alabaster bottle had a certain value. You have value. You matter to God, and regardless of what people have to say, you have something to offer and something to say that is costly and precious. When Mary came into the room, they talked about her because they believed she had mistakes in her past that made her unworthy to approach Jesus. Maybe someone or several people have said things like that about you. Maybe people feel that you have done some things in your past that make you unfit to be a servant of God, and therefore, believe that you do not have a right to be in ministry. Maybe it is just the fact that people feel you are too young.

No matter what you may have said or done, your life and your witness is the ointment in your alabaster box. When they talked about Mary, Jesus came to her defense and Christ will do the same for you. He will stand beside you and protect you when people want to tell you all the things you can't do. You can take the bad things from your past and turn them around for your good. Use those things to encourage other people, and give them hope that they can make it through certain obstacles because you made it through it. Never be afraid to share your testimony about what God has done in your life because you never know how it will save or change lives. Your desire to please the Lord and to share the love and good news of Christ to those without hope is a precious gift that you can offer. Your ministry is a sweet fragrance that is not only pleasing to the Lord, but it is the fragrance of your life that can linger like perfume.

What is your ministry? Your ministry may not be my ministry and vice versa, but if you haven't already figured it out, begin to pray and ask God what it is that you can offer. What costly offering will fill your alabaster jar, so that when it is broken before the Lord, it will release a sweet fragrance that might be a blessing to others? You have made it this far and have overcome so many obstacles in your life for a reason, so that you can be like Mary, pressing your way through the stumbling blocks and using them to create stepping stones. Your ministry is the ointment in the alabaster jar, and as you come to bring this costly gift to the Lord, you may begin to say…

> I've come to pour my praise on Him like oil from Mary's Alabaster Box.
> Don't be angry if I wash His feet with my tears and I dry them with my hair.
> You weren't there the night He found me
> You did not feel what I felt when He wrapped His loving arms around me
> And you don't know the cost of the oil in my alabaster box.

Amen!

48

"A BEAUTIFUL THING"
Matthew 26:6-13

Lucas Rice

In 1990, the men's magazine *Esquire* ran an extraordinarily popular cover of one of the most popular actresses of the day, Michelle Pfeiffer.[1] She was absolutely stunning in it: head cocked back, skin flawless, her features symmetrical, her hair absolutely angelic. She was the epitome of beauty.

A few years later, it was revealed that the magazine spent over $1,500 just in touchups alone. Beauty, it seems, may not always be skin deep.[2]

In the gospel of Matthew, we hear of another woman who was the bearer of profound beauty. Her beauty, however, was of a different sort. Hers was not a beauty of symmetry, neither was it the comeliness of her skin, nor the gracefulness of her hair–and yet, the beauty that she bore was the epitome of Christian aesthetics. Hers was a beauty of faith, and we see this in one significant and utterly impressive act.

What was so remarkable about this act? Why does Jesus want us to remember it? I want to propose three different reasons that this was a beautiful act of faith.

First, this was a beautiful thing because it was an act of great personal expense. Matthew tells us that Mary sought out Jesus in the home of Simon the Leper. Many commentators assume that Simon had been healed by Christ. This, however, is an informed guess–we really don't know. There is the possibility that Mary traveled to Christ with a real fear of contracting a disfiguring disease.

More tangible is the financial expense associated with this act of faith. John's account of this story says that Mary brought an exorbitant amount of ointment–costing roughly the equivalent a day laborer's annual salary.

---

[1] *Esquire,* December, 1990.

[2] *Adjuster's Quarterly,* Summer 1995, Vol. 3, No. 4.

Perhaps most important, Mary's gift carried with it a tremendous emotional expense. Church tradition teaches us the Mary was a harlot, a prostitute.[3] How could someone with such a bad reputation, someone so damaged–so stained–dare approach the healing messiah?

Although forgiveness of others is woven into the very fabric of the gospel message, for many, opening one's self up to forgiveness is among the most difficult of spiritual endeavors. Don't believe me? Go to an Alcoholics Anonymous meeting. Pull up a chair and listen to the testimonies of despair, guilt, and brokenness. One need not be an addict to experience the oppression of isolation. It is something we have all experienced. And yet God desires the sacrifice of the meek. To quote the psalmist: "The sacrifice acceptable to God is a broken spirit; a broken and contrite heart, O God, you will not despise" (Psalm 51:17).

This highlights a second aspect of the beauty of Mary's act of faith. This was a beautiful thing because God exalts the lowly. He had done this before. He condescended to the shores of the Jordan River and submitted to baptism by his first cousin–but then again, Jesus calls John one of the greatest human beings ever born. He even knelt down and washed the dirty feet of his disciples, but these were men who were hand-picked by him to do his ministry. But here the story is different. In this text, Jesus submits himself to an undesirable...a harlot! How does he do this? How does he submit himself to her and–in so doing–exalt her?

Jesus, seated at the table of fellowship, allows her to pour oil on his head. John terms this to be what it unmistakably is–*an anointing.*

There are three clear applications in the Old Testament of the anointing of oil. First, kings were anointed to rule. Second, priests were anointed to offer sacrifices on behalf of sins. Third, altars were anointed as places of sacrifice. Each of these connotes "a setting apart" of a person for a particular office or ministry. The gospel states with great clarity the purpose of this particular anointing. Jesus is being anointing for his burial.

---

[3]John Chrysostom, "Homily 80: Matthew 26:6-7 in *Homilies on the Gospel of St. Matthew,* A Select Library of the Nicene and Post-Nicene Fathers of the Christian Church, v. 10 (Grand Rapids: Erdmann, 1956), 462.

But who does the anointing? Not a prophet. Not a high priest. Definitely not a king. Who anoints Jesus? A harlot, a prostitute. . . a conspicuous sinner! The lowest of the low would prepare the Son of God for death. She came to him in loving humility and washed his feet with her tears and dried them with her own hair.

In this act, we see the third way in which this is a beautiful thing: Mary cherished the person of Jesus. The disciples had a good point. It was a lot of money. It could have done a lot of good for the poor. Think of all the food, water, and shelter that a year's salary could pay? And yet, in this moment, the disciples had lost sight of what was really important. They had lost what our Orthodox liturgy refers to as a "sacrifice of praise." Their concerns, though admirable, were still worldly. Mary's concern was for Jesus.

Mary demonstrated her love for Christ in a profound way: she was willing to let him die. In one episode of the sitcom *Northern Exposure*, the show's protagonist–a neurotic, out-of-place New Yorker named Dr. Joel Fleishman–is on a road to self-discovery. In his surrealistic journey, he wanders through the snow-covered forest while he questions everything: work, love, and purpose. He comes to a locked bridge which is guarded by a snarly man. In front of the bridge is a trapper. The trapper is burly, decked in plaid, and seems perfectly suited to this environment.

Well, the trapper is not up to the challenge posed to him by the gatekeeper: "You wanna cross this bridge, you're gonna have to answer the riddle." The riddle is this, "How do you keep the one you love?" The trapper replies, "A dozen roses, a box of chocolates"? Obviously wrong. Then Fleishman pauses and answers correctly: you don't. He says, "Love is selfless, non-possessive. If you truly love somebody, then you have no desire to possess them. You don't keep them."[4]

Mary of Bethany is the only person in the gospels who truly accepts the death of Christ. She, like most other Jewish people in the first century, was looking for the Messiah. She was eagerly awaiting the person who would come and right the political, economic, and religious wrongs of her people. She was awaiting the person who would make a better world possible–the kind of place where women did not have to sell themselves on the street just to get by.

---

[4] *Northern Exposure,* Season 6, Episode 14, "The Quest."

And yet, she comes to Jesus, says nothing worth mentioning, washes Jesus' feet with her tears, and dries them with hair. She cried tears of mourning and loss. Someone she loved dearly would be leaving. As her tears ran down his feet, she saw her hopes rolling off his skin and muddling onto the dirt floor below. Despite all this, she let him go. She did not objectify Jesus with his office of Messiah; she loved him as a person. She loved him so much she was willing to let him do what he must–die.

In closing, I would like to share a story about how this divine beauty became real to me.

In my first job out of college, I worked in a children's home. All of these children were removed from their homes for various reasons. Almost all were abused. Some had criminal records. Some were just "too much" for their parents to raise. This was the case with Nathan.

Nathan had severe autism. Our job was to teach life skills to the residents: to help them eat, get dressed, and practice good hygiene. When they struggled, it was our job to help them. Nathan, perhaps more than any other child there, needed special care.

One sweltering day in the middle of July, word came to me that Nathan had defecated on himself. My supervisor informed me that it was my job to make sure he got cleaned up. Common sense and a good deal of training made me leery of the situation. We were never supposed to be in this position alone, but we were short-staffed that day and I had been assigned to care for him.

Slowly, we walked up the old steps of the dormitory. I knew I would have to walk him through every process of the bath. I walked him through how to disrobe and how to dispose of soiled clothes. At this time, I was arrested by something that one could not help but notice. Nathan was not anatomically male. Why am I telling you this? Because at that phase of my life, I was questioning my calling. More importantly, I was questioning my faith. I was at the crest of unbelief. I wondered intensely, "What is the purpose of faith or religion or spirituality?"

In the middle of the summer, in an unconditioned wing of an old building, I found my answer. Nathan, still covered in his own feces, just stood then in there in the shower. He was not a handsome boy. He was not even a boy in some people's eyes. He was not a savant. He was not even nice. He would never have a job. Never pay taxes. Probably never be married. Definitely never have children.

In the eyes of many, he was useless. He was the epitome of all that is undesirable, all that is unwanted and all that is unbeautiful.

There I was in my crisis of faith. If there is no God, then he is of no value. Nathan would live as a leech on society. It would be better for everyone if he were dead. Right?

And yet, when viewed through the lens of Christ, Nathan is a person of inestimable worth. Nathan is beautiful in the eyes of our benevolent Creator. Though the world will never love him, Jesus does. Though he will never have power or influence, our Lord says that "the meek will inherit the earth." Nathan matters to God. He is beautiful in the eyes of God.

We are caught in world of aesthetic extremes: Nathan and Michelle Pfeiffer. Most of us are somewhere in the middle. We are confronted with the choice of the beauty of this world or the beauty of the world to come. We, like Mary of Bethany, have a choice. Are we going to be content with our harlotry–that is, our own sinfulness which for most of us is our lack of love? Or will we, like Mary, seek after Christ?

Let us follow in her footsteps of Mary and anoint Christ in our own hearts. Let us bring him our gifts, allow him to be the king who leads our lives, the priest who sacrifices for our shortcomings, and the very altar of loving sacrifice on which we are saved. In the name of the Father and the Son and the Holy Spirit. Amen.

49

"PASTOR JESUS"
Psalm 23

Jonathan Scott

As I began to prepare my message for the Festival, I quickly became overwhelmed. One of the first steps in sermon preparation is to know and understand who your audience is. But that was the whole problem: I had no idea who might be listening to me today. The possible audience ranged from young people being called into ministry, to lay people who have heard a message on about every scripture there is, and then to the seasoned pastors who have preached on just about every scripture in the Bible. To top it all off, I chose the most familiar passage of scripture in the Bible: Psalm 23. If we know nothing of the Bible we have heard this scripture. If we know the Bible well, we hold this psalm in our hearts. So I asked myself: what in the world can I say that will speak to each person's heart?

Then it hit me; preach about a pastor. Preach about the greatest pastor to ever minister on this earth. Regardless of who we are, whether a young person being called into the ministry, a lay person in the church, or a seasoned pastor, each of us needs a pastor. Each one of us needs someone to lead and guide our life. Regardless of our profession and the stage of our life, each of us needs the care of a shepherd. We all need the Wonderful Counselor, Mighty God, Everlasting Father, and Prince of Peace! We need the Great I Am, the Alpha and Omega, the First and the Last, the Beginning and the End! We are dependent on the Good Shepherd, the Light of the World, the Bread of Life. We call him the Rock of our Salvation, the Redeemer of our Souls, and the Ransom for our Sins! He is our Deliverer and Defender! He is the Way, the Truth, and the Life! He is our Savior and friend today. He is Immanuel, God with us!

There are many names we can use to describe Jesus. In fact, scholars have identified over 700 different names and titles in the Bible trying to portray who our Savior is. Yet I believe that out of those 700 names comes only one. We will understand Jesus the best when we understand him as a *pastor.* Jesus is indeed every 700+ names used to describe him, but the name that captures the character of Jesus the best is *pastor.* It is through his character that each name was given to him. It is through the character and ministry of Jesus that the name pastor can be given to the Savior of the World. Jesus Christ is indeed our heavenly pastor!

The word pastor is defined as a shepherd. When God calls us into ministry, he is calling us to be a shepherd. When Jesus ordained Peter into ministry, he told him to be a shepherd. This is our call. This is the command of Christ for our lives. The example has been set before us. But remember this: there is a shepherd for our souls. There is a pastor to minister to our hearts. If you are a young person being called into ministry, there is a divine mentor for you. If you are a lay person in the church, there is a perfect pastor; one who never makes a mistake and one who is always available to you. If you are a seasoned pastor, there is a heavenly pastor who meets your needs and encourages your soul. There is a pastor's pastor. Have you met Pastor Jesus?

The Shepherd meets our needs. Pastor Jesus knows our inmost being. There is not a day that goes by without Jesus knowing how to satisfy our souls. As pastors, as lay people, and as young men and women being called into the ministry, we are and will always be trying to meet the needs of people. There is not a day that goes by without us having to meet someone's needs. Those teachers at school always want us to do homework, take tests, and write papers. Every day it seems they need something from us. Our bosses and supervisors always need us to do just a little more. They need us to come in on Saturday. They need us to work overtime for some new project. As pastors, someone always needs us for something. Will you come preach at this? Will you prayer over the meal tonight? Hospital visits, funerals, phone calls, sporting events, and meetings fill up our agendas. We are always trying to meet someone's needs. Yet, we can't do it. There are times we just have to say, "No." There are times we can't be two places at once. We are not always able to meet the need.

Pastor Jesus never misses the needs of his people. A shepherd would have to be capable of seeing the needs of his sheep. Sheep are helpless animals without someone to take care of them. They have no way of telling their shepherd exactly what is going on. The shepherd must be able to look at his sheep and see the need. But more than that, the shepherd must be able to meet each one of their needs. That is what our Shepherd does for us. We as humans are helpless spiritual souls without the tender care of Jesus. Even when we do not know what is going on, there is one who does. There is one who sees our needs before we even know them. As humans we cannot meet every need someone has, but Pastor Jesus can.

Pastor Jesus is reliable, capable, and available! He is seeing, meeting, and redeeming our needs. He supplies our needs by leading us to a place where we can thrive. When a shepherd is leading his sheep he is always on the alert. He is always watching out for wild animals, rough terrain, and the weak sheep who struggle to keep up with the rest. Yet a shepherd is also on the offensive. He is always looking for green pastures and quiet waters. He looks for a place in which the sheep can thrive. A shepherd leads his sheep to green pastures to satisfy their hunger. He leads them to quiet waters to satisfy their thirst. It is the shepherd who supplies every need for his sheep.

Pastor Jesus supplies every need for his parishioners. He provides encouragement for the young preacher, places of service for the lay person, and refreshment for the seasoned pastor. He leads us to our needs. The shepherd leads his sheep to their needs. For the sheep they probably didn't even realize they were hungry or thirsty until it was placed right in front of them. But it was still up to the sheep to eat and drink from the shepherd's hand. What need is our Shepherd supplying before us? Maybe today you need the Academy of Preachers. You need a support group to help you overcome the fear of being called. Maybe today you need to be a mentor for some young preacher. Or just maybe you need rest for your soul. Jesus has placed our need right before us. Will we eat from the Shepherd's hand?

At this point, if it were up to the sheep, they would never leave this place of nourishment. But the shepherd knows it will soon run dry. The journey must continue. If it were up to me, I would never leave the Festival of Young Preachers. I would never leave the place of spiritual refreshment. I have the nourishment my soul needs right here in this place. But Pastor Jesus knows if we stay in the same spiritual place too long, we too will dry up. The green pastures and quiet waters are only pit stops on the road of life. Our Shepherd has something better in store for us. We must continue to follow on the journey.

A shepherd not only meets the needs of his sheep, but he also leads them on the path. In verse three, "paths" mean "well worn paths, ruts." A shepherd does not attempt to travel along a new trail. The risk of his sheep going astray is too great. Instead, the shepherd leads his sheep down a well worn path, a path of righteousness. He leads his sheep in the right direction. All the sheep have to do is follow the footsteps of their shepherd. Pastor Jesus wants to lead each one of our lives. He is walking before us leading us in the right direction. All we must do is follow in his footsteps.

Young preacher, don't second guess your calling. Jesus is leading you. Follow his footsteps. Young person who doesn't know what you want to do in life, Jesus is leading you. Follow him. Lay person who fills unused and without a purpose, Jesus has one for you. Take a step in his direction. Seasoned pastor searching for a vision again, Jesus has already seen it. Take one step in his presence. Each step the sheep take is a step of faith. They have no idea where they are going. They simply have to trust the shepherd. Each step we take is a step of faith. We have no idea where we are going. We must trust our Shepherd. He is leading us in the right direction, the path of righteousness, the path that Jesus walked 2,000 years ago. The footprints are before us. Will we walk where Jesus walked?

The path of a good shepherd is a path leading to the mountains. There comes a time each year that the pasture is left bare and the shepherd must seek new fields. The good shepherd will lead his sheep to the rich hillside grass of a mountain. Not every shepherd will take the risk. Not every shepherd will make the journey. But the good shepherd will. However, in order to get there, he has to take his sheep through the valley. Every mountain has its valleys. Every mountain has steep sides with rough ravines and difficult terrain. The best way to the mountain is to go through the valleys, and the good shepherd knows the journey is well worth it. Our Shepherd has done the same for us.

The Good Shepherd had to seek out new fields. He had to make a way directly to the Father. Not every shepherd would have taken the risk. Not every shepherd would have made the journey. Yet our Shepherd did. He knew what was waiting beyond the cross: an empty grave to prove our Savior lives! But he had to walk through valley to get to the mountain. The path has already been traveled. The footprints have already been left. They lead to the only safe haven and assurance of spiritual blessing: the cross of Jesus Christ.

The shepherd meets the needs, he leads, and finally he blesses his sheep. Pastor Jesus is here to do same thing for us. As we walk through the valleys of life–the valley of fear and doubt, the valley of discouragement and temptation, the valley of sorrow and grief–he is leading us to the Promised Land. Young preacher, follow the call of Jesus. He is leading you to a place of harvest where you can save and sanctify souls; a place to break the chains and set people free, a place to minister and change lives through the gospel message of Jesus Christ. Lay person, he is leading you to a place of service, a place where you can lead people to Christ, a place where you can nourish these young preachers in their calling and ministry. Seasoned pastor, he is leading you to a place to continue to minister. He is leading you to a place to heal the brokenhearted, bind up the captives, bring peace to troubled, rest to the weary, and hope to the hopeless. He is leading each of us to life everlasting. Pastor Jesus is speaking. Will you answer the call?

Resurrection

50

"EMBRACING THE FEAR OF NEW LIFE"

Mark 16:1-8

Scott Claybrook

How could they do it? How could they say nothing to anyone? Their fear is understandable, but surely their silence is unforgiveable? Isn't it? This is a troubling passage, a worrisome end to the gospel.

Before we proceed, we must pause and address the issue of how exactly the gospel of Mark ends. In most bibles today, we will see a note following Mark 16:8. The most ancient copies of the gospel end with verse eight. For this reason and others, individuals later added verses nine to twenty to provide a more proper conclusion to this worrisome end.

The real question for readers today becomes whether the original author intended verse eight to conclude the gospel or whether the intended ending was somehow lost. To discuss and answer this question would be beyond the scope of this sermon and this preacher. For our purposes, this passage, verses one through eight, will serve as the end of the gospel no matter how worrisome that may be.

We are left, therefore, with a gospel that ends with the terror in the tomb and the silence of the faithful. And we are left asking, "How could they do it? How could they say nothing to anyone?"

Less than a week ago, we celebrated the birth of a new year and a new decade. From Tokyo to New York and from Oslo to Sydney, millions of people celebrated the beginning of 2010. While I am not sure of the figures, I would be willing to bet New Year's Day is one of the most widely celebrated holidays in the world. More so than Christmas, Ramadan, or Yom Kippur, New Year's transcends religious distinctions and cultural barriers.

Newness often brings with it hope. Each New Year brings with it a process of saying goodbye and saying hello. Many of us look to each New Year as something almost magical. In 2010, we can finally lose that weight, start that workout, pay off that debt, and be that better spouse, that better human being. Recent surveys show nearly two-thirds of Americans will make a New Year's resolution during their lifetime. In addition, forty-five percent of Americans will do so on a regular basis. We need newness. We need hope.

Once the ball finally drops, we turn towards the dawn of the New Year, a year pregnant with possibility, and think that for at least one night anything is possible. Perhaps it is for that reason the end of the gospel of Mark remains so disturbing, why the silence of the women is so deafening. To paraphrase the angel in the tomb, he says to the women, "Do not be alarmed. Jesus has been raised and he is not here. Go tell his disciples and even Peter – that disciple who betrayed Jesus and betrayed his own calling – that he has gone ahead of you to Galilee."

The gospel of Mark tells us, "The women went out and fled from the tomb, for trembling and astonishment had seized them, and they said nothing to anyone, for they were afraid" (Mark 16:8). How could they say nothing to anyone? These women were witnesses not to the dawn of a new year but a new era. The Lord has been raised! Death has been defeated, and hope has come in a new and miraculous way. We need newness. We need hope.

This ending to the gospel of Mark leaves something to be desired. It is as if the New Year's Eve ball began to drop only for the telecast to cut out before it reached the bottom. Everything seems out of place, and yet, if we look close enough, you and I might just find our own place as preachers of the gospel.

What we are doing here, what this Festival is doing, is recognizing the fact that we are all preachers. Big or small, male or female, young or old, we are all preachers–whether by vocation or by virtue of our faith–we all must preach. The text dares the reader to examine the women's silence, because in the process, the reader must examine his or her own silence too.

The women most likely set out for the tomb in the twilight of morning. They wrapped their cloaks tight about them, but the coolness of night clung still tighter. They probably said very little to one another in these early morning hours. What was there to say? Jesus was dead. The sights and smells of his crucifixion were seared into their memories. His disciples most likely scattered. Jesus' movement and message has been laid to rest with him. All that remained were three women, three faithful disciples.

They set out that morning to offer one last gift of service to Jesus, their friend and fallen Lord. Anointing a body with spices served a very practical purpose: to keep the smell down. In life, Jesus might have been special. Simon Peter even said he was the Christ. But for these women that would have seemed like a lifetime ago. Jesus was dead three days now, and he smelled like the rest of us.

As preachers, we have much to learn from their example. For one, their audacity was astounding. We must not forget Jesus was a convicted criminal. Crucified by the Romans–in reality, lynched by a mob–these women marched to a felon's tomb and maintained that he deserved a burial the same as any Jew. But more importantly for us, they went to the tomb with a measure of faith.

They set out that early morning with cloaks wrapped, sandals tied, and spices in hand. The gospel records only one question they discussed among themselves: "Who will roll away the stone for us from the entrance to the tomb?" These stones were fairly large and these women were undoubtedly fairly small. Stones served to keep people out of tombs, and this was foremost in their minds; however, they did not turn back. It was the third day and the body must be anointed. They remained faithful to their charge.

Quite often as preachers, the stone looms foremost in our minds too. The way to people's souls seems all but blocked. "Who will move these people?" we ask. We wonder, "How can what I say make a difference? How can what I say bring new life?" The women continued to the tomb with their questions unanswered. So too should we continue to our pulpits and our preparation with the same determination. Those women never did move that stone. In the end, something far greater did. Likewise, we may never move a single person by the advent of our great stories or beautiful language, and yet if we remain faithful to our calling, something far greater than us just might change the world.

While their faith might be most inspirational, their fear and silence is most puzzling. The women come to the tomb and find the stone already rolled away. Immediately, we can feel their hearts begin to thump. Who could have moved it? Robbers? Romans? Desecrators? The first feelings of alarm begin to take hold. As the women stoop into the small opening of the tomb, their shock and amazement grow. They see an angelic figure next to where Christ's body once rested. The gospel simply says, "They were alarmed" (Mark 16:5*b*). And seeing their panic, the young man's first words to them are, "Do not be alarmed" (Mark 16:6*a*). As the young man explains what has occurred, however, their alarm turns to fear and silence.

We might be quick to assume that the encounter with the angelic figure is to blame for their fear, but to do so would fail to appreciate the scandal of the empty tomb. For at the time of Jesus' burial, a Roman law existed which made the removing of a body from a tomb a capital offense. Under pane of death, no one was to remove the dead from their resting place. The alarm of the women turns to fear because they become responsible for the empty tomb! They did not move Jesus' body, but who would believe them? You can imagine the conversation: "Resurrected, really? That 'King of the Jews'? Right, sure he was."

This is where the text stands against us, challenging us, and indicting us all as preachers. We offer grace and even sympathy to the predicament of the women. "We are not in their shoes," we say, "Sure, it is definitely scary, even alarming." But we still ask, "How could they do it? How could they say nothing to anyone?" In response the gospel of Mark simply replies, "How could you say nothing to anyone?" This does not necessarily entail a literal silence. What is our responsibility to preach the fullness of the gospel, the dangerous parts of the gospel?

At times, we all stand guilty of silencing some part of the gospel. At times, we preach the good points and neglect the pointed questions. We make the Christian life something easily consumable rather than something all consuming. We cast Jesus in our image, making him more a white workaholic than a Palestinian peasant. At times, we too stay silent.

As preachers of the gospel, like these women at the tomb, an encounter with the resurrection is an acceptance of responsibility. While the resurrection leaves everyone with a measure of trembling and astonishment, I do not believe we need to leave in silence. This text challenges us to speak and speak fully about the resurrection, but beyond this challenge the gospel leaves us with good news.

And the angel said to them, "Do not be alarmed; you are looking for Jesus of Nazareth, who was crucified. He has been raised; he is not here. Look, there is the place they laid him. But go, tell his disciples and Peter that he is going ahead of you to Galilee; there you see him, just as he told you" (Mark 16:6*b*-7). For preachers, particularly for us young preachers, there are few more liberating passages than this.

Not only has Jesus been raised, but he has gone on before us. As preachers, we serve a living and active God. We dare not forget it.

It is all too easy to bear the burden of ministry alone. If we do not challenge these people, who will? If we do not change these people, who will? If we do not raise Jesus from the dead, who will?

We serve a savior who chooses to will and to work in this world, a savior who to this day is still going ahead of us. It is not our job, therefore, to raise Jesus from the dead but to bring the dead to the living Jesus. We do not save souls; we only care for them. Too often we fail to realize the power does not reside in our hands. Salvation is not our possession. We join with Jesus in the work of the kingdom of God. Do not let your hearts be troubled or your souls burdened–Jesus is going ahead of you and me. He is risen, alive, and among us today. That is our gospel, our good news.

The resurrection rests at the heart of our faith, and it should rest at the heart of our ministry. As we part ways this weekend, may we all be encouraged as preachers, and may we not forget the example of these women, these final disciples. As the women headed towards the tomb that early morning, the spices in their hands probably felt like an insufficient gift for a dead Lord. Often as we head toward our pulpits in the early morning hours, the sermon in our hands may feel like an insufficient gift for a living Lord. But do not fear, for something far greater than us remains at work.

Once the women entered the tomb, their lives were never the same; likewise, by accepting the call to preach, we too are never the same. There is faith and fear and new life.

To this day, new life in Jesus Christ remains a scary endeavor. Experiencing the gospel also entails accepting responsibility for it, for all of it. But by embracing this fear of new life, we also embrace a savior who rolls away stones, offers the world new life, and goes ahead of us just as he promised. We are privileged to preach.

"Do not be alarmed. Jesus has risen. Go and tell."

51

"FROM DOUBT TO FAITH"
John 20:19-29

Aaron Flucke

It is a tremendous honor to not only be a part of the inaugural Festival of Preachers, but it is humbling to be one preacher among such a great group who will be the next preachers, teachers and leaders of our sacred faith. This opportunity will not only benefit my colleagues, but also the future of Christianity. We all come from different backgrounds and traditions with varying levels of experience, but all of us come and participate in this event because we all see room for improvement. Some of us come with great confidence while some come questioning our abilities. All of us come hoping to find ways to improve our ability and to hone our craft as we use it for God's glory and to advance his Kingdom. As we move towards the fulfillment of God's call on our lives, we all come with the hope that Jesus will lead us from any and all of our doubts into faith in his plan, his promise, and his truth.

Early in my high school career I had a desire to go away to college. I wanted to get out of my home town, see what it was like to live somewhere else, and see a different part of the world. By the end of my high school career I wanted to stay as close to home as possible. I realized that I was a bit more of a "momma's boy" than my macho male ego would have liked to admit. After two years of Bible College in Louisville, Kentucky, the Lord led me to transfer to Oral Roberts University in Tulsa, Oklahoma, nearly 700 miles from my hometown.

Moving that far from home was the toughest thing I had ever done. Even though I did not enjoy making this move and the first couple of months were really tough, I knew that I knew that I knew this was where God wanted me to be. But for the life of me I could not understand why. In spite of this deep conviction that I was where God wanted me to be, I had my doubts that God really knew what he was doing. I was mad at God, and I questioned what he was up to every step of the way for those first few months away from home. This is often how we are as humans. We are full of doubts and questions, and we constantly question if God knows what he is doing as he leads and directs our lives. Sadly, we are not alone in our doubts.

Our text takes place after Jesus' resurrection, and verse 19 tells us that all of these events took place on the first day of the week, Sunday. Just before this passage, we read about one of Jesus' followers named Mary Magdalene (along with Peter and a disciple that is nameless) going to Jesus' tomb and finding it empty. Later, Mary will have an encounter with Jesus himself. This verse tells us that later that same day Jesus appears in a room where the disciples had assembled. Obviously, the disciples are without Judas, but for an unknown reason this passage tells us that Thomas is not there either. The author then makes a point in verse 19 to mention that the doors of this room had been shut yet Jesus appears in their midst and says, "Peace be with you."

What beautiful words for the disciples to hear at this point. Not only are they most likely quite startled, but I wonder if they might be feeling guilt or remorse at the sight of Jesus. They did not exactly handle the events of Jesus' trial and crucifixion well, especially Peter. Even at this point the disciples appear to be in fear as the author tells us that the door of this room is shut.

What comforting words to hear from Jesus, "Peace be with you." In my own life I tend to be a worrier of sorts about numerous things. I find myself worrying if I made the right decision about certain things and wondering if things will work out well or if I heard God correctly or made a poor choice. Thankfully, my wife has been a tremendous compliment to me in this area because she has a very calm and peaceful attitude about things. Whenever I start to get worried about things, her peaceful confidence becomes very reassuring that everything will be okay and that is immensely helpful for me. How much more reassuring and comforting is it for us when we hear those kinds of words from Jesus, "Peace be with you." When we feel bad or worried or ashamed for the way we have acted or didn't act, we don't hear a voice of condemnation from our God, we hear the sweet words, "Peace be with you" from Jesus. How reassuring is this for us?

The author then tells us that as Jesus shows them his hands, letting them look at the scars from the nails, and then he shows them his side. The disciples appear to be glad that Jesus is with them and he tells them once again, "Peace to you." With this second saying of peace, Jesus adds a commission, telling the disciples that "as the Father has sent me I am sending you." Instead of reprimanding the disciples, he sent them into the world to share this good news of his resurrection. With that John 20:22 tells us that Jesus breathes on them and tells them to receive the Holy Spirit. As Jesus commissions the disciples to go out into the world in John 20:21-22 there is a sense that all believers are privileged to share in this mission as they receive the Holy Spirit like the disciples. This is something that sets our God apart from every other god. As Christians we serve a God who loves us as we are and though we are all sinners and we all have our problems and our baggage, Christ still says to us comes follow me, there is much work to be done.

I was 17 years old when I first had a sense that God was calling me into the ministry, and growing up as a "PK" I wasn't thrilled about God's choice of vocation for me. I had a wonderful experience growing up as the minister's son, and I truly loved this experience and my childhood, but seeing all that my father had to do never gave me the desire to follow in his footsteps. As I wrestled with this call and began to grow up and mature, I really began to struggle with the prospect of going into ministry because the thought of being the spiritual leader of a congregation was a heavy responsibility that I found a bit intimidating. I know myself. I know my problems and my struggles, and I certainly don't feel worthy of this calling. I would often have a conversation with God telling him that it would not be a good idea for me to be in the ministry. I would say, "God if you really knew me you would know that I really wouldn't be good at this." But all of that is ridiculous because God knows me more than I know myself. If we are all honest, who among us is really worthy of this calling? Were the disciples worthy, as Peter denied Christ and the other disciples run and scatter? Are any of us really worthy of this calling?

Yes! We are worthy of this calling God places on our lives because Christ died for us and rose again defeating sin's curse over us. He then gave us the gift of the Holy Spirit to help us in this calling to go and do his work, fulfilling this commission. It is very easy for me to begin doubting myself, doubting that I can participate in the work of ministry with Christ. How easy is it for any of us to doubt ourselves and doubt God's plan for us? As a culture we tend to be very negative in the way we speak. In the words we use, we rarely are a positive people. It is very easy for us to be a doubting and negative people. Often times we use the word hope, but within the idea of hope is an element of doubt.

We say things like, "I hope Wal-Mart won't be too crowded today. I hope when we get to Wal-Mart that I don't get that cart that only goes left. I hope this week at work goes well. I hope we win the game." Within all of this usage of the word hope is an element of doubt. As human beings who have fallen victim to the temptations of sin in this world, doubting often times becomes part of our nature.

As we read on in this passage we see an interesting interaction between Jesus and the disciple named Thomas. John 20:24 tells us that Thomas was not with the other disciples when Jesus appeared to them, and by the time Thomas arrives Jesus is already gone. Of course, the disciples tell Thomas what happened as they say in John 20:25, "We have seen the Lord." In spite of their excitement at this wonderful news, Thomas does not believe. He doubts that any of this is true. Thomas says, "Unless I see in His hands the print of the nails, and put my finger into the print of the nails, and put my hand into his side, I will not believe."

This passage tells us that it is not until eight days later that Jesus once again appears to the disciples and this time Thomas was with them. Jesus came into what John says is a room with "shut doors" once again, and once again Jesus says, "Peace to you!"

How easy is it for us to read Thomas' words and look down on him for his doubting attitude? Is Thomas really any different than the other disciples? Earlier in John 20, Mary Magdalene goes to the disciples and tells them that she has seen Jesus and they spoke with him. Yet John 20:20 tells us "it is not until the disciples see Jesus for themselves and see his scars that they become filled with joy." All of the disciples doubt at one point or another in this story, so why do we only call Thomas the "doubting disciple" and not all the others?

Up to this point I have portrayed doubt to be something that is negative and harmful and often times it certainly can be. There must come a point in our lives, especially as believers, when we are able to trust God no matter what we wade through in this life. But doubting can be a good thing if it is not a lifestyle, because doubt encourages rethinking. I read one author who said, "Doubt is one foot lifted, poised to step forward or backward. There is no motion until the foot comes down." Doubt can and should lead us to a decision but it should never be a permanent condition we find ourselves in.

One of my heroes in the Christian faith is C.S. Lewis. Lewis was an agnostic, but through his relationship with men like G.K. Chesterton and J.R. Tolkien many of his questions and doubts of the existence of God were answered. Lewis' doubt in God led him as he says, "from believing in God to definitely believing in Christ and Christianity." The good example we see with Thomas' doubts, much like those of Lewis, is his willingness to allow Jesus to bring him to belief. Thomas' doubts encouraged him to do some rethinking which lead him to a decision that would change the future course of his life.

In John 20:27 Jesus says to Thomas, "Put your finger here and see my hands. Reach out your hand and put it in my side. Do not doubt but believe." Thomas has a profound reply after this experience. He answers Jesus by saying, "My Lord and my God!"

We cannot say for sure what happens to Thomas later in his life, but there are numerous accounts that he sailed east to the Southwestern Coast of India where he started several churches until his martyrdom. India's Syro-Malabar Catholic Church, with its three million members, claims Thomas as its founding minister. In any case, it appears that Thomas' doubts led him to belief, and he apparently went on in some form or fashion fulfilling the mission Christ gave the disciples to go out into the world and reach others with this good news.

As a seminary student I look ahead to Hebrew and Greek classes, countless papers and lost hours of sleep. There will be ordination exams and countless other steps I must take before I am able to fulfill God's call upon my life, the same call Christ gave to his disciples. Standing where I am, the "to do" list seems almost insurmountable. As someone who has never been an academic type of person, the challenge seems great and doubt enters in. But like Thomas, I have the opportunity to allow Jesus to take my doubts and lead me to into belief.

For a number of years I served in a church as the youth director. And just before I started my work, the church experienced a difficult loss. A very beloved member of the community was diagnosed with terminal cancer, and the doctors only gave her a brief time to live.

Immediately, the church began praying and doing all they knew how to do to see that God would touch her body and restore her to health and wholeness.

Sadly, she was not healed in the manner we had hoped, and many in the church began to doubt the very existence of God. After all, if God was a good God who loved them and this dear sister, how could he let cancer take her in the prime of her life, leaving behind three young children and a husband? Many in the church began to allow their doubts to move them in the opposite direction from God. Many of those people ended up leaving the church entirely. Their faith was tested, much like Thomas' was, and they walked away and turned their backs on God.

Now I'm not sure where any of you are in your journey with Christ or what you may be going through, but I know that as we live our lives striving to fulfill God's purpose, doubts and questions will come up. As we face difficult times in life and encounter situations that can't be explained, doubts will creep in. And when they do, we have an opportunity. As the doubts arise we stand with one foot raised, poised to take a step backward or a step forward with Christ. We have the opportunity to allow Jesus to lead us from our doubts into belief, and in so doing, Jesus will take us by the arm in the midst of the ups and downs and storms of this life and say to us, "Peace be with you."

52

"THE MISFORTUNE OF A MISPLACED MESSIAH"

John 20:13-14

Willie Francois

What a dilemma we have seated in this text. A church, the disciples, with amnesia about the throbbing heart of its burgeoning influence and the provisions and power availed to them by God. In this text, we discover that the disciples are oblivious to the whereabouts of their Lord. This text demonstrates the divergent responses to the Resurrection of Jesus. Although the Resurrection marks a moment in Christian history designated as a time of commemoration, confirmation and celebration, it duly posed a time of chronic confusion. While the empty tomb was meant to incite celebration, our text conveys how it catalyzed confusion. Nonetheless, Christological confusion transcends the constituents of the first century movement of Jesus. This biblical community maintained presuppositions about the methodology of the salvific work of Jesus as the Christ, which caused them to miss the triumphant reality to which the empty tomb pointed. They ascertained sociopolitical import of the long awaited Messiah and expected Jesus' triumphant project over death. However, the biblical characters misconceived Jesus' methods. In a real sense, the disciples momentarily lived with broken promises based on their confused orientation. They saw the vacant tomb as a sign of Jesus' broken promise and the Messiah's failure. We too bemoan unanswered prayers, pending promises, and unrealized prophecies because of our own preconceived and misconceived notions of the methods of the Divine. What a tragedy it is to know the promises of the Lord but miss them when they are immediately before you–Christological confusion.

In the 21st century, as proven in preceding centuries, Christological confusion generally yields ecclesiological extortion and institutional impotence in society. It is imperative for us to explore the point where Christology intersects with the social situation of people. H. Richard Niebuhr aids us in handling the pervading culture. He avers that

Christ, through human agency, must be a transformer of corrupting culture. Our cause is crippled by our concern with keeping the culture from co-opting the church that we've rendered futile. Martin Luther King, Jr. suggested that only a "dry as dust" religion prompts a minister to extol the glories of Heaven while ignoring the social conditions that cause men an earthly hell. The empty tomb should have incited celebration because God in Christ kept his promise, but it incited trepidation and anxiety. Our prayers have been answered, but we lack the intuition to realize them.

The Johannine community's rendering of the resurrection of Jesus occurs in the heat of crisis for the movement. The hero is dead, and his body is missing. However, something brought Mary back to the tomb. Something kept her in the garden, functionally confused. Although verse 8 typically conveys to average readers that the disciples believed, verse 9 explicitly denotes that they failed to remember the promises of the scriptures. "They did not believe the scripture" does not connote that they believed a resurrection transpired, but that they believe in Mary's report of an empty tomb. The disciples, all of them, are confused about Christ. For the disciples, the resurrection did not immediately incite celebration and strength to fight on; it caught them in their tracks and induced fear and confusion. As we witness a display of communal confusion, we locate three effects of the Resurrection.

Initially, this text communicates that the resurrection poses unsettling new assumptions. This text conveys a strange assumption about the meaning of this empty tomb. Mary, the lone disciple in this garden, perceives the empty tomb to speak of the malicious engagement of humanity instead of the transformative potency of Divinity. She determined that the scarred, mutilated body of Jesus was laid elsewhere. Many Christians demonstratively indicated their disapproval of the prohibition against prayer in schools, but an aspect of greater criticality is not the absence of Jesus, but the misappropriation of Jesus. How Jesus is being employed causes graver problems for society and the global reputation of the Church. Mary bemoans where he is more so than where he is not. Her assumption feasts on the idea that humanity controlled the whereabouts of Jesus as opposed to Jesus fulfilling his storied promise of Resurrection.

As devout Christians, we often find ourselves disheartened, unnerved, in deep consternation because factions, parties and organizations distort what we feel is the integrity of Christ and his spiritual and social project of redemption. However, Harry Emerson

Fosdick avers that Christianity is not an idea we can use, but it is an idea that uses us. We often fall victim to the false assumption that we own the brand of Christ and can use it as we please. Our understanding, our assumptions bespeak humanity's autonomy to misappropriate or distort the character of Christ. They have taken his name and conflated it with political messages that hurt the masses. They have taken his name and endorsed tyrants and exploitative practices of the weak. They have taken his name and masked senseless wars over unclaimed territory. They have taken his name and raped a people's land of its natural and human resources. People have attempted to lay him down, employ him in service of a lie leading to selfish military flexing. Churches lower their prophetic voices to raise their profits. "They have taken my Lord, and I don't know where they laid him." Obery Hendricks posits, "In today's religiously charged political environment, there can be grave consequences when the name of Jesus is invoked in politics as if his teachings are being used as a guide when, in fact, they are not."[1]

Instead of ascertaining the independent power of Jesus in the Resurrection, Mary responded under the assumption that humanity possessed the power to control, to misappropriate him. They will never wholly distort and thwart his agenda of truth. When people misappropriate, distort and lay down the message of Jesus, a group emerges, like the Academy, willing to carry the sacred cargo despite the pressure. Mary pleads with the unidentified person to relinquish the body of Jesus. Although willing, in reality, Mary could not carry the weightiness of a dead Christ alone. However, Jesus as the Christ was not deceased. Yet, the reality of her insufficient strength remains relevant. We cannot, indeed, mantle the reality of Jesus and all he represents, but we ought to be willing. When the fragility of our mortality and the limited capacities of our intellectual resources fail to communicate the unfettered truth of Christ, he finds a means of communicating his integrity through the willing. Although rooted in her confusion about the reality of Jesus and despite her physical limitations, Mary was willing to take on the task of carrying the body of the Lord. Although it's an inscrutable and daunting task, we must have the volition to mantle love in a habitat of hate, tote peace in a militaristic milieu, shoulder hope in the midst of nihilism, and carry the candor of Christ in the midst of a multifarious culture of

---

[1]Obery Hendricks, *The Politics of Jesus: Rediscovering the True Revolutionary Nature of Jesus' Teachings and How They Have Been Corrupted* (New York: Doubleday, 2006) 195.

corruption. Mary acknowledges that someone has taken the Lord and laid him somewhere, but she wants to carry him away–shoulder his cause. They laid him down. Society, factions, and governments lay him down, but Mary wants to carry him on. In essence, instead of laying him down, I hear the clarion call to lift him up. The hymnist penned, "Lift him up. Lift him up until he speaks from eternity. If I be lifted up, I will draw all men and women unto me."[2]

Not only does it cede ground for unsettling assumptions, the resurrection proved they were/we are unconscious of new realities. Societal structures and entities are not the only ones culpable of functional Christological confusion. Jesus announced to his disciples and more enigmatically to the crowd that called for his crucifixion. Verse nine communicates that the scriptures spoke of this resurrection reality, but Mary and the disciples were perplexed by the vacant sepulcher. Jesus' resurrection meant he wouldn't be in a tomb, but they failed to realize the resurrection. If they sincerely awaited a resurrection, she wouldn't have visited the tomb that morning and the disciples would not have given in to the frenzy of confusion.

The Johannine community essentially syncretizes the other three gospels in this account. One portrait says that the women followed and saw the place where they laid Jesus. The tomb represented the last place she saw the body of Jesus. She lingered at the tomb, because she figured this was the place he was supposed to be. She failed to embrace the new realities, because she was preoccupied with the familiar. She searched an old space, expecting things in the same fashion. Psychologically tied to the tomb, because that was the last place she saw him. The familiarity, which inhibits the realization of freshness, relegated Christ's Resurrection to old methodologies and conceptions. However, the Resurrection intends to prod us from old place into new realities. That is my diagnosis of the Church's futility, too consumed with old spaces like Mary. Despite our psychological attachments, God cannot be relegated, confined to the familiar, the routine and the ways of the past. Serene Jones distinguishes, "Tradition is the living faith of the dead, while traditionalism is the dead faith of the living." What stands in the way is a lot of outworn traditions, moth-eaten slogans and catchwords that substitute duty for thought, as well as our entrenched predatory self-interest.[2] We keep searching in the antediluvian, archaic spaces for God's Glory, but there are emerging forms of love, compassion and economic justice. Concurring with

---

[2]B.B. Beall. "Lift Him Up" in *Songs of Zion* (Nashville: Abingdon Press, 1981) 59.

Richard Lischer, "Religion is being synthesized into something deeper and more comprehensive than the formulas that had been drummed into our heads; it transcends creeds and recited covenants."[3]

In a phrase, I am endorsing Bonhoeffer's "religionless Christianity." We must interpret the empty tomb and the resurrected Lord as the end to deadly, marginalizing religiosity and politics. Jesus did a new thing. He was resurrected something fresh, in a new way but she (Mary) was preoccupied with and psychologically attached to old ideas. She did not recognize Jesus when she gandered at his glory. We get so caught up in our limiting, old ideas about Jesus that we miss him even when we see him and his works. We miss our evolving spiritual enlightenment, because we fail to embrace and explore Jesus as the Christ in his totality. He was flesh and spirit, some amalgam of these two realities. Mary grasped his identity by hearing his words. Jesus' words are always personal with communal affects. His teachings and his words remain constant amidst the incessantly fading fads and corrupting culture and customs of the day. The Ramah of Jesus, the teachings and promises of the Christ, outlive the maiming materialism of the modernity and the false security of titles. He calms her anxieties and invigorates her ambitions with the calling of her name. What healing we find in the words of Jesus. People's hearts are hard or uncomprehending, but through Word and Sacrament, through presence and even avuncular advice, the Lord is made known to us.[4]

In addition to engendering unsettling assumptions and proving we're unconscious of the new realities of Jesus, the resurrection offers unadulterated hope in a new order. After seemingly shattered dreams and a broken promise, Jesus' words reignited the energy and momentum of the movement. The thought-world of the Gospel was not wholly insulated from the thought-world of synagogues and rabbinic schools. As I am reminded of Fosdick's sermon, "The Ideas that Use Us," I concur that when we cannot cling to hope, hope holds on to us. The crucifixion advertised the temerity and tentative victory of imperialism, violence and economic exploitation, but the Resurrection of Christ is God's insurrection against these moral, spiritual and social injustices–God's nonviolent, unarmed terrorism against institutional iniquities and systemic sins. Reinhold Niebuhr intimates that [oppressors] do not recognize that when

---

[3]John Dewey, *Philosophy and Civilization* (New York: Minton, Balch, 1931), 329.
[4]Craig Barnes, "Savior at Large," *Christian Century*, 2002.

collective power, whether in the form of imperialism or class domination, exploits weakness, it can never be dislodged unless power is raised against it.[5] Polarizing policies imposed by the state, crippling customs cherished by our country, but the Resurrection inaugurates the triumph of another way of being in the world. The resurrection points to an impending reality of something new, fresh and inclusive. This hope conspires to materialize the perpetual advent of the love-based politics of Jesus. Our solution is embedded in the realization of God's Kingdom on earth, a Kingdom that critiques and transcends Caesar's Rome, Napoleon's France, Hitler's Nazi Germany, Ferdinand's Spain, Elizabeth's England, Hussein's Iraq, Castro's Cuba, and Obama's America.

Our demonstration of compassion further affects the advent of a greater empire, the egalitarian empire of the Prince of Peace. This new way of being in the world is wrapped up in the Way, tied to Truth and linked to Life. Systemic poverty does not have the last word. Reckless militarism and a culture of violence are not the closing curtains. Hunger, sickness and subprime lending are not the singing fat ladies on the issues that occupy our existential concerns. As God's insurrection against iniquity, Christ's resurrection plows the way and nerves the hearts of all who believe the kingdom is manifesting. In the shadow of his resurrection, we espouse the strength to echo the slave song composed in the brush arbors of antebellum America, "I ain't gonna let nobody (thing, system, concept) turn me around." Those bond persons also sung "Were you there when they crucified my Lord? It caused me to tremble." But now, we shall know him in the power of his resurrection, a power that opens agitates the social equilibrium, corrects moral mediocrity, extinguishes spiritual apathy, and opens avenues of hope. I agree with the hymnist,

> My hope is built on nothing less
> than Jesus' blood and righteousness.
> I dare not trust the sweetest frame,
> but wholly trust in Jesus' Name.
> On Christ the solid Rock I stand,
> all other ground is sinking sand;
> all other ground is sinking sand.[6]

---

[5]Reinhold Niebuhr, *Moral Man and Immoral Society,* (New York: Charles Scribner's Sons, 1960) xii.

[6]J. Jefferson Cleveland. "Were You There?" in *Songs of Zion,* 126.

53

"FOLLOWING A CHRIST WHO REMAINED IN THE TOMB"

Mark 16:1-8

Carra Hughes Greer

From across my desk, a teenager glared at me through watery eyes. I was shocked and confused. This student was one of my "tough guys" who put more thought into his social life than his spiritual one. What was going on? We sat in silence for several seconds before words erupted from his soul, "Carra," he asked, "Would you still follow Jesus if he had never been resurrected?"

I sat and wondered if this was some cruel joke this student was playing on me. Had he gotten into my office and rambled through some of my personal writings? My palms started to sweat and the color drained from my face. I waited before answering his question to see if a smile would appear across his face with the admission that he had been snooping in my office. But it became all too clear to me, as tears began to stream from his doubting eyes, this kid was searching for truth.

While many good, Christian, church-going folks I know would have quickly dismissed his question or simply assured him that that wasn't the way the story panned out, I could not bear to so easily spout out an answer. I was not going to answer this teenager as I had been answered so many times as a teen. My doubts and fears and questions as a teenager always got me in trouble. If there had been a principal's office for Sunday school children, I would have been there on many occasions. Teachers dreaded having me in class, all because I questioned scripture. I questioned the writers of the Biblical text; I questioned my teachers; and sometimes, yes, I even questioned my God.

I was not in any way disturbed by this teenager's theological inquiry; instead, I felt a sense of accomplishment that my students were finally thinking outside the box. Finally, they were making their faith their own instead of just taking on their parent's faith or their teacher's faith. My conversation with the teenager was indeed one of the best theological discussions I have had, not just with a teenager, but with any congregant. It is one I will not forget and one that spurred me on to tackle such a topic through a sermon.

"Would you still follow Jesus if he had never been resurrected?" You may find the question silly since the answer is clearly documented in our scripture. We are told the stone was rolled away, the tomb was empty, and Jesus appeared to his disciples. For me, the question is not so silly. It is a serious one, and one that can give us a new perspective on life. The first time one hears such a question it seems so absurd, but with a second listen it begs us to ponder, to answer. Would you still follow Jesus if he had never been resurrected?

We are so fortunate to have this holy book of scriptures. In this book, we find several accounts of Jesus' resurrection. What wonderful knowledge and faith we have in the resurrection of Christ. Consider the story in Mark 16. Christians find such comfort in these verses. After all, these verses take away the mystery and fear of what happened to Jesus. Jesus indeed died, but we read it right here that the stone was rolled away and the man sitting inside, robed in white, tells us Jesus the Christ has been raised. And then, included in an alternate ending of Mark 16, the gospel writer tells of Jesus' proclamation of eternal salvation.

All my life I was told to follow Christ so that I may receive eternal salvation. All my life, Sunday school teachers and preachers pounded their pulpits and proclaimed the importance of Jesus' death and resurrection for me to receive eternal salvation in heaven. All my life, I heard grizzly stories of the death of Christ, stories of how sinful I was as a human being, stories laden with guilt and fear leading to self-deprecation. All my life, I felt as if I were on some quest to be accepted by Christ but given a salvation I wasn't worthy of receiving. I'm not so sure that's what Jesus had in mind. I'm not so sure that's how Jesus wanted his death and resurrection to impact the world.

Peter Rollins is one of my very favorite modern theologians, if you will. In his book *The Orthodox Heretic*, he has written a collection of parables that pushes his readers to think in new ways about their faith. One parable in particular really grabbed hold of my soul and nurtured my faith in ways I never imagined. The parable, "Being the Resurrection," is about a small following of Christ.[1] After his

[1]Peter Rollins, *The Orthodox Heretic: And Other Impossible Tasks* (Paraclete Press: Brewster, MA, 2009), 67-74.

crucifixion, this community was so devastated by his death they were unable to take the immense pain and sorrow they felt, so they moved far away to a land they could call home. It was an isolated place where this new community sought refuge. Their primary focus was "to keep the memory of Christ alive and live in simplicity, love, and forgiveness, just as Jesus had taught them."[2] They spent the next hundred years living this way, remembering Christ and living as he did, but their community was disrupted one day by missionaries.

These missionaries brought startling but joyous news to this community about the resurrection of Christ. This was something they knew nothing of because of their departure after Jesus' death. The community wanted to celebrate the resurrection of Christ with a great festival, so they gathered one evening in the center of their village to celebrate with the missionaries.

One of the missionaries realized, after the celebration had ensued, that the leader of the community was not present so he went out to find him. He eventually found the wise leader on the outskirts of the village, weeping and praying. Rollins then gives us their poignant dialogue:

"Why are you in such sorrow?"asked the missionary in amusement. "Today is a time for great celebration."

"It may indeed be a day for great celebration, but this is also a day of sorrow," replied the elder. "Since the founding of this community we have followed the ways taught to us by Christ. We pursued his ways faithfully even though it cost us dearly, and we remained resolute despite the belief that death had defeated him and would one day defeat us also."

The elder slowly got to his feet and looked the missionary compassionately in the eyes.

"Each day we have forsaken our very lives for him because we judged him wholly worthy of the sacrifice, wholly worthy of our being. But now, following your news, I am concerned that my children and my children's children may follow him, not because of his radical life and supreme sacrifice, but selfishly, because his sacrifice will ensure their personal salvation and eternal life."[3]

It still gets me; it still stirs every fiber of my being, the elder's words, "I am concerned that my children and my children's children may follow Jesus, not because of his radical life and supreme sacrifice,

[2]Ibid., 67.

but selfishly, because his sacrifice will ensure their personal salvation and eternal life."[3] What did Christ want us to gain from his death and resurrection?

I am ashamed but so grateful that it took reading this fable, this parable before I could truly understand what Jesus' resurrection means for me. It is my hope that each of you walk away today inspired and empowered by Jesus' death and resurrection rather than wounded and scarred as my pastor unintentionally left me. Shame on us for ever selfishly following Christ only to ensure our salvation and eternal life. The resurrection was so much more than that. Shame on us for encouraging others to accept Jesus in order to have "fire insurance," as I have heard it so casually and humorously called. We owe it to people to share with them the significant life and ministry of Christ. Shame on us for placing more importance on our own salvation than the lives of the orphan, the widow, the stranger, the sick, the addict, the blind, the depressed, and the marginalized. If there is anything we can learn from Jesus, it is to think of others before ourselves.

Oh, but what hope we can have; what hope there is in knowing that each day we get out of our beds and decide to follow Christ. We decide to live lives reflecting the love, the grace, the mercy, the simplicity, and the compassion of Christ. And each day we live as Christ, each day we shine the light of Jesus to our communities, we are being the resurrection. The resurrection of Christ was not a onetime event. The resurrection happens every day, many times a day, as we live out the teachings of Christ in our lives. The resurrection happens when we speak words of encouragement to those who are struggling. The resurrection happens when we cloth the naked, feed the hungry, and visit the sick. The resurrection happens when my mama and daddy kiss their sweet, adopted child on her cheek and tuck her safe into her bed. The resurrection happens when our congregation gathers around the graveside of a member and holds his spouse in our arms. The resurrection happens when our youth spend a week in the middle of nowhere working tirelessly on a home for an elderly couple they don't know. The resurrection happens when the least of these teach us a little about what it means to be grateful, to be thankful, to be humble. The resurrection happens when those

---

[3]Ibid., 69.

of us who deal with depression, illness, abuse, grief, or addiction feel nurtured and loved and hopeful again.

The resurrection happens when you and I let Christ's life and ministry and death and resurrection change us. No, Christ is not dead. He is alive in each of us and calls each of us to do our part, no matter how small or how large. We choose every day whether we will be the resurrection in our world or not. Don't let the resurrection be an event that stays in the pages of your Bible, let the resurrection of Christ live on.

The student who sat before me teary-eyed and full of doubt, held captive by his theological inquiries, left my office feeling redeemed by a faith that encourages exploration, as did I. While this teenager's question could have been quickly answered with scripture and swept under the theological rug, we decided to face the doubts and fears and "what if's" of our faith head on. We discovered, just as scripture supports, that we follow a Christ who did not remain in the tomb. And we follow a Christ that was resurrected. We learned a valuable lesson not so clearly printed in the pages of scripture. We learned it is up to each of us to be the resurrection in a dying world.

Be the resurrection. Amen.

54

"A HEART BURNING"
Luke 24:13-32

Taylor Lewis Guthrie

I hate waiting in line, especially when other people are taking such a long time. Like this woman standing in front of me–I could tell she was going to take forever once she got to the front. I saw her start to fidget with something hanging around her neck. I could see that it was a pass for the Boston train system. It had her name and the words "THE RIDE" printed across the top. Ah, "THE RIDE." That meant this woman had a disability. I wondered what kind. I wondered if it would hold me up. When she was called to the counter, the pharmacist asked for her name and she showed her badge. The pharmacist started to talk and then, before she could say much, we all realized the woman was deaf. So the pharmacist called over another pharmacist and the two started talking really loudly and slowly to the woman. The woman tried to speak back and used as many gestures as she could, but it was rather useless. Ensuring that this woman had no sense of privacy, the pharmacists basically yelled that she had three prescriptions to pick up, which totaled $41.48. The woman reached for her wallet and pulled out two twenties. One pharmacist yelled back, "You need $1.48 more!" The woman took both hands and opened them, showing she had nothing left. Both pharmacists looked exhausted, frustrated. One rolled her eyes and said, "Well, you can have these two, but you'll just have to come back when you have the rest of the money for the last one." I stood two feet away. I felt my heart burn with the most stinging of flames. I was so close but yet…

They said to each other, "Were not our hearts burning within us while he was talking to us on the road, while he was opening scriptures to us?" Cleopas and his friend turn to each other, shocked now for the third time this week: first, by the crucifixion of their beloved rabbi, Jesus; second, that their friends–the two Marys and Joanna–told them that when they went to Jesus' tomb, he was gone; and third, they just realized that their fellow traveler on the road to

Emmaus had been Jesus the Risen Christ himself and as soon as they recognized him in the breaking of the bread, he *vanished.*

So, with Jesus gone, the disciples turn to one another for an explanation. They turn to each other and ask if it was possible that maybe their hearts knew that Christ was in their midst even if their eyes, minds, and ears did not. Can you imagine their heartbreak? Can you imagine how these two disciples must feel? They'd walked with this man they thought was just a stranger, this man who asked them questions, and then who called them out and told them every single piece of Scripture that proved his existence and yet they still didn't realize who he is. This is the same man who they've been walking with and talking to everyday, seeing perform miracles, the same man for whom they dropped everything to follow, the same man who had just hung on a cross in front of them. And they didn't recognize him. They wondered if maybe it was possible for their hearts to react to the presence of Christ in a way so innate, so natural, so internal – they asked, "Did you feel that? Did you feel the flames? Did you feel the burning?" How could they ignore words they thought they knew so well, lessons they had heard before, stories they had lived with their teacher? Their hearts were burning, but instead of paying attention to their heartburn, these disciples realized they had just downed a bottle of Tums and went along their way. And I don't blame them. Who wants heartburn? Who wants to have to feel all that stuff?

So we turn our attention to our minds, to our heads, don't we? It's like we're all just heads walking around without bodies. We keep our heads in separate hemispheres from our bodies, an equator between what we think and what we feel. On the walk to Emmaus, these two disciples were doing the same thing. As they journeyed away from Jerusalem, away from all the trauma and prophecy come true, Cleopas and his friend divide themselves from what they had felt the days before–it was a lot–death, possible resurrection. They had a lot on their plate–why add something more? They were so wrapped up in their own heads, in their own interests, they ignore that their hearts are reaching from deep inside–their hearts are reaching out towards a familiar voice, a familiar demeanor, a familiar teacher. Instead, the disciples keep talking, keep walking. And then, even when Jesus starts to tell them the stories of the prophets, even when he starts to tell them the great story beginning with Moses, they have no idea. Inside the disciples hearts, these Scriptures swirl around like mad, jumping up and down on their hearts like little children, holding a megaphone up and screaming, "Hey you! You know me! You know my message! You know my lessons!" But, the disciples just walk along like everything's normal, like the Scriptures are just words, just stories about a people they've never met. The disciples ignore their burning hearts. They ignore the familiar words coming out of the familiar mouth of their Messiah, Jesus.

Maybe it was all too familiar and all too normal. Maybe hearing Scripture explained yet again felt like the same old game. Maybe the disciples we're falling into a routine of ignoring Scripture – ignoring it as it is lived out before them, ignoring it lived out before their very eyes, their very bodies. Maybe the disciples just want to separate themselves, draw the line between their heads and their hearts. Maybe the disciples are desperately trying to throw water on the fire that is building inside of them. Maybe they're afraid that the fire will consume them and they will have to deal with yet one more thing this week. Maybe they're just exhausted, frustrated. Maybe they're just done. Maybe it's just all too much.

Her hands opened up, revealing she had no more money to pay for her prescriptions. I thought, "Oh, I have $1.48. I also know a little sign language. Hmmm…maybe I should help her." My heart felt like it was beating so loudly that everyone in line could hear it, it felt on fire. I thought, I could just tap her on the shoulder but no…I don't want to startle her. I thought, I will just walk to the counter and stand next to her. Would that embarrass her? I thought, I'll raise my hand? Who was I kidding? The woman shook her head and made a gesture that seemed to say, "Well, ok. I guess I'll come back tomorrow." And like that, she walked away and out the door. And finally it was my turn. Everyone around me seemed to breathe a sigh of relief, but I felt more and more engulfed in a fire I had no idea how to put out. I hurried to pay for my medicine, and I ran out the door as fast as I could thinking that if I could just catch her, if I could just give her the measly $1.48, I would feel better, the fire charring my insides would just stop and I could breathe again, my heart would slow down again. Flinging open the doors, I looked to my left, to my right, and I saw nothing. I saw the bodies of people I had never seen before. I looked for the body of the woman who had been standing in front of me, right next to me, but she had vanished. The fire that burned inside began to close in on my heart, encircling it, squeezing it tightly and consuming every bit of composure I had. I opened my mouth and with a sigh, tears began to flow down my face, flowing like a river, flowing like a flood. I stood in the middle of Harvard Square feeling as if my heart just broke open and that fire, that heartburn was filling it, that fire was burning now deep within my heart. It felt like my heart was no longer beating and instead, my heart was burning, burning from within.

The disciples' hearts knew Christ and knew the Scriptures, knew the stories he revealed. Their hearts burned with a most glorious, passionate fire because their hearts wanted to be broken, broken open. And this is different from their earlier heartbreak. This is different from feeling sad and depressed, feeling like there is no answer. This is different from feeling confused or like you just missed someone or you've not seen the obvious. No, their hearts were burning, burning from recognition, burning when they saw Christ, when they felt his presence next to them, when they heard him in the promise of Scripture. Their hearts were burning because their hearts begged to be broken. Their hearts demanded to be broken open. Their hearts desired to be broken and then filled and sustained with something the disciples already possessed.

There is a Hasidic folk tale about a rabbi and his students. One of his students asks, "Rebbe, why does Scripture tell us to write the Word of God on our hearts? Why does it not tell us to write the holy words in our hearts?" The rabbi answered, "Only God can write Scripture in your hearts. You must write Scripture on your hearts so that when you heart breaks, the sacred text will fall inside." When Jesus met the disciples on the road to Emmaus, he knew that they already had the words of Scripture, the words of promise and hope and grace and love. They had those words written all over their hearts. He had taught them the living Word himself, but Jesus also knew that letting those words in takes a bit of coaxing, a bit of massaging, a bit of the most clear-cut obvious examples. Jesus knew that he had to teach his disciples to let their hearts be broken, be broken open so that the heartburn they feel becomes the burning truth of their every heartbeat.

When Jesus meets us on the road, on our way, in line, in the obvious, in the subtle, Jesus is meeting us the same way. He is trying to break our hearts open. This is the promise of the resurrection; this is the promise of the Scriptures we know so well. We are called to break our hearts open and let the fire of all those most sacred and beautiful words fall in, feeding us every step of the way. Pretending it's just heartburn, ignoring it, casting it aside because it is too much, it is too exhausting, it is terrifying, it is ugly, it is poor, it is unlike me is only going to make that heartburn worse. It's only going to make Jesus knock harder at the doors of your heart and say, "Hey, I'm here. You know my message. Let me in. Let me feed you with fire so you can do my work in the world. Hey, I'm right here, right next to you. Recognize me." Amen.

55

"SPEAK LIFE"
Ezekiel 37:1-14

ElBonita Hawkins

Today we meet Ezekiel. Ezekiel and God are walking and talking and they come to a valley of dry bones. God says, "Ezekiel, look at these bones! Can these bones live?" Ezekiel looks around – probably thinking it's a trick question. But he answers, "Well God, you know!" God says, "Ezekiel, speak life to these bones." Ezekiel takes another look around and speaks life into the bones. The bones start to rattle and come together, but there is no breath in them. So God says, "Speak life into them again." Ezekiel did what God asked and breath entered their bodies. Ezekiel stands in amazement at the work of God. God says, "Ezekiel, these bones are a symbol of hope and dreams. Although these bones were dry, I can restore all things." Ezekiel says, "Wow!"

The valley of dry bones was such a great story it had to be recorded. But what about the modern day stories? Is life still being spoken?

There is one modern story about a girl named Elizabeth. She was a very bright child, full of life and innocence. However, as the years progressed, the light became very dim as a result of abuse from different people she should have been able to trust. While other children were able to laugh and play, Elizabeth suffered in silence. The comfort of love that should have been in her life was replaced by depression, oppression, fear, and silence. She reached out to some of her family and friends, but they rejected her confessions and broke her trust. She looked to the church for help, but instead of praying for her, death and fear were spoken into her life. Years of crying in silence brought years of guilt, shame, loneliness, and brokenness. Elizabeth tried several ways of escape including three failed suicide attempts. She eventually discovered self-mutilation, but even that couldn't comfort her. At the age of 21, she hit rock bottom emotionally and spiritually. She came to a valley of no hope and lost dreams, and she decided she was too tired to continue on. Elizabeth reached a point of desperation, and with one last attempt, she prayed to God for healing deliverance.

With that one last attempt, God moved on her behalf. God sent someone Elizabeth's way who was willing to stand in the gap, pray for her, and speak life into her situation. Although the healing process hasn't been easy, joy and innocence have gradually been restored. Elizabeth is now living, breathing, and filled with the love of God. Like Ezekiel in the valley, someone was given instructions by God to speak life into Elizabeth. With the help of God, she was able to live again.

How many of you are standing in a valley of no hope and lost dreams? How many of you have given up on life and on God? How many of you know people who have been through a valley but didn't make it? Who will be their Ezekiel?

When you come to a valley experience and it seems like there is no hope and no faith that anything can change, will you choose to speak life or will you accept defeat? Imagine you are Ezekiel and this room is the valley of dry bones. What would you be thinking? Could you bring these bones back to life? If it were me, I would say, "Really God, are you serious? Look at these bones! Wait a minute; I'm being tricked. Okay, the joke's on me. You can't be serious. This situation looks impossible. How could these old dry bones lives?" But Ezekiel knew of God's work, and he placed his faith completely in God. He did not limit God or what God could do. He knew God was able.

So I ask you today, "What is your valley of dry bones?" For some of you it may be you're struggling to make it through college. For some of you it may be you're struggling financially, and you have no idea how you will get your bills paid. For others it may be you return to an empty house and you're reminded everyday that you're lonely. For others it may be you're addicted to drugs or alcohol and can't seem to break free. Whatever your valley is, trust that you can make it. You may be terrified and feel helpless, but God is able! With the help of God, you can speak life into your situation.

So how do you do this? How do you speak life into your valley of dry bones? First, it's important to understand that life has many battles, but God says the battle is not yours… it's mine. So when fear sets in, you say… "Greater is God in me than the evil that is in the world." When trials and tests come, you say… "I can do all things through Christ who strengthens me." If you find yourself in a valley of depression, you say… "I shall live and not die." When you're in a valley of persecution, you say… "No weapon formed against me shall prosper." Claim victory and not defeat! You are not a victim but a victor in Christ!

So when you come to a valley, find someone that can help you. Get plugged into a ministry. Get a prayer partner. Add your name to a prayer list. Seek God for yourself. If you can't believe in who you are, believe in whose you are. You belong to the King of Kings and the Lord of Lords, the Alpha and the Omega, the Beginning and the End! God says you can do all things through me, and I will be your strength!

Finally, after life has been spoken into you and your valley experience is over, remember that the valley isn't just a onetime thing. Just as the seasons change, so do the challenges of life. Discouragement and uncertainty may come, but God's mercy and grace are sure. God will collect the bones again and again and again. There is comfort in knowing that God is there.

56

"THE ROAD TO EMMAUS"
Luke 24:13-35

Jeremy Shoulta

I'm going to show you the silhouette of a man, a man that I assume all of you know about. He's a well-known figure, a man who was very effective at what he did for a living. He has been recognized multiple times and has received countless awards for the things he accomplished during his career. He has given a good amount to charity, and his career is not entirely without scandal. Now that I've given you all those hints, can anyone tell me who the man is in this silhouette? No? We'll, let me show you another silhouette and we'll see if you can figure it out. (Hold up silhouette of "Air Jordan"). How about now? Indeed, it is the greatest basketball player of all time, Michael Jordan, soaring through the air preparing to dunk the basketball. We seemed to have a little trouble knowing it was Jordan in the image of the man standing regularly. But when we see the iconic symbol of Jordan which encapsulates what his career was all about, we immediately recognize the man who has become the symbol of dominance in professional basketball.

There are probably a few silhouettes of famous figures I could have shown you that you would have no trouble identifying: the Heisman Trophy (which is actually modeled after a 1930's football player named Ed Smith), James Bond in a stance after having drawn his gun, Michael Jackson in the middle of one of his signature dance moves. Each of these figures' silhouettes might not look much different than you or me if we were all to pose while standing upright in a normal, casual position. But there is something so unique about them that can be captured in a particular act that we are able to recognize them instantaneously.

This afternoon we look at a passage in the Gospel of Luke where two disciples are met on the road to Emmaus by the silhouette of a man–a man who at first was unrecognizable by them. But after seeing this man do something that completely captured what He was all about, the disciples' eyes were immediately opened and they recognized him as the Christ, the Christ who had died on the cross but was now sitting with them at the Table. And when they miraculously began to see that he was indeed the very Messiah they had been talking about on the road to Emmaus, the disciples waste no time in sharing the news that Jesus is alive. As we examine this passage today, I hope that our hearts and minds will be enlightened by the words of the scriptures, and that we can be moved to tell others about the Christ and show them the love and grace which makes him unique and immediately recognizable.

When Jesus first encounters the two disciples on the road, they are discussing all of the events of the past few days–events that anyone in Jerusalem would have known about–and through just a bit of prodding, the unknown Jesus discovers that the disciples have just about given up hope because they themselves had not yet seen him alive. We read that concerning Jesus, they said, "He was a prophet, powerful in word and deed before God and all the people. The chief priests and our rulers handed him over to be sentenced to death, and they crucified him; but we had hoped that he was the one who was going to redeem Israel. And what is more, it is the third day since all this took place. In addition, some of our women amazed us. They went to the tomb early this morning but didn't find his body. They came and told us that they had seen a vision of angels, who said he was alive. Then some of our companions went to the tomb and found it just as the women had said, but him they did not see" (Luke 24:19-24).

Doubt and sadness clouded their hearts, so much so that they did not recognize him. Now I don't know if the disciples' eyes were somehow veiled by the hand of God or if they were blinded enough by their own troubled thoughts. In my younger days, I remember thinking that Jesus had shaved his beard, or cut his hair, or put on a different robe, or looked so terrible from the crucifixion that the two disciples were unable to recognize him at that point. But that's clearly not what this verse is about. Jesus' words in verse 25 strongly suggest that these disciples did not believe that their Lord and Savior had been resurrected. In a sense, they had stopped waiting and watching out for the risen savior. It just seemed that nothing good could come out of the terrible things they saw just a few days earlier. Their master had been mocked, tortured, and put to death in the most shameful way possible. How does one come out on the other side of such an event feeling hopeful or encouraged?

And before we shake our heads too much at the doubt and shortsightedness of the disciples, which we often do, let's ask ourselves,

"How often as Jesus disciples do we doubt the power and the miraculous work of God even in the midst of dire situations? How often do we forget the words of scripture telling us that God loves us even then? How often do we not recognize the presence of Christ as he walks with us on the paths of life that we trod every day?" Maybe we're not all that different from the two disciples walking on the Road to Emmaus on that first Resurrection Sunday. Sure we may have encountered Jesus and may recognize him as the Messiah, but even after extensive discipleship, worship, fellowship, and mission in his name, we can still become blind through doubt and fear which can easily can cloud our faith and dampen our spirits. We should know, even in times when we feel abandoned as we walk down the paths of life, that God is there and that Jesus is alive and present with us touching our hearts, and the Holy Spirit moves among us in our fellowship.

As we move forward in this passage we read with anticipation like we would in any story, wondering if there will be a resolution to the problem at hand–the problem the disciples have in failing to recognize Jesus. We read that the disciples invite this man to stay with them because it was getting late and the day was almost over–a providential act, wouldn't you agree? And as they dine, we read of something truly miraculous. Through the breaking of bread, the disciples were able to see that the man dining with them was the Lord Jesus Christ, alive and risen from the dead. The breaking of bread–the same action the disciples had witnessed during their last supper prior to Jesus' execution–the act signifying the grace of God – gave the disciples the means to see what was behind that silhouette of a man, for it is in what Jesus does, rather than what he looks like, that we recognize Him as Savior, Lord, Messiah. Through this act, disciples (that includes us) experience community with God and with each other, disciples experience the peace of God even in the most troubling of times as we gather together around the table, and most of all disciples experience the love of God as we see the picture, or the image, of his sacrificial death in the breaking of bread and also in the drinking of the wine.

Of course, the Lord's Supper does not end with the breaking of bread. It goes on and we consume the bread. When we eat and drink, we fulfill our most basic needs for physical well-being, and when dining at the table of the Lord we fulfill our need for reconciliation made possible through the life, death, and resurrection of Christ Jesus. Daniel Migliore, the man behind the words of the textbook which guided me through two seemingly long semesters of Christian theology, summed this moment up well when he wrote that the Lord's Supper is "a meal of thanksgiving to God for the gifts of creation and redemption; a meal of communion with the crucified and living Christ who is God's gift to the world; and a meal of joy and hope in the power of the Spirit who gives us a new life and provides a foretaste of the great messianic banquet of the end time, when God's liberating and reconciling activity will be completed. " The disciples would have realized this, and what a joyous time it is when we feel refreshed and reinvigorated after dining at the Table of the Lord.[1]

We come to the end of our passage today, and lucky for this young preacher, and maybe even lucky for you, I didn't have to spend a ton of time asking, "So what do we do now? How does this text call us to respond? What do we do when we finally recognize the presence of Christ and experience the grace that has been given to us, made known especially through the breaking of bread in communion with God and fellow believers?" We read in the final three verses that the disciples "got up and returned at once to Jerusalem. There they found the Eleven and those with them, assembled together and saying, 'It is true! The Lord has risen and has appeared to Simon.' Then the two told what had happened on the way, and how Jesus was recognized by them when he broke the bread."

Like the disciples who witnessed the miraculous work of Jesus, we are inclined to tell others about the one who was dead but is now alive. It is the result of receiving the free gift of grace. And that requires more than a simple image in black and white. If we only choose to show a silhouette of a stationary man, no one will really get the picture. They may not recognize him; their eyes may be veiled. But if we work to portray Jesus in the act of what he is all about – sacrificially giving of himself so that we may experience salvation, I trust that God will work. By this, of course, I mean that not only do we tell others about the Savior, but we show others the essence of the Savior by loving the Lord our God with all our heart, soul, mind, and strength, and loving our neighbors as ourselves. I ask you in closing: How will you be the presence of Christ as you walk alongside those who think that all hope is lost? How will you be the image of Christ to all of those who are in need of such marvelous grace?

---

[1]Daniel Migliore, *Faith Seeking Understanding: An Introduction to Christian Theology* (Grand Rapids, MI: Wm. B. Eerdmans, 2004), 292.

57

"FINDING MY FAMILY"
Luke 24:13-35

Darnell Tingle

I have always loved this story but have never understood why this particular resurrection appearance is so much richer in detail than those in other accounts. In my opinion, this is one of Luke's most vivid and dramatic accounts about Jesus, and he tells the event with great skill and drama. The account begins with Cleopas and his companion setting out in a state of anxiety, or even depression: they have lost their savior and don't know what to make of reports that his corpse has vanished. They are in a state of disbelief. This is the state in which they meet the Risen Christ, whom they fail to recognize. No doubt we are meant to conclude that their failure of recognition is owing to their disbelief. As they proceed along the way, Jesus explains the scripture to them: there can be no doubt that they know the texts, as good Jews would, but they have failed to understand the scriptures' significance. Finally, they arrive at their destination, and at the meal, Jesus gives a blessing and breaks the bread. At this point they recognize the Lord, but the Lord is no longer visible. It was not until Jesus had broken bread with Cleopas and his companion that their eyes were opened and they recognized who Jesus was.

A stranger drew alongside them. Isn't it odd how we can so often find ourselves unburdening ourselves to a complete stranger? How many times on a bus or a train or at a party have you blurted it all out to someone you've never met before and are never likely to meet again? Perhaps that's part of the attraction–we will never meet them again and so our honesty about ourselves and our lives and those around us will have no come-back, no repercussions, and we will never be held accountable for what we have said. But just for the length of that journey, or as long as the party lasts, that person, that confidante is a valuable companion walking alongside us. As they walk, their companion begins to explain the scriptures to them, pointing out the footprints of God through the history of their people, and especially the footsteps of God that would lead to the coming of Jesus into the world. Then he went over the scriptures again and explained what the coming of God into the world must be like–not a coming in power and might and majesty, but a coming into the world that embraced the whole of human life, fear and loneliness, suffering and pain, even death.

What makes the story remarkable is how unremarkable it is. I can understand Jesus appearing to the disciples, to the faithful women who followed him, and even to Paul. All of them were very practical appearances in terms of establishing the church and its mission. Yes, the story resonates with a sense of the church and its mission and of the tremendous power of the Word and the sacraments to connect us with the presence of God. But what stands out to me is that the Emmaus story is a story of a God who will not leave us alone. When we are hurt and disappointed, even when it seems that the brightest and the best in life has been destroyed, God will not leave us alone. The death of Jesus could no more stop God from loving us than night can keep the sun from coming up every morning. In moments when we least expect it, the sounds of soft footsteps come up behind us. We turn around, wondering who it could be. Then we hope that no one caught us maybe looking foolish. And those times when we're not necessarily trying to be religious, we feel his presence at the table. Like the two disciples, we try to get away from it all in Emmaus and on our way, Jesus comes, unexpected and uninvited and vanishes as quickly as he has come. Because Jesus cannot be held down, cannot be possessed any more than he could be confined to a tomb.

The road to Emmaus is a symbol of God seeking to reunite with his children. This story is about ordinary despair, and ordinary, Monday-morning drudgery. It is a story about meeting a stranger, hearing his words of comfort, sitting down at table and sharing a meal. This is a story about the meaning of the resurrection. It enables us to see the world, not as a place of death, decay, and defeat, but as a place of waiting, groaning toward God's final victory. It enables us to see that the risen Lord gives hope and joy, when all we see is disappointment, discouragement and despair. My brothers and sisters, we have the opportunity to be together again with God in his kingdom. What happened at the cross was not the end, but a new beginning. The future is not a funeral but a feast, a family reunion if you will.

ABC airs a television series called *Find My Family.* The show centers on finding and reuniting family members that have lost contact with each other. The show relies on a team of researchers and the hosts, Tim Green and Lisa Joyner, to help people searching for lost family members. Each episode covers the story and search for mothers, fathers, daughters and sons who have lost contact for years and are reunited again. After gathering the background information, the *Find My Family* research team begins the difficult task of searching through public archives and records to find the missing family. Host Lisa Joyner makes the initial contact with the found family members to inform them that someone from their biological family is searching for them, and the individuals are reunited with their lost family.

Hello, my name is Darnell Tingle and I am the host of *Light and Salt Inc.* I have been given the honor of informing you that your father and big brother have been looking for you. You see, I've looked through the public archives (the Bible) and it says here how you were stolen out of a place called Eden by something called sin (Genesis 3) and ever since God has been trying to find a way to get you back. But God found a way, you see, for it says right here in the record book (the Bible) that this is how much God loved the world: He gave his Son, his one and only Son. And this is why: so that no one need be destroyed; by believing in him, anyone can have a whole and lasting life. God didn't go to all the trouble of sending his Son merely to point an accusing finger, telling the world how bad it was. He came to help, to put the world right again (John 3:16-17).

He sent his son, our big brother Jesus, to earth where Jesus went to a place called Calvary. He was nailed to a cross to die for our sins so that we could have the opportunity to reunite with our Father. Jesus was humiliated, Jesus' blood was shed, and ultimately Jesus rose and conquered death.

You see, to most people death is final. But Jesus was looking beyond that next 24 hours of suffering – beyond the arrest, beyond the humiliation and, yes, even beyond the crucifixion. You see, Jesus was looking to the resurrection. He was looking forward to when he would descend into the depths of hell and proclaim the mystery of the gospel, declaring death was swallowed by triumphant life! Who got the last word? Oh death, who's afraid of you now? It was sin that made death so frightening and law-code guilt that gave sin its leverage, its destructive power. But now in a single victorious stroke of life, all three–sin, guilt, death–are gone because of the death and resurrection of Jesus Christ (1 Corinthians 15:55-57).

Jesus also did this so that these things would be written and made public record, so that we might find him. Now is the perfect to time to reach out to your heavenly family, your father, God and big brother, Jesus Christ, who have been waiting for you. Will you respond? Here is your chance right now, the decision will change your life forever, and once you've done that, I have three words for you: WELCOME BACK HOME!!

Plenary Session Sermons

January 8 & 9, 2010

58

"THE TREE OF LIFE"
Revelation 22:1-2

Brad Braxton

"Bless the Lord, O my soul, and all that is within me. Bless God's holy name." Grace and peace to you, my sisters and brothers in the family of faith. It is a joy to participate in this inaugural Festival of Young Preachers. I applaud Dr. Dwight Moody and his extensive network of supporters for casting and implementing such a creative vision that will enrich the body of Christ and the body politic for generations to come.

I also congratulate all the Festival participants for exploring and embodying the call to preach the glorious gospel of Jesus Christ. As a homiletics professor and pastor, I have spoken this mantra over countless seminarians and fledgling preachers: "Serious preaching makes a serious difference and arouses serious opposition." Please allow the supportive context in this Festival to propel you along your journey to be a *serious* preacher. As you go, however, remember that you represent a Christ who was condemned as a criminal and crucified by a cruel empire. Yet since Sunday's empty tomb triumphs over Friday's blood-soaked cross, you can overcome every opposition through Christ! The Apostle Paul rightly declared, "We are more than conquerors through Christ who loved us."

I live in a neighborhood on the south side of Chicago where there are several magnificent trees. Their wide trunks and towering branches indicate that they are ancient residents of our neighborhood. Decades, maybe even centuries, before we moved in, they were already there.

As I stood recently gazing at some of those towering trees, I was reminded that trees play a central role in Christianity. Trees serve as landmarks on the journey of fallen and redeemed humanity. According to the scriptures, the first tree in the history of salvation was in the Garden of Eden. As Dr. Gardner Taylor, the Dean of Preachers, once suggested, Eden's divine landlord told Adam and Eve that they had the run of the whole place–except for one tree.

Adam and Eve were explicitly instructed not to touch the tree of the knowledge of good and evil. But temptation crawled on its belly into the precincts of paradise, placing before Adam and Eve an offer they could not or would not refuse.

Because of their disobedience at the first tree, Adam and Eve broke the conditions of their lease, and God evicted them from paradise. The first tree was in Eden. It was the tree of shame. At that tree, our feet stumbled, and we fell from grace.

Because of the tragedy at the first tree, there would eventually be a second tree. On a dark Friday, on a skull-shaped hill outside the city walls of Jerusalem, Jesus hung from the sixth to the ninth hour on a tree. His bruised body, convulsing with pain, stood affixed between heaven and hell on that tree.

Humanity's disobedience at the first tree would be consummated generations later at the second tree as Rome visited unspeakable violence upon Jesus. The second tree was a heinous spectacle of imperial violence, demonstrating how costly it is when prophets *justly* challenge *injustice.* Christians believe that in the second tree God somehow was secretly subverting the ungodly politics of empires past and present.

While the first two trees are vitally important, it is really a third tree that captures my imagination this evening, as we celebrate the power and promise of young preachers of the gospel. The good news of the third tree speaks powerfully to those of us longing for a world of justice, peace, and social inclusiveness.

In Revelation 21-22, John poetically paints a portrait of a new heaven and a new earth. More specifically in Revelation 22:1, an angel takes John to the river of the water of life. This river in the New Jerusalem flows right down the middle of the street. The primary purpose of the river is to irrigate a tree. John calls it *the tree of life.* Permit me to talk about this tree for a moment.

First, the tree of life bears twelve kinds of fruit, and there is never an "off season." Every month, the tree produces an abundance of fruit. In other words, in God's new world, there is an abundance of what we need. This is a remarkable word of hope for a world where an alarming number of children–especially black and brown children–are born in poverty and never have a chance to escape poverty.

In the nearly ten years that have passed since September 11, 2001, we have heard much rhetoric about the immorality of terrorism. Certainly, there is no moral justification for the heinous violence that terrorists have enacted against our country and other countries. Yet by the same token, it is also immoral for the richest nation in the world to be so callous about the poverty of its own citizens and the citizens of the world community.

The tree of life, with its monthly yield of hunger-satisfying fruit, would have a hard time growing in our country and world. In our domineering quest for more money and better technology, we have contaminated the soil with toxic waste. More tragic than the *soil pollution*, however, is our *soul pollution*. Our souls have been polluted with the poisonous run-off of a mean-spirited capitalism that is more interested in the creation of profit than in the salvation of people. The only tree that matters to many in our world is the money tree whose green leaves have printed on them ironically "In God We Trust."

The tree that symbolizes God's future for the world is the tree of life. This tree teaches us that healing and hope will occur in this world when the vast majority of the world's resources are not consumed greedily by a small percentage of people who reside primarily in the United States. God's promise is that a day will come when abundance, not scarcity, will be the order of the day for all the world's inhabitants–and not just those with American passports. So many people are hurting and need healing because in a land of plenty, a few have too much while so many can't get enough to survive.

The miracle of the tree of life will ultimately be God's doing. Nevertheless, we are called right now to plant a seed for the tree of life to grow in this world. We are called to water that seed so that the tree of life might produce some fruit for impoverished people in the present even while we wait for God's future. I have met so many "religious" people who are waiting to go *up* to heaven. But the book of Revelation teaches us that God is waiting on us to bring heaven *down* to earth through our loving sacrifice and courageous action. The tree of life has an abundance of fruit.

Also, according to John's vision, the tree of life is irrigated by the river of life that flows right down the middle of the street in the New Jerusalem. In fact, the tree of life is actually not one tree, but at least two trees or maybe many trees. The river flows down the middle of the street, and on both sides of the river, the tree of life stands. There is a tree of life on the right side and a tree of life on the left side. In other words, God imagines a future for us where there will be unlimited and unrestricted access to privilege.

This is a mighty word of hope for people stuck in the old order still riddled by networks of nepotism that favor the friends and cronies of a powerful elite, while denying access to necessary goods and services to whole segments of the world. In this nation, those who live on the right side of the tracks have state of the art schooling. Those who live on the wrong side are regularly enrolled in the school of hard knocks and missed opportunities. While we should gratefully acknowledge the grand strides our country has made, we also must acknowledge that America still perpetuates a subtle, sophisticated system of racial and economic apartheid.

Our world is characterized by unfair restrictions to privilege. But John declares that a future is coming when those ungodly restrictions will be removed. In the new city, the river sustaining the tree of life flows right down the middle of the street. There is a tree of life on the right side and a tree of life on the left side of the river. In God's glorious future, there will be no wrong side of the river; no wrong side of the tracks.

Everybody who has served God and embodied the truth of the gospel will have access to privilege. In God's future, there will be no sign on the tree of life that reads:

only whites allowed;
only middle class allowed;
only men allowed;
only Christians allowed;
only people with college degrees allowed;
only heterosexuals allowed;
only English-speakers allowed;
only the young and able-bodied allowed;
only the mentally well-adjusted allowed.

When God's future is fully manifest, we will discover that many of the barriers that religious people have created do not represent God's inclusive intentions. The good news in Revelation 22 is the *promise of abundance* symbolized by the fruit of the tree of life, and the *promise of access* symbolized by there being trees on both sides of the river.

There is one final feature of the tree of life that must be described. The tree has special leaves on it. Thanks be to God for the leaves on the tree of life! For the leaves of that tree are good for the healing of the nations. The final promise of the tree of life is the *promise of healing.*

Healing is what God's future will entail. God graciously allows us to get enough of heaven's healing now to make it through this troubled world. But our healing will not fully come until God's future has finally come. The full and final manifestation of God's future–some call it heaven–will be the time and place where our ultimate healing is granted. The longer I live the more convinced I am that heaven will not be a classroom where our questions will be answered. It will be a hospital where our hurts will be healed.

It is so exciting to witness the passion and potential of all you young preachers. For some of you, concerns about healing might seem irrelevant at this point in your journey, since you are dashing toward your dreams with the winds of energy and enthusiasm at your back. Having now turned 40 and been around the block a few times, I can confidently declare that none of us will sprint into eternity. All of us will limp into eternity, having been wounded by some tragedy, some disease, some disappointment, some miscalculation, some misstep. Thus, God will spend the first epoch of eternity simply applying healing balm to our hurting hearts.

The hope that keeps me struggling along is that some day we will be healed. Surely our world needs healing:

healing between women and men;
healing between husbands and wives;
healing between parents and children;
healing among the races and religions;
healing among the nations;
healing among gays, lesbians, and heterosexuals;
healing between conservatives and liberals;
healing between red states and blue states;
healing for persons infected with HIV-AIDS;
healing for the entire world that has been affected by HIV-AIDS.

Our ultimate healing will come in God's future, but I believe that we can reach up and grab a leaf on the tree of life right now. On behalf of a hurting world, young preachers, you should reach up into the heavenly world and pull down one of those leaves and apply its healing balm:

Reach up; grab a leaf, and heal someone. The 1 billion people in our world lacking clean drinking water need you to grab a leaf on their behalf.

Reach up; grab a leaf, and heal someone. The 400 million people in our world infected with malaria need you to grab a leaf on their behalf.

Reach up; grab a leaf, and heal someone. More than 30 million people in our world living with HIV-AIDS need you to grab a leaf on their behalf.

Reach up; grab a leaf, and heal someone. The thousands of lonely children across this country need you to grab a leaf on their behalf before they turn to gangs and suicide.

The tree of life grows in another world, but through our faith, generosity, and advocacy, we can reach up to heaven, pull down a leaf, and heal somebody right here, right now. Young preachers, reach up...reach up...reach up...and then reach out. Amen.

59

"HEADING OUT FOR THE DEEP WATER"

Luke 5:1-11

Stephanie Paulsell

Well, young preachers.If the walls of this sanctuary could talk–if the walls of the fellowship hall and the chapel and the choir room could tell us what is on their minds this morning–I believe they would testify to the goodness and mercy of God. For who could hear the preaching that has filled this building in the last few days and not be filled with hope? Who could hear such preaching and not be changed?

Yesterday, there were moments when a preacher would step down from the pulpit, and I would think: ok, that's it. I'm full. And just as I had decided that I was so full of good things that I couldn't possibly receive one more word, a new preacher would step into the pulpit and open my heart a little wider. Thank you, young preachers, so much, for your ministry among us these past three days. I think I speak for the other mentors here when I say that our roles have been turned upside down this week, and I don't know if we can go back to the way things were. You have mentored *us* this week, you have taught *us* about what passionate commitment to preaching means, and you have reminded us how very much this practice matters. Our own commitments have been reawakened and renewed by your proclamation of the gospel. We are so grateful to you.

You blessed us this week with the gift of scripture, interpreted through your stories, your studies, your bodies, your lives. And the living word of scripture is what I have to offer you in return, in thanksgiving for your ministry. I'm going to read you an old story, a familiar story, one I'm sure you know well. But I want you to find a special place to tuck it away so that when the day comes when you need it, it will be close at hand. Luke, chapter 5, verses 1-11.

I saw the Sea of Galilee for the first time in my life just a few weeks ago. It's so beautiful. I was staying with my family at a kibbutz called Nof Ginosar–the modern name of Genneserat, where this story takes place. It was dark when we arrived, and I couldn't see the water, but the first thing I did when I woke up the next morning was to walk down to the shore with my daughter. And there it was: the beach where Jesus called his disciples, the lake where he preached from the deck of Peter's boat, the landscape of his ministry. "Oh mama," my daughter said. "Here's where Jesus made history."

Two decades ago, during a drought that caused the waters of the Sea of Galilee to recede, two brothers from the kibbutz in Ginosar–two brothers who had grown up on the lake and had fished in it all their lives–found an ancient boat, buried in mud. After careful excavation, experts dated the boat to the first century, the time of Jesus' ministry in Galilee. It was the kind of boat he would have preached from, the kind of boat Peter, James and John would have left behind on the shore when they heard Jesus' call.

I visited this boat it in climate-controlled room where it is carefully held in a cradle of metal supports–an ancient, fragile, precious thing, preserved with devotion. That boat is a testimony to those who made their living, and fed their families, and supported their communities through fishing on the Sea of Galilee, 2000 years ago. And it was a physical reminder for me of what a powerful image for ministry the hard work of fishing has been for the church over the centuries. "Do not be afraid," Jesus tells Peter from the deck of just such a boat. "From now on you will be catching people."

I imagine Jesus smiling as he says this. Jesus seemed to love hanging out with fishermen. He must have enjoyed their company because he spent so much time with them, going out with them in their boats, sitting and talking with them on the shore as they washed and mended their nets. What do you suppose drew him to fishermen?

Maybe Jesus loved the hard work of fishing, the lowering of the nets over the side of the boat and the hauling them back up, hand over hand. It was impossible for one person to handle those heavy nets alone; maybe he loved the shared work, the labor done side by side. Maybe he figured that people who could work that hard day after day would be good partners in the work of building up the kingdom of God.

Maybe Jesus loved the moments of solitude and silence that fisherman experience when the sea is quiet, or when they are fishing at night. Maybe he liked the feeling of being alone together, crossing the lake in silence under the wide, wide sky.

Maybe he just loved being out on the water, feeling the sun on his skin and listening to the slap of the water against the sides of the boat.

Any of this could be true, I suppose, or all of it. But here's what I think. I think Jesus loved fishermen because their business is with what lives below the surface, and their work is an act of faith. Every day, they lower their nets into the water, hoping that there will be something there. And on good days, the best days, when they heave up those nets, they find it full of just what they and their community need to flourish.

I think Jesus recognized his own vocation in theirs. And I hope that you recognize yours in this story as well.

In a little book on religious education, the great fourth-century African bishop, Augustine of Hippo, described a problem that every preacher faces. When I teach or preach, Augustine writes, I can feel what I want to say inside of me. But when it comes to putting the truth I know inside myself into words, my words cannot suffice to my heart. I love this phrase, because it is so true. *My words cannot suffice to my heart.*

Now, you all are very gifted preachers. And your words, even if they don't match precisely what is in your hearts, have certainly spoken to the hearts of your listeners. But you know what Augustine means, I think. There is a certain impossibility about our preaching vocation. As preachers, we stand on the fragile bridge of language, and we toss out our lifeline of words across all that divides us, and we hope those words will make a difference in someone's life a difference in the world. But no matter how carefully we prepare, there is so much about preaching that is out of our control. It is a leap of faith, every time.

Because this is so, it can be tempting to try to domesticate the practice of preaching, to "master" it. And for good reasons! When I was a young preacher just starting out, my husband coined a term for the Saturday nights when I struggled with my sermon: *sermo inferno*. And truly, who wants to spend Saturday night tearing her hair out over a scripture passage that will not yield up its wisdom or trying to argue her way out of the theological corner into which she painted herself on page three or measuring the distance between what is in her heart and what she has managed to get onto the page? *Sermo inferno* is a real thing. If it weren't, preachers wouldn't steal each other's sermons off the internet.

But stealing another preacher's sermon isn't the only temptation that will present itself to you at those times when the work of preaching seems impossible or at least too unpredictable to bear. There are many more subtle temptations than that. And that's why I want you to keep the story of Jesus and Peter fishing together on the Sea of Galilee close.

After Jesus finished preaching to the crowds on the shore, he said to Peter, "Put out into the deep water and let down your nets for a catch." Peter protested: "But Lord, we've been letting down our nets all night long, and we have caught nothing. But if you really want me to, I'll do it." Peter steers his boat into the deep water, and he and Jesus lift up those heavy nets and heave them over the side. And the nets fill up with so many fish so fast that the nets begin to strain and break. Peter calls out to James and John in their boat that he and Jesus need help, and together they pull and pull on those nets until the decks of both boats are covered in fish, their fins and scales flashing in the sunlight–so many fish that the boats start to sink.

There will be times in your preaching life when you will feel that you cannot lower your net one more time. Maybe you have struggled with a sermon for days and the distance between what is in your heart and what you're able to say remains vast. You're good with words, though, and you know you could just paper over your difficulties with language that is beautiful but isn't really saying anything.

Put out into the deeper water, and let down your nets.

Or maybe you've gotten comfortable with a certain approach to preaching. Maybe you've got a system–a story from your life, three points, a conclusion–that is working for you, a system that gets the wild practice of preaching under control. But maybe your devotion to your system is starting to get in the way of your preaching the gospel, which resists all our systems and can break through their nets in an instant.

Put out into the deeper water, and let down your nets.

Or maybe you feel most comfortable preaching on the gospels, or the psalms, or the book of Genesis. Week after week you return to these bedrock texts of our faith that are themselves so deep we could swim in them our whole lives long and never touch the bottom. But don't just stay where you're comfortable. We need a word about sexual intimacy, about the goodness of our bodies: preach to us from the Song of Songs too. We need a word about how to live with hope in a fearful time: preach to us, as Rev. Braxton did last night, from the book of Revelation. We need a word about brokenness–deep, deep brokenness when it feels like that there is no mending mercy in this world: preach to us sometimes from the book of Lamentations.

Put out into the deep water, preachers, and let down your nets.

Maybe you'll find one day that God has written a word on your heart that you know would arouse what Brad Braxton called *serious opposition* in your community if you spoke it aloud. This is not a word that will earn you a handshake and effusive praise at the back of the church when the service is over. But maybe your heart is burning with the effort of keeping that word inside.

Steer your boat into that deep water, preachers, and let down your nets.

When I was just starting out in ministry, my mentor was an Episcopal priest named Bernard Brown, who took me on, even though I was radically unqualified, as his associate minister at the university chapel where he served as dean. After several weeks of assisting him at the altar, where he celebrated the Eucharist according to the Book of Common Prayer, he asked me to serve as the celebrant.

Now, I admired the ritual of the Eucharist Bernie celebrated each week–it was lovely and strange and really different from the Lord's Supper I grew up with in the Disciples of Christ. I thought it over, and then I told my mentor, "In my tradition, we share a meal around a table, not a sacrifice at an altar. I don't think I can lead this ritual, because I don't really know what it means."

And Bernie replied to me in words that I have carried with me ever since: "We don't do this," he said, "because we know what it means. We do it in order to find out what it means."

We do it in order to find out what it means. This is as true of preaching as it is of anything else we do in church. Preachers and congregations together find out, week after week, what preaching means. Sometimes you'll preach an entire sermon about something very close to your heart, and someone in the congregation will hear an entirely different sermon. The place where the sermon you thought you preached and the sermon your listener thought she heard meet is the place where the meaning of your sermon comes to life.

Is there any more thrilling work to be done in this world? I can't think of any–not even fishing! And this is why: the meaning of our preaching does not belong to us alone. Preaching comes to life in community. Preaching comes to life in the presence of God. We preach our sermons in order to find out what they mean.

This must be why Barbara Brown Taylor compares watching a preacher enter a pulpit with watching a tightrope walker take that first step on the wire. We can try to make preaching safer. But Jesus calls us into in the deeper water.

Don't be afraid, preachers. Take your place with Jesus near the edge of the boat. He will help you lift that heavy net over the side, and he will help you haul it up again. Steer your boat into deeper waters, and have faith: faith in yourself, faith in the work of preaching that you share with those with whom you minister and with God, faith in the one who gives all our work its meaning. Have faith that the fish are there, moving through the dark water, covered in their intricate patterns and colors, even when they are hidden from our eyes.

List of Contributors

John Jay Alvaro is a student at Duke Divinity School in Durham, North Carolina, and attends The Gathering Church in Durham. His mentor is Chuck Gaines.

Jake Caldwell is a graduate of Lexington Theological Seminary in Lexington, Kentucky, and Minister in Residence at Central Christian Church in Lexington. His mentor is Michael Mooty.

C. J. Childs is a student at Trevecca Nazarene University in Nashville, Tennessee, and attends Shurlington Church of the Nazarene in Macon, Georgia. Her mentor is Heather Daugherty.

Andrew Fiser is a student at Vanderbilt Divinity School in Nashville, Tennessee, and attends Edgehill United Methodist Church in Nashville. His mentor is Rich Voelz.

Ryan Gilbert is a graduate of the University of Chicago Divinity School in Chicago, Illinois, and the pastor of First Presbyterian Church in Prestonsburg, Kentucky. His mentor is David Carr.

Adam Graham is a student at Vanderbilt Divinity School in Nashville, Tennessee, and attends Howell Hill Church of Christ in Fayette, Tennessee. His mentor is Paul Prill.

Allison Hicks is a graduate of McAfee School of Theology (Mercer University) in Atlanta, Georgia, and is the associate pastor of First Baptist Church in Middlesboro, Kentucky. Her mentor is Matthew DuVall.

Jeffrey Hood is a student at Candler School of Theology (Emory University) in Atlanta, Georgia, and attends Wadley Baptist Church in Wadley, Alabama. His mentor is David Key.

Roger Jasper is a student at the Baptist Seminary of Kentucky in Lexington, Kentucky, and attends First Christian Church in Winchester, Kentucky.

Matthew Kelley is a student at Vanderbilt Divinity School in Nashville, Tennessee, and attends Bethlehem United Methodist Church in Nashville. His mentor is Thomas Gildemeister.

James Kinnard is a student at Howard University in Washington, D.C., and attends First Baptist Church in Jeffersontown, Kentucky. His mentor is Kevin Nelson.

Sarah Lewis is a student at Multnomah Seminary in Portland, Oregon, and attends Veritas Church in Federal Way, Washington. Her mentor is Mike Fuhrman.

Cody Maynus is a student at St. John's University in Collegeville, Minnesota. His mentor is Dee Lundberg.

J. Barrett Owen is a student at McAfee School of Theology (Mercer University) in Atlanta, Georgia, and the pastor of Union Baptist Church in West Point, Georgia. His mentor is Jim King.

Steve Rhodes is a student at Asbury Theological Seminary in Wilmore, Kentucky, and the pastor of Wyoming Baptist Church in Cincinnati, Ohio. His mentor is Steve Cummins.

Nicholas Richards is a graduate of Morehouse College in Atlanta, Georgia, and an associate pastor of Abyssinian Baptist Church in New York, New York.

Adam Quine is a student at Northern Kentucky University in Highland Heights, Kentucky and attends First Presbyterian Church in Owensboro, Kentucky. His mentor is Jonathan Carroll.

Katie Anderson is a student at the Baptist Seminary of Kentucky in Lexington, Kentucky, and attends Buechel Park Baptist Church in Louisville, Kentucky. Her mentor is Don Rogers.

Katie Beachy is a student at Eastern Kentucky University in Richmond, Kentucky, and attends Middletown Christian Church in Louisville, Kentucky. Her mentor is David Emery.

Mary Alice Birdwhistell is a student at Truett Divinity School (Baylor University) in Waco, Texas, and attends Calvary Baptist Church in Lexington, Kentucky. Her mentor is Dwight A. Moody.

Paul Booth is a student at the Candler School of Theology (Emory University) in Atlanta, Georgia, and an associate pastor at Zion Hill Baptist Church in Atlanta. His mentor is Howard Creecy.

Neal Brooks is a student at Southwest Baptist University in Bolivar, Missouri, and attends First Baptist Church in Shawnee, Kansas. His mentor is Mike Fuhrman.

David Depoister is a student at Oakland City University in Oakland City, Indiana, and attends Enon General Baptist Church in Enon, IN. His mentor is Tammy Scheller.

Christine Coy Fohr is a student at Louisville Presbyterian Theological Seminary in Louisville, Kentucky, and attends First Presbyterian Church in Owensboro, Kentucky. Her mentor is Jonathan Carroll.

Patrick Garcia is a student at Cincinnati Christian University in Cincinnati, Ohio, and attends Southeast Christian Church in Louisville, Kentucky. His mentor is Steve Yeaton.

Brandon Grady is a graduate of Bethany Theological Seminary in Richmond, Indiana, and the pastor of Ambler Church of the Brethren in Ambler, Pennsylvania. His mentor is Bennett Poage.

Alyssa Haller is a student at Ball State University in Muncie, Indiana, and attends Bethel United Church of Christ in Evansville, Indiana. Her mentor is Michael Erwin.

Kara Hildebrandt is a graduate of Vanderbilt Divinity School in Nashville, Tennessee, and an associate pastor at First Presbyterian Church in Bowling Green, Kentucky. Her mentor is Sally Hughes.

Joshua Johannes is a student at Southwest Baptist University in Bolivar, Missouri, and attends Sardis General Baptist Church in Forsyth, Missouri. His mentor is Mike Fuhrman.

Katie Lynde is a student at West Chester University in West Chester, Pennsylvania, and attends Ridgeway Community Church in Harrisburg, Pennsylvania. Her mentor is Elizabeth Bidgood-Enders.

Michael Oellig is a student at Millersburg University in Millersburg, Pennsylvania, and attends Ambler Church of the Brethren in Ambler, Pennsylvania. His mentor is Brandon Grady.

T. J. Pancake is a student at Zionsville High School in Zionsville, Indiana, and attends Traders Point Christian Church in Indianapolis, Indiana. His mentor is Jake Barker.

Brandon Perkins is a student at Trevecca Nazarene University in Nashville, Tennessee, and attends Fisk Memorial Chapel in Nashville.

Krista Phillips is a student at Hanover College in Hanover, Indiana, and attends Trinity Presbyterian Church in Hanover. Her mentor is Robyn Abel.

Anne Marie Roderick is a student at Earlham College in Richmond, Indiana, and attends Judson Memorial Church in New York, New York. Her mentor is Kelly Burke.

Daniel Rudy is a student at Bethany Theological Seminary in Richmond, Indiana, and attends Glade Valley Church of the Brethren in Walkersville, Maryland. His mentor is Paula Bowser.

Christian Smith is a student at Northern Kentucky University in Highland Heights, Kentucky, and attends East Second Street Baptist Church in Lexington, Kentucky. His mentor is Don Gillett.

Kevin Stamps is a student at Asbury Theological Seminary in Wilmore, Kentucky, and attends Sonora United Methodist Church in Sonora, Kentucky. His mentor is Kent Lewis.

Brooks Talbott is a student at Cincinnati Christian University in Cincinnati, Ohio, and attends Southeast Christian Church in Louisville, Kentucky. His mentor is Max Semenick.

Alex Williams is a graduate of Cincinnati Christian University in Cincinnati, Ohio, and attends Southeast Christian Church in Louisville, Kentucky. His mentor is L.D. Campbell.

Lonnie Winston is a student at Grand Rapids Theological Seminary in Grand Rapids, Michigan, and the pastor of Cedar Grove Missionary Baptist Church in Brownsville, Kentucky. His mentor is Keith Hackett.

Zachary Bailes is a student at Wake Forest University Divinity School in Winston-Salem, North Carolina, and attends Third Baptist Church in Owensboro, Kentucky. His mentor is James Byrd.

J. C. Campbell is a student at Georgetown College in Georgetown, Kentucky, and attends First Gethsemane Baptist Church in Louisville, Kentucky. His mentor is T. Vaughn Walker.

Chris Dodson is a student at Truett Seminary (Baylor University) in Waco, Texas, and attends First Baptist Church in Kearny, Missouri. His mentor is Mike Fuhrman.

Thomas Gricoski is a graduate of St. Meinrad Archabbey in St. Meinrad, Indiana. His mentor is Brendan Moss.

David Malcolm McGruder is a student at Morehouse College in Atlanta, Georgia, and attends Total Grace Christian Center in Decatur, Georgia. His mentor is Lawrence Carter.

Kimberly Proctor is a student at Lexington Theological Seminary in Lexington, Kentucky, and attends East Second Street Christian Church in Lexington, Kentucky. Her mentor is Don Gillett.

Lucas Rice is a student at St. Vladimir's Orthodox Seminary in Crestwood, New York. His mentor is Chad Harfield.

Jonathan Scott is a student at Oakland City University in Oakland City, Indiana, and the pastor of Francisco Church of the Nazarene in Francisco, Indiana. His mentor is Darin Nossett.

Scott Claybrook is a student at McAfee School of Theology (Mercer University) in Atlanta, Georgia, and attends Northwest Baptist Church in Atlanta. His mentor is Brian Wright.

Aaron Flucke is a student at Louisville Presbyterian Theological Seminary in Louisville, Kentucky, and attends Community Presbyterian Church in Charlestown, Indiana. His mentor is David Flucke.

Willie Francois is a student at Harvard Divinity School in Cambridge, Massachusetts. His mentor is Lawrence Carter.

Carra Hughes Greer is a graduate of McAfee School of Theology (Emory University) in Atlanta, Georgia, and an associate pastor at Smoke Rise Baptist Church in Stone Mountain, Georgia. Her mentor is Bob Browning.

Taylor Lewis Guthrie is a graduate of Harvard Divinity School in Cambridge, Massachusetts, and attends Harvey Browne Presbyterian Church in Louisville, Kentucky. Her mentor is Stephanie Paulsell.

ElBonita Hawkins is a student at Eastern Kentucky University in Richmond, Kentucky, and attends the Berea College Campus Ministry Center in Berea, Kentucky. Her mentor is Loretta Reynolds.

Jeremy Shoulta is a student at the Baptist Seminary of Kentucky in Lexington, Kentucky, and attends Deer Park Baptist Church in Louisville, Kentucky. His mentor is Bill Turner.

Darnell Tingle is a student at United Theological Seminary in Dayton, Ohio, and attends Wesley Center A.M.E. Zion Church in Pittsburgh, Pennsylvania. His mentor is Glenn Grayson.

Brad Braxton is the Distinguished Visiting Scholar at McCormick Theological Seminary in Chicago, Illinois. He has also taught at Vanderbilt Divinity School in Nashville, Tennessee and Wake Forest Divinity School in Winston-Salem, North Carolina. His books include *Preaching Paul* (Abingdon Press, 2004) and *No Longer Slaves: Galatians and African American Experience* (Liturgical Press, 2002).

Stephanie Paulsell is the Houghton Professor of the Practice of Ministry Studies at Harvard Divinity School in Cambridge, Massachusetts. She has also taught at the University of Chicago Divinity School in Chicago, Illinois. Her books include *Honoring the Body: Meditations on a Christian Practice* (Jossey-Bass, 2003) and *The Scope of Our Art: The Vocation of the Theological Teacher* (Wm B. Eerdmans Publishing Co., 2001).

LaVergne, TN USA
17 December 2010
209202LV00004B/2/P

9 780827 20272